Praise for *Surviv...*

D0661716

"Successful startups require courage an[d ...] for taking the time to share these insi[...] entrepreneur!"
—Carol Sands Langensand,
Managing Partner of The Angels' Forum

"Don't run a company without reading this book. It will save you time, direct your energies, and sharpen your ability to execute. Hoffman's writing is clear, smart, and important."   —David Eagleman, PhD,
Neuroscientist at Stanford,
Bestselling Author, Entrepreneur

"The book provides a wealth of practical information and inspiration."
—Jonathan Littman,
Coauthor of the international bestsellers
The Art of Innovation and *Ten Faces of Innovation*

"*Surviving a Startup* takes you into the specifics of what a real business needs to go through. Flowing sweat and tears, both practical and spiritual, have a very big, guiding significance for entrepreneurs to highlight the encirclement, exceed the limit, and give birth to the next commercial unicorn."   —Bowen Zhou, Vice President of JD.com

"Entrepreneurship requires not only courage but also methods. This book is the secret of Mr. Hoffman's investment and thinking in Silicon Valley. With these methods, you will make fewer mistakes, improve your probability of success, and make your enterprise bigger. It is worth reading carefully!"   —David Xu Yong, CEO of Angel Camp

"*Surviving a Startup* recognizes the character and traits of risk in entrepreneurship so that we can better understand the mystery of successful entrepreneurs and venture capitalists."   —Yuan Yue,
Cofounder of Pegasus Brigade

"*Surviving a Startup* unveils a wholly new world about everything an entrepreneur needs to run a successful startup."   —Mike Xu,
Managing Director of Fosun Capital

"This book will not only broaden your horizons, it will help you break through obstacles and realize your dreams."   —Sam Gui,
Founder of Jingbei Investment and Angel Teahouse

"With *Surviving a Startup*, Steve Hoffman has captured what it's really like to be a founder and the traits that separate out the good ones from the run-of-the-mill ones."
—Larry Namer,
Cofounder of E! Entertainment Television

"I believe entrepreneurs will find spiritual resonance, direction, and guidance from this book while enjoying every chapter on the way to realizing their dreams."
—Hu Yu,
President of China University of
Science and Technology and iFLYTEK

"Brilliant and authentic. Hoffman provides a window and perspective to simplify and humanize the tumultuous journey of entrepreneurship. It is a great read for every aspiring individual and team daring to embark on such a journey."
—Tae Hea Nahm,
Managing Director of Storm Ventures

"So direct and real yet still able to feel and see the lightness of it all and remain engaging throughout. This may become the essential compendium for all entrepreneurs and executives."
—Roland Van der Meer,
Managing Director of Ultra Capital

"In this book, Steve Hoffman tells entrepreneurs all the elements needed for successful entrepreneurship."
—Jia Junxin,
Chairman of Shenzhen Xinheng Lida Capital Management

"The art of entrepreneurship is to acknowledge that a startup is a process, and success only comes by doing it and continuously learning from failures and mistakes."
—Ronald Chwang, Chairman of iD Ventures

"*Surviving a Startup* is an important guide for today's entrepreneurs, filled with practical knowledge for those who need to understand the real mechanics of startup funding, avoid mistakes, and break through to commercial success."
—Alex Chompff,
Managing Director of Evolution Accelerator

"As an entrepreneur and investor, Captain Hoff accepts the challenge to put into words the harsh reality of being an entrepreneur."
—Ricardo Politi,
General Partner at Mindset Ventures, *Forbes* 30 Under 30

STEVEN S. HOFFMAN

SURVIVING A STARTUP

Practical Strategies

for Starting a Business,

Overcoming Obstacles, and

Coming Out on Top

Fountaindale Public Library District
300 W. Briarcliff Rd.
Bolingbrook, IL 60440

To Douglas, Zachary, and Skylar Hoffman
Special thanks to Naomi Kokubo

© 2021 Steven S. Hoffman

All rights reserved. No portion of this book may be reproduced, stored in a re-
trieval system, or transmitted in any form or by any means—electronic, mechan-
ical, photocopy, recording, scanning, or other—except for brief quotations in
critical reviews or articles, without the prior written permission of the publisher.

Published by HarperCollins Leadership, an imprint of HarperCollins Focus LLC.

Any internet addresses, phone numbers, or company or product information
printed in this book are offered as a resource and are not intended in any way to
be or to imply an endorsement by HarperCollins Leadership, nor does Harper-
Collins Leadership vouch for the existence, content, or services of these sites,
phone numbers, companies, or products beyond the life of this book.

ISBN 978-1-4002-2321-3 (eBook)
ISBN 978-1-4002-2319-0 (PBK)

Library of Congress Control Number: 2020950411

Printed in the United States of America
20 21 22 23 LSC 10 9 8 7 6 5 4 3 2 1

"I'm convinced that about half of what
separates the successful entrepreneurs from
the non-successful ones is pure perseverance."[1]
—Steve Jobs, cofounder and CEO of Apple

"When starting a company,
I'd advise people to have a high pain tolerance."[2]
—Elon Musk, cofounder of Tesla and SpaceX

Contents

SECTION 2 Raising Venture Capital

SECTION 3 Bootstrapping It

SECTION 4   Unicorn Hunters

SECTION 5   Scaling Up

SECTION 6   Rules to Win By

SECTION 7   Startup Life

Captain's Log

LET ME INTRODUCE MYSELF. MY name is Steve Hoffman, but in Silicon Valley, they call me Captain Hoff, because I'm the captain and CEO of Founders Space, one of the world's leading startup incubators and accelerators.

I've learned a lot over the past two decades launching, mentoring, and accelerating new businesses. I've been in the trenches and seen it all. Having founded three venture-funded startups and two bootstrapped ones, I know what it's like to be on the front lines. I know how tough it can get when the battle turns against you. But I also know what it's like to taste victory and overcome impossible odds.

I wrote this book to help you learn not only from my experience but also from what I've seen firsthand coaching hundreds of entrepreneurs. Some have gone down in flames, while others blazed a path into new territory that even they did not know existed. I will help you navigate the minefields. I will show you strategies that work. And I'll dive deep into the tactics smart founders use to maximize their chances of success, while minimizing the inherent risks.

People see me now and think it all came easily. But it was brutal getting here. I learned a lot the hard way, and I want to share those insights with you. I want to show you the nuts and bolts and sweat and tears of running a real business. It's about dealing with dysfunctional teams; hitting dead ends; messing up half the time; losing money, motivation, and self-confidence; and then moving forward. It's about what it's actually like to be an entrepreneur when things go wrong. It's about becoming a survivor.

By the time you're done with this book, I hope you will learn both how to survive your startup and how to embrace the unpredictability, never-ending challenges, and pure chaos of running your own company.

Devil's Candy

Launching a Startup

Let's begin by addressing the concerns every founder must face when launching a startup. It's no easy decision to quit your day job, risk your life savings (and possibly your marriage), and embark on a voyage that has a 90 percent or higher chance of failure. But that's what entrepreneurs do every day, and that's what makes them special.

So, how do you know if it's the right choice for you? Are you cut out to be an entrepreneur? Is your idea even good enough? If so, when should you take the leap? Should you borrow money from friends and family? How do you build the right team? What's the most important thing to do first? And why do most startups fail?

By the time you're done with this section, I hope you'll be a lot wiser than I was when I began, or at the very least, a lot better prepared for what lies ahead.

Taking the Leap

I SPEAK AT STARTUP EVENTS around the world, and eager young people often come up to me and ask, "Should I start a company or get more work experience first?"

I always respond by asking them a question in return: Why do you want to do it? Often, I can see that they are thinking of launching a startup only because everyone else is doing one. Or they're afraid they'll miss out. Or they read about how exciting it can be. Or they think they'll get rich quick. None of these are good reasons. What I want to hear is that they have a burning passion to solve a problem and have identified a strong business opportunity they believe in.

For most people, I recommend not starting a company if they are on the fence. Why? Because it's no fun if you're not 100 percent committed. In fact, it can be torture. Being an entrepreneur means you will be taking on a lot of risk and a lot of stress. Do you enjoy working all the time? Are you happy giving up your weekends and nights? Do you want to suffer under the worst, most tyrannical boss in the world: yourself? Do you think it's wise to gamble away your life's savings on a wild dream? Do you revel in alienating, annoying, and neglecting your family and friends? Do you like being short on money and fretting over the next payroll? Can you tolerate relying on underpaid employees who may quit at any time? Are you ready to jump on the biggest emotional roller coaster of your life and not be able to get off? If so, then by all means, do a startup.

Seriously, you have to be a special type of person to appreciate this. It's not for everyone, and if you lack the conviction, you probably won't survive. You have to ask yourself: Is it worth the pain? If you hesitate, then you'll regret it. So, get a real job and never look back. Let other fools suffer while you enjoy dinners with your family, weekends at the spa, long lunches, and watercooler banter, all while earning a steady paycheck. That's not a bad life.

※

You have to ask yourself: Is it worth the pain?

Most of the time, the people who ask me the question about starting a company or getting more work experience first are college students who have no idea what they want to do with their lives. For college students, the answer is obvious. You are young, you don't know much, and you can clearly benefit from experience in the workplace; so why not get some real-world exposure first? It can't hurt to learn how companies actually operate. The same advice applies to everyone, whether you are twenty-two or fifty-two years old, whether you have no experience or have worked for someone else your entire life. If you want to do a startup, begin by thinking like an entrepreneur and acquiring the necessary skills before taking the leap.

To do this, you need to find or create the right job. If you feel your current job is a dead end, with no room for growth and experimentation, and you want to become an entrepreneur, then you need to identify the type of job that can become your ideal training ground. Your number one goal should be to learn as much as you can as fast as you can. Whatever job you decide to take, it should be one in which you can maximize your learning. Choose a job not based on salary, title, or security, but on where you think you can grow the fastest. Look at what responsibilities, resources, and latitude you'll be given. Once you take the job, don't wait for anyone to teach you. You must own your job—just like you own a company. You need to constantly be finding ways to add more value, move the business forward, navigate around obstacles, and come up with innovative solutions.

Don't worry about upsetting your boss. It's fine to rock the boat. It's fine to fail. It's fine to act like a fool. That's an essential part of being an entrepreneur. It's even fine to get fired. You'll find another job. What's not fine is sitting at your desk doing the same repetitive tasks day in and day out. If you do this, you are not cut out to be a startup founder. It might be easy and comfortable, but you won't go anywhere.

Mark Cuban, the host of the popular TV show *Shark Tank* and owner of the Dallas Mavericks, knows a lot about when to quit a job. His first real job was at Mellon Bank in Pittsburgh. "A lot of my peers at Mellon were just happy to have a job," says Cuban. "I wanted to be more entrepreneurial. I took the initiative." He started a group called the Rookie Club, where he'd invite senior executives to a happy hour to talk with the younger employees. Then he went a little further. He started writing a newsletter. He did updates on current projects. He even tried to inject a little humor into the staid banking atmosphere. He thought his boss would love him for doing these things.

Instead, Cuban's boss called him into his office one day and ripped him a new one. "Who the f**k do you think you are?" yelled the bank manager.

"I told him I was trying to help Mellon make more money," says Cuban. "He told me I was never to go over him or around him, or he'd crush me. I knew then it was time to get out of there."

After tending bar for a while in Dallas, Cuban landed a job at Your Business Software, which sold PC software to businesses and consumers. At the time, this seemed like the ideal job to him. It paid $18,000 a year plus commission.

"I was happy," recalls Cuban. "I was selling, making money. More importantly, I was learning about the PC and software industry and building a client base."

About nine months in, he got an opportunity to make a $15,000 sale. He was going to make a $1,500 commission, which was a big deal to him at the time. Cuban asked a coworker to cover him at the office. He called his boss and told him that he was going to pick up the check. Cuban thought his boss would be thrilled. He wasn't. He told Cuban not to do it.

"I thought, *Are you kidding me?* I decided to do it anyway," says Cuban. "I thought when I showed up with a $15,000 check, he'd be cool with it. Instead, when I came back to the office, he fired me on the spot. I had disobeyed him."[1]

That's when Cuban decided to start his own company, and he never looked back. He knew that everything he'd done up until that point was about learning as much as possible. He understood the computer industry, what it needed, and how to make sales. He used that knowledge to grow MicroSolutions into a company with $30 million in revenues. A few years later, he sold it to CompuServe. He used this windfall to launch an internet radio startup, which he later named Broadcast.com. The startup grew like crazy. This time around, he wound up selling his company for $5.7 billion to Yahoo!

Take Cuban as your role model. Keep pushing yourself. Don't settle for mediocrity. It's better to work for free at a job that challenges you than to get paid to squander your most precious resource: your time. Time is what matters most. Time should equal growth. That's the only way to progress. Your brain is the most important asset you have. You can't let it atrophy. You need to exercise it daily, pushing its limits so you can see just how far you can go.

※

Time is what matters most. Time should equal growth.
That's the only way to progress.
Your brain is the most important asset you have.

Look for those opportunities where you feel you can make a real difference. Then dive right in. Don't worry if you don't know what you're doing. You may flounder around, but you can't swim if you won't get wet. Find someone you truly respect to mentor you. Go out of your way to befriend those exceptional people who have the ability to change everything and everyone around them. Offer to help them for free—even if it means staying up late and working weekends. That's how you compress the learning curve.

Before taking the leap to launch your own startup, try a variety of different jobs. Make a plan to learn as much as you can about all aspects of business. How does the company scale? What makes it so successful? Why do customers buy the products? Position yourself to interact with various departments—from engineering and logistics to sales and marketing. Understand exactly what they do and how they do it. How does the company acquire customers? Who's in charge of the procurement? Is there a search engine optimization guru on the team? Who are the top salespeople, and what are they doing right? How did the company build its brand? Go as deep as you can.

The size of the company doesn't matter. There are always opportunities for you to learn. Consider it your MBA in how enterprises work. You have a chance to dissect the organization, like you would a frog in science class, and understand it from the inside out. No matter what you decide to do with your future, whether it's to rise up the corporate ladder or start your own business, this approach will benefit you. You'll discover what you like doing and what you're naturally good at. You'll also figure out the types of jobs you shouldn't be doing.

If you do decide to take the leap and actually launch your startup, you will discover that the most obscure pieces of knowledge can suddenly come in handy. It's hard to predict what you'll need to know in the future, but every little bit of experience helps. Most entrepreneurs I work with lack at least one or two key areas of expertise when they launch their companies, and sometimes this can lead to problems.

For instance, I mentored a group of engineers who founded a startup. They were brilliant at coding but knew nothing about generating business. These engineers believed coding was the hard part, and that business development, marketing, and public relations was the easy part. They thought that all they needed to do was build a better product, and the customers would come. Only, the customers never came because no one knew their product even existed. The engineers hadn't brought anyone onboard who could help them with marketing or public relations because they didn't believe it mattered. Even worse, they thought it was a waste of money and time. So, they ignored the problem and continued coding. They added new features, optimized the servers, and scaled the back end. But, sadly, none of this helped, and their startup failed.

This is an extreme case, but even assuming the founders of a startup understand that they need help in marketing, PR, and sales, they often don't know enough to hire the right people. The best way to hire someone is to have done the job yourself, so you know what to look for. If you have no clue as to what the job entails, it's hard to find the right people. This is all the more reason to have tried a lot of different things. You will know when to fill certain positions, what qualities to look for, and what the work entails.

Nearly every job affords a learning opportunity if you look for it. If you can't find it, then quit. And while you're searching for your next job, learn on your own. Remember, everything you do in life adds up, so your goal should be to make sure you are exposed to as much as possible each step of the way. This is how to best prepare to take the leap.

2

The Right Reasons to Launch a Startup

FIRST, LET'S START BY REVIEWING the ten reasons not to launch a startup:

1. **To be your own boss.** This isn't a reason to launch a company. If you think you have problems now with your existing boss, wait until you become the boss. It's ten times worse.
2. **To become famous (or rich) quick.** Yes, we all read about becoming a Zuckerberg overnight and reaping the glory, but it seldom happens. You're far more likely to wake up broke or, worse, hopelessly in debt. If you want to lose what little money you have, there's no surer way than doing a startup.
3. **To escape a boring job.** If your job isn't exciting, change your job. Don't start a company.
4. **To solve an emotional problem.** If you're unhappy with your life and have emotional issues, a startup won't help. It will only make things worse. I guarantee that. The stress from running a startup will exacerbate any psychological problems you have. Please deal with your hang-ups first, and then you can better focus on building a company and managing other people.
5. **To satisfy someone else.** Don't ever launch a startup because other people, like your spouse, peers, or parents, are

pressuring you. The need to create a company shouldn't be tied to pleasing someone else. If you don't really want to do it, you're better off choosing your own path.

6. **To be like everyone else.** This is the number one reason people start companies in Silicon Valley. They see everyone around them doing it. Just because others are doing something doesn't mean it's right for you. You need to know yourself and what the right fit for your personality is.

7. **To avoid missing out.** I have heard many people say, "If I don't do it now, I'll miss my chance!" This simply isn't true. There will always be another opportunity. New technology is constantly emerging, and with each new invention, there are thousands of new business opportunities.

8. **To add a bit of excitement to your life.** There are plenty of ways to add excitement to your life. A startup isn't one of them. What it will add is a lot of anxiety and work. If you want excitement, go parachuting or whitewater rafting.

9. **To make your life meaningful.** Startups don't create meaning. You do. You need to look into your soul and ask yourself what matters. Relationships? Religion? Community? Country? Where you invest your time and effort will determine the meaning you derive from it. There are many ways to give purpose to your life, and you should begin exploring them. Remember, a startup is, first and foremost, a business. Anything meaningful must come from within you.

10. **To change the world.** Now you're getting close, but still no cigar. This is too general. I know a lot of people who would love to change the world, but that doesn't mean they should start a business. You can change the world by joining a nonprofit, donating to cancer research, protecting the environment, inspiring people to action, and so on. You don't have to launch a startup. In fact, most startups don't actually change the world in a meaningful way. That's just a trendy thing people from Silicon Valley like to say to make themselves feel good.

I believe the right reason to launch a startup is because you have a specific problem you want to solve. You may not know how to solve the problem, but you know the solution would be enormously valuable as a business. You have a burning desire to figure it out. You want to challenge yourself. You can handle extreme uncertainty. You know your strengths and weaknesses. You have the support of your spouse or significant other. You don't mind gambling everything on this project. You have enough money to survive at least a year without needing a job. And you enjoy building and running businesses. If you can honestly check all of these boxes, then go for it. You've passed the test and are ready to roll.

Taking on Debt

I WAS BROUGHT UP TO believe that debt is dangerous. You don't want any debts, other than maybe your home mortgage, because that's unavoidable for most people. However, as an entrepreneur, cash is the fuel of your business, and without fuel, you're left sitting by the side of the road cursing. You need money, and when angels and venture capitalists are nowhere in sight, using your credit card to refill your tank is more than tempting.

"Wait, don't do it! Credit cards will destroy you." That's my gut reaction. I personally have never taken on credit card debt that I couldn't pay off without incurring interest or fees. I know how quickly credit card interest can compound and make a bad situation worse. I've seen my friends drowning in it. It took them years to resurface, and all of them swore off credit cards for life. That said, when doing a startup, you often don't have a choice. You'll need money to prove out your idea, and that money has to come from somewhere.

The key is figuring out a way to validate your assumptions while spending as little money and time as possible. It may surprise you, but there are a lot of ideas out there that don't require millions of dollars, or even hundreds of thousands, to test. Most of us own a laptop, and cloud hosting is cheap when you don't have many users. Getting people to work for you for equity, not cash, is not only possible, it's better because they are investing their time right alongside you.

At Google, they have a rule: If you want to do a project, you don't need management's approval. All you need is to convince your coworkers to drop what they are doing and commit to your project.

For a startup, I think the same rule should apply. If you can't convince at least two of your most brilliant, talented, and charming friends to quit their jobs and join you, then you probably aren't ready.

✳

If you can't convince at least two of your most brilliant, talented, and charming friends to quit their jobs and join you, then you probably aren't ready.

This seems like simple advice, but you'd be surprised at how many startup founders don't line up a team. Overcome with enthusiasm, they just plunge right in, only to discover much later that their genius idea can't seem to get off the ground. They often wind up hiring people to help out, but that gets expensive fast. You can easily wind up burning through your life's savings in no time, which brings me to another point.

It's better not to raid your retirement account or your kid's college fund to pay for your magnificent but totally unproven dream. Another thing to avoid is your friends' and relatives' money. This is the true devil's candy. It's tempting but dangerous. Do you care about your friends and relatives? Do you value these relationships? Do you want to be on speaking terms in the future? If you don't, by all means, grab the cash. But if you want to keep your friends and continue showing your face at family gatherings, avoid borrowing money from them, if at all possible.

Let me give you some perspective. According to Gust, one of the largest angel-funding sites in the world, only 2.5 percent of the companies listed actually obtain funding through the site. This is relatively high compared to venture capitalists, who fund fewer than one in four hundred business plans on average, according to the US Small Business Administration.

Assuming you obtain funding, the outcome is far from certain. According to a study conducted by professors from Harvard University, MIT, and NBER, only 17 percent of angel-funded startups in their sample group were still doing well after four years, while 34.6 percent had closed or had an unsuccessful exit during the same time period. The rest were struggling.

The Startup Genome Report, coauthored by Berkeley and Stanford faculty members, did a much more extensive study. They gathered data from more than 3,200 high-growth technology startups. The data indicates that more than 90 percent of startups fail. Of the less than 10 percent that do succeed, most encounter several near-death experiences along the way.

Let's get back to borrowing money from friends and family. I do have one exception, and that is your parents and grandparents. If you have an exceptionally strong relationship with them, where they are used to supporting you and would gladly give you money, even if there were no chance of ever getting it back, then it shouldn't be a problem. But take it as a gift. Don't ask them to invest. This is the test. If they're willing to give you the money as an advanced inheritance, then they aren't expecting anything from it. Their sole motivation is to support you in your dream, and you're probably not going to damage your relationship.

If you don't have wealthy relatives, you can look into inventory loans, equipment loans, loans tied to accounts receivables, and payday loans. Some of these won't apply to you, and others may charge usurious rates. High-interest-rate loans can come back to bite you, especially if the loan is tied to your personal credit. If it's only tied to your business, that may be okay. In the United States, you can always shut down a corporation and walk away if things go badly. That won't be the case, however, if you borrow from a loan shark. If you can't pay, say goodbye to your kneecaps.

Another option is to go to your local bank for funding, but don't get your hopes up. Banks are conservative. They are not venture capitalists, and they want to minimize risk, not maximize returns. That's why banks almost always avoid startups at an early stage. They want to see cash flow. They want predictability. At the very least, they want to see top-tier venture capital firms in the deal.

I've had friends take out a personal bank loan that they guaranteed with hard assets, like their homes. Is this a good idea? Well, it's better than a credit card, and it's certainly better than your friends and family. It's your home, after all, and if you end up losing it, you can always rent. Just don't do it later in life. If you're young, it's easy to bounce back. The bottom line comes down to whether you believe enough in your business. But before you do this, please get the buy-in from your spouse, or you will live to regret it.

There are many other ways to get money, but I have issues with most of them. A lot of entrepreneurs have used ICOs (initial coin offerings). This has been a wildly successful way to raise billions, but it's looking more like a Ponzi scheme every day. Unfortunately, some bad apples have abused the system, pumping up the value of the coins and siphoning off the money, instead of using the funds to launch real businesses. Even those where no fraud is committed are still far from proven. At this stage, the whole idea of betting on cryptocurrencies is more like gambling than investing. I'm not sure ICOs are good for society or startups in the long run.

There are other crowdfunding options, but they also come with risks and liabilities. You have to look carefully into each one and remember that your reputation is on the line. You can always earn back lost money, but it's much harder to earn back a lost reputation. I recommend erring on the side of caution.

Now for the really hard part. When do you know if your business is worth the bet? The fact is, you will never know for sure until you try it. But let me tell you, it's not how you feel that counts. It's not how passionate you are and how much you believe in yourself. You need to be more objective than that. It's easy to get carried away by passion. We've heard the stories of how Elon Musk put his personal fortune into Tesla at the darkest hour and saved the company from certain death. We all want to believe we are made of the same stuff.

It's fine if you're Elon Musk, but life usually doesn't work that way. Don't expect a fairy-tale ending. You need more than a dream to base your decision on. What you need is outside confirmation. You need someone who isn't wed to your fantasy of being the next genius to take a cold, hard look at your business plan and let you know if you should be sinking your life's savings into it. And don't rely on your best friend, Billy, who works in the local burger barn for advice. You need someone experienced in startups to take a look at all the evidence and weigh in on the decision.

Don't stop there. Get second, third, and fourth opinions. Ask as many smart people as you can if they would recommend that you risk your money on this venture. Even better, ask potential customers and investors. Tell them it's your life's savings and walk them through the entire business plan. If they love the idea, ask them if they are willing to invest. If they are a potential customer, ask for a preorder or a letter of intent. The more they commit, the more confident you can be that you're onto something. Don't let anyone off the hook with just a nod of the head. The more data you can gather and the more qualified opinions you can solicit, the better you'll be able to assess the risks.

What type of data do you need? Well, it's simple: all the same data you would present to a venture capitalist. After all, you are also the investor. You are investing your time, your money, your relationships, and your reputation. You can't go into this blindly. You need to know as much as possible before taking the plunge. Otherwise, you may wind up diving into an empty swimming pool.

Now, I'm going to completely contradict myself. I've given you the sound counsel of an experienced hand. I've seen hundreds of startups fail, and it's not pretty. So, naturally, I'm jaded. I'm cautious. I have my own battle scars. But I'm not here to give you only practical advice. I also want to inspire you to take big chances.

There are many entrepreneurs who don't always follow this practical advice, and a small percentage of them actually succeed. Those are the stories we thrive on. Those are the people we remember. That's what makes life so exciting. We can't help but love it when our hero does something incredibly daring, even foolhardy, beats all the odds, and comes out on top. Humans don't want to read about the cautious entrepreneur who was prudent, carefully managed risk, worked hard for twenty years, and gradually built a prosperous business. That's boring. When we open *Fast Company* or the *Wall Street Journal*, we want to hear about the crazy fool who bet the farm and won big-time.

That's what gets us entrepreneurs out of bed in the morning. Doing a startup is hard, and if you can't indulge in some unbridled fantasies, then what's the point?

So, let me tell you a story that contradicts all my sagacious advice above. It's the story of an ice cream entrepreneur. Yes, someone who believed he could create a better dessert than anyone else, even the big guys, like good old Ben & Jerry's and Baskin-Robbins. But his ice cream would be different. It would be healthy. And it would make him millions.

The words *ice cream* and *healthy* seem like an oxymoron, but this was Justin Woolverton's dream. He was a corporate lawyer who loved ice cream so much, he became obsessed with it. His vision was to create an ice cream that would be low calorie, healthy, and still taste like ice cream—a seemingly impossible task. That didn't stop him. He was a mad scientist with no formal training. He would mix stevia, a low-calorie sweetener, with Greek yogurt, berries, cream, eggs, protein concentrate, chocolate chips, and a host of other ingredients in varying combinations, and then freeze it.

The verdict came after it was frozen, and Woolverton took the first bite. Did it taste like ice cream? Was it any good? It wasn't until thousands of bites later, through sheer trial and error, that he managed to come up with a combination that tasted like ice cream. Once he hit upon the magic formula, he could hardly sleep at night.

Making ice cream in your kitchen is one thing. Manufacturing ice cream for sale in supermarkets across the country is another. This is where he transitioned from wacky inventor to entrepreneur. He didn't have a factory or any knowledge of what it took to actually produce a commercially viable product. After a bunch of phone calls, he managed to convince a local manufacturer to let him come in on the weekend and use the six-gallon mixer to create a batch of his special ice cream. It turned out to be absolute garbage. It didn't even freeze.

Back to the drawing board. It took an entire year for Woolverton to finally crack the code. He managed to perfect a formula for an ice cream that was only three hundred calories per pint, tasted great, and had the right consistency when frozen. The next problem was that he needed money. He paid a graphic designer $30,000 to develop the logo and packaging. Then he needed more than $100,000 for more ingredients. He quickly burned through his paychecks and savings in an attempt to launch his product, only to discover that his brand name, Eden Creamery, infringed on another company's trademark. This meant he had to scrap everything and come up with a new name: Halo Top.

Woolverton targeted natural food stores whose clientele didn't mind paying higher prices for healthier foods. He was making progress but needed help. That's when he brought in another lawyer, Doug Bouton. That's right, you can't have too many lawyers in an ice cream startup. But this lawyer had a different skill set than Woolverton. Bouton was a natural at operations. He took over the financial spreadsheets, supply chain, and sales, letting Woolverton focus on the food and guerrilla marketing.

The dynamic duo set out to conquer the freezers of America. Bouton visited seventy-five buyers and landed three of them, with Whole Foods being the biggest. All was great, except for their finances. They desperately needed money, and so they broke every rule I told you about. First, they raised $500,000 from family, friends, and former colleagues. They anticipated this would keep them afloat until business took off and they were cash-flow positive.

There was just one problem: They didn't realize how much the slotting fees would be. The stores wanted them to pay for shelf space, and for large chains, this came to hundreds of thousands of dollars. Ouch! They also had quality-control issues, and some stores canceled their orders. The red ink mounted, and the idea of reaching profitability was out of the question.

With no other way to fund his business, Woolverton broke my next rule. He ran up $150,000 on five credit cards. But this wasn't enough to cover the growing expenses. So, in an act of sheer desperation, he went a step further and reached for more devil's candy: a predatory loan, which had a 24.9 percent interest rate. Only he got turned down! He wasn't even credible enough for loan sharks. So, his partner, Bouton, applied for the loan instead and secured a $35,000 loan, which gave them two more months.

You can imagine how stressful this was, but when you're in this deep, there is no turning back. Luckily, at the last minute, they heard of the crowdfunding site CircleUp, and before their cash ran out, they managed to raise $1 million. This was enough to buy them sixteen months of runway. It was their make or break. The process was so agonizing that both Woolverton and Bouton agreed that if they couldn't make it with this funding, they would close down the company. It was just too painful.

Fortunately, by this time, they'd learned a lot. They discovered that they could negotiate a discount on the slotting fees if they agreed to advertise on their own and drive traffic to the stores. Through a clever use of hyper-targeted ads on Facebook and Instagram, where they targeted ice cream lovers in ZIP codes near the stores, they got customers to the shelves much more effectively than in-store demonstrations.

The real breakthrough came when a writer from GQ.com tried Halo Top and fell in love with it. He wrote an article titled, "What It's Like to Eat Nothing but This Magical, Healthy Ice Cream for 10 Days,"[1] which chronicles how the journalist ate only Halo Top for ten straight days. This article went viral, and it was followed with more articles on Halo Top. This happened just as Halo Top hit nearly five thousand grocery stores nationwide. The combination sent sales soaring.

To add icing to the ice cream cake, people felt comfortable eating more Halo Top than regular ice cream, because it was supposedly healthy and low calorie. So, instead of just taking a single scoop of ice cream, many Halo Top fans began indulging in a pint a night. That meant more ice cream sales and bigger profits. Halo Top now has more than $100 million in sales, and none of this would have happened if they didn't try the devil's candy. Sometimes you have to go all in, even if it means taking insane risks.

Now let me back up and clarify. These guys weren't delusional. Woolverton and Bouton knew they had something real. They understood that there was a market for their product. There is nothing Americans love more than their desserts, and ice cream is the all-time favorite. The problem is that desserts make you fat, and America is suffering from an obesity epidemic. As a result, everyone is trying to be more health conscious, which makes it the perfect time for healthy ice cream. They discovered the holy grail of desserts. The promise was that anyone could eat a pint of ice cream every night without gaining weight. Who can resist that? It was a gold mine, and they were sitting on it. But they needed money to get the gold out.

If you're in this position and have the conviction and evidence to back up your beliefs, then you can go ahead and break all my rules. I give you permission. If you don't bet big, you can't win big. Just be sure you're making the right bet.

4

Does Your Idea Suck?

MANY ENTREPRENEURS START WITH AN idea. They spend weeks, months, or even years trying to think of the perfect business concept. But you know what? The majority of startups end up discarding their initial ideas. Rarely do they work. Why is that? Because an idea without data to back it up is just a fantasy. You may think you have the most brilliant business in the world, but until you can show some evidence that it provides real value to the customer, it's only a dream.

Don't worry. You are not alone. Many of the most successful startups in Silicon Valley started off with the wrong idea. LinkedIn began as a dating site called SocialNet, which failed miserably. But without this failure, Reid Hoffman, the cofounder, says he wouldn't have launched LinkedIn. SocialNet taught him a tremendous amount about how social networks function, which formed the basis for LinkedIn's phenomenal success and profitable IPO (initial public offering).

Nick Woodman also started off with the wrong idea: a gaming and marketing platform that gave users the chance to win cash prizes. He called it Funbug and launched the startup in 1999. Two years and $3.9 million later, he had to shut it down because users simply weren't coming back. No one cared about Funbug. Depressed, he took a surfing vacation, and that's when he came up with the idea for GoPro and pioneered wearable cameras for recording everything from skydiving to surfing and shark riding.

This isn't unusual. Google started as a tool for finding academic research papers online before switching to general search. YouTube was a video dating site. Groupon was a site for social causes called The Point. Slack was a game. And Twitter began as a podcasting company. None of these startups had it all figured out in the beginning, so why do you think you should be any smarter?

Even more surprising, many of the most successful entrepreneurs didn't even come up with the concept for their startups. Elon Musk didn't come up with the idea for Tesla. He wasn't even a cofounder. He was an investor who assumed the CEO role when the electric car company began to stall out. Similarly, Travis Kalanick didn't come up with the idea for Uber. He was also an early investor who jumped in once he saw the potential. As an entrepreneur, your job isn't necessarily to come up with the world's most brilliant idea. Your job is to recognize the opportunity and run with it.

Your job isn't necessarily to come up with the world's most brilliant idea. Your job is to recognize the opportunity and run with it.

Focusing too much on the idea at the very beginning is not only a waste of time; it puts you on the wrong track. I've seen entrepreneurs spend months, even years, working on an idea by themselves, and it's only when they get stuck that they start casting about for cofounders. The problem is that, by then, they don't want to give a newcomer much in the way of equity. After all, they already spent a lot of time and money on their idea. So, giving up any equity is painful. This turns off the best cofounders who don't want to receive a tiny amount of equity to work on someone else's project. They might as well do their own thing.

For this reason alone, most solo entrepreneurs who focus on their idea at the expense of team building wind up failing. I always tell entrepreneurs to forget about their ideas. Ideas don't matter. They're just a starting point. Instead, focus all your energy on bringing in the best possible talent. People are what matters. Nothing will have a greater impact on your success. In fact, if you toss your initial idea out the window, you'll be better off. Instead of thinking of ideas, think of the direction you want to head. Focus on an area or problem that really interests you. Then look for other people who are fascinated by this same thing. Together, you can figure out what works and what doesn't. In the end, it doesn't matter whose idea it is as long as it's the right idea.

⚹

Focus all your energy on bringing in the
best possible talent—nothing will have
a greater impact on your success.

This approach instantly empowers your cofounders. They aren't being asked to work on your idea. Instead, they are being asked to contribute their own ideas and work together to figure out how to build the business. Now they have ownership, and it's not just equity. It's psychological ownership. You're enabling them to give birth to the company with you and raise the baby together. So, hold off on developing your ideas until you've built the best possible team.

5

What's the Right Team?

LET ME BEGIN BY POINTING out that it's incredibly difficult to launch a startup when you're alone. I've seen this firsthand with many companies that I have mentored. For a solo founder, it's easy to give up when you hit a low point. There's no one there to lift you up when you stumble. However, if you have cofounders to whom you've committed, you're much more likely to stick it out. You owe it to them. It's like the Marines. You're in the trenches with your buddies. They're counting on you, and even if you're scared to death, you're not about to let them down. When you're faced with an impossible situation, they have your back, and you have theirs. You're going to make it out together.

Most entrepreneurs are short on money, so it's difficult to hire the right people. You need to have a team willing to work like crazy because they believe in the mission and are vested in the company—not because you're paying them. Even if you have enough cash, it's better to pay in equity. It binds them to your vision. It also allows you to save your cash for those unavoidable expenses that always come up.

Another problem with paying cash is that it sets the wrong expectations. Most startups run out of money at some point, and the employees who are used to receiving regular paychecks often get discouraged and leave the company. I've seen this happen countless times. With startups, the initial idea often doesn't work, so the entrepreneur has to redo it—not once, but several times. What seems like a manageable budget can quickly spiral out of control, until the bank account is dry. At this point, the startup can get stalled and die a slow, painful death.

When the going gets tough and you're out of cash, all you typically have are your cofounders. Without them, you're sunk. The importance of having dedicated cofounders is evident in the number of founders that make up most unicorns (startups valued at $1 billion or more). Here's the data from an early crop of unicorns:

- Four unicorns had one founder each.
- Thirteen unicorns had two founders each.
- Fourteen unicorns had three founders each.
- Four unicorns had four founders each.
- Three unicorns had five founders each.
- Only one unicorn had six founders.

As you can see, there's a direct correlation between the success of the startups and the number of cofounders. The optimal number tends to be two or three. If you don't have cofounders, at least bring on dedicated employees and compensate them mostly in equity. Think of them and treat them as cofounders. Everyone on the core team should be given equity and responsibility. If these first employees aren't good enough to be treated as cofounders, then they definitely aren't good enough for your startup.

※

There's a direct correlation between the success of startups and the number of cofounders.

That brings me back to contractors. They are the opposite of cofounders in how they think and act, especially if they're being paid in cash, not equity. Fixed-fee contractors want to get the work done in the minimum time possible because completing the work early maximizes their returns. This results in goal misalignment. Not only that, even if they don't tell you, they are probably juggling multiple jobs at the same time. They do this in order to even out their erratic income. This means they can't spend too long laboring on any one project. They have to keep bouncing between projects, which scatters their attention. Don't expect your typical contractor to come up with many light-bulb moments. They are focused on completion, not invention, but it's precisely these epiphanies that a startup needs to break through.

If you want to increase your odds of success, you should build a team that's 100 percent committed to the project and nothing else. You need everyone, from customer service to engineering, obsessed with how to make your company number one. On the weekends, during commutes, in the shower, and in the wee hours of the night, each member of your team should be thinking of how to do things faster, smarter, and better. If you're going to invest your time in them, they need to be fully invested in the business. Otherwise, you're diminishing your own power.

Think of the team as an extension of yourself. You are all parts of a single being. If one part isn't performing well, it limits the performance of the whole. In the early stages, everyone needs to live and breathe the startup in order to come up with that one special insight that changes everything. Having half your mind in hyperdrive, while the other half is distracted, doesn't cut it. Innovation is about going further than anyone else, and a team can't do that if everyone isn't working toward the same goal.

I have a rule: Never bring on a cofounder or early employee who isn't willing to drop everything else he or she is doing and commit heart and soul to the mission.

I remember with my third startup, my cofounder, Adam Zbar, kept asking: "Are we all in? Are we all in?" He wouldn't stop until we all pledged that we were 110 percent committed. He knew that without the commitment, we had nothing.

I've seen so many founders fumble the ball because each member of their team wasn't committed to the same play. You may have found one of the best people in the world, but if this person isn't truly committed, you can run into problems.

One CEO whom I coached found a brilliant engineer at Google who was interested in what his startup was doing, but this engineer would only commit to working nights and weekends. He didn't want to give up his Google lifestyle. This was fine in the beginning. The engineer was motivated. It was an interesting project, and things were humming along. But eventually the fun turned into hard work, and the engineer had a deadline at Google as well as personal obligations. Guess what? He stopped responding. At first, they didn't hear from him for a few days at a time, then a week, then a few weeks. The entire time, their startup was on hold. It was excruciating for the CEO. What could he do? He'd already invested months with this engineer. The guy had written the entire code base. The startup couldn't afford to switch and start over. *Arrgghh!*

Try not to put yourself in this position. Nothing is worse than struggling to get someone to do something when they don't care as much as you do. So, when you're bringing on cofounders or early employees, ask them one question: "Are you interested or committed?" If they're interested, you can stop right there. They are of little or no use to you. Yes, they can be a part-time advisor, but don't fool yourself into thinking they're going to be there when you really need them. If they say they're committed, find out just how committed they are. Are they willing to quit their job? Do they have a problem working nights and weekends? Are they planning a long vacation this summer? How far are they willing to go to make this startup succeed?

*Ask cofounders and early employees if they're
interested or committed? If they're interested,
you can stop right there.*

Being committed is more of a mindset than anything else. Not everyone can quit a day job at first, but everyone must be prepared to do whatever it takes to make the company succeed. If someone doesn't have this mindset, it's going to cause problems down the road. You must promise me that you'll follow this rule. Only bring people on the team if you believe they're mentally prepared to go all the way. If you don't get this commitment, don't let them on the team. Keep searching. A startup is just too hard to have people with one foot out the door.

My next rule for team building: Never, ever settle on a person you feel is not absolutely, positively the best. You can only afford excellence. I don't care if you don't have any money. I don't care if the person you just interviewed seems like they can do the job. If they aren't exceptional, you're wasting your time. The early team members will make or break your company. Finding them is the first test as to whether you're CEO material or not. If you cannot find them and convince them to work for you for equity, you don't have what it takes to run a startup. Go get a job. You'll be happier.

The reason you should never bring on someone you don't think is incredible is that you'll likely regret it. Firing someone is awful. You wind up wasting so much time and money. There are two types of people: amplifiers and diminishers. Amplifiers take whatever energy you put into them and make it ten times bigger. You spend one hour with them, and they produce exponentially more and better work. Diminishers are the opposite. Whatever time and energy you invest in them winds up yielding less. In a startup, you need amplifiers. You need teammates who are outrunning you. Even before you think of what they should be doing next, they're already all over it.

The ideal engineer for an early-stage startup is a full-stack developer. When you only have one or two coders, it's good if they can tackle a wide array of problems. I always look for engineers whose idea of fun is spending the weekend contributing to open-source projects, attending hackathons, tweaking servers, and scouring the local electronics store for just the right parts for the new gizmo thingy they are building. Having a freak who dreams in hexadecimal and pontificates about the merits of proper coding syntax can be a blessing when it comes to solving hard problems.

The same is true for every single person on your core team. Whether it's marketing, sales, or design, you need full-stack personalities. They must all own their job so completely that nothing seems impossible to them. If you have the slightest doubt, run in the other direction. When building a team, especially in the early stages, anyone who is not best of breed is not an option. There's no room for mediocrity. Anyone less than excellent will just slow down the rest of your team. Unless you have an incredible team, you have nothing but an idea. And ideas alone are worthless without execution.

Ideas without execution are worthless.

Last, get people who aren't exactly like you. You don't want to be surrounded with clones of yourself. That doesn't give you any competitive advantage. You want people who see the world differently and will challenge your ideas and inject their own thoughts and perspective into the process. We see this time and again in successful teams. At Salesforce, the CEO, Marc Benioff, is a three-hundred-pound, six-foot-five, fist-pounding force of nature with an oversized personality, while his cofounder, Parker Harris, is a modest, good-natured listener.

"They're the yin and yang," says Chuck Dietrich, who spent nine years at Salesforce. "It's not the optimist-pessimist, but more like a futurist and reality."[1]

A similar dynamic played out at Apple, with Steve Jobs being the outgoing, creative visionary, and Steve Wozniak the thoughtful pragmatist. If you look at the most successful teams, they tend to be made up of opposites who manage to work well together and complement one another.

6

Paying for Talent

ONCE YOU FIND THESE PEOPLE, give them a giant bear hug and never let go. I mean it. These folks are the soul of your company. They will take you all the way to the Promised Land. But you have to treat them well.

By this, I mean don't be cheap. Make them real cofounders—not glorified employees. If you're offering them less than 5 percent equity at the early stages, they are nothing but hired hands. If they're going to be true cofounders, they should have 5 percent or more, depending on their role and value. In my early startups, all of the cofounders received equal equity. That isn't a requirement. A lot of times the CEO gets more, but we felt it was right for us.

What I'm describing is true for Silicon Valley, but it's not the case in countries like China, where investors feel the CEO should retain absolute control over the company and give out as few shares as possible to anyone else. This is a cultural difference. China is a hierarchical society, and people are accustomed to having the big boss in complete control. In fact, Chinese investors get worried if the CEO doesn't own the majority of shares. They are betting on the CEO, and they want to make sure he doesn't lose power.

The cultural differences go even deeper. In Silicon Valley, most people believe the generosity shouldn't stop with the cofounders. Everyone on the team, from early employees to advisors, should get their fair share. I see a lot of startup founders fretting over equity. They don't want to get diluted too quickly, so they begin hoarding shares. I can understand the feeling. I've felt that way, too. But it's counterproductive. Remember, doing a startup is an all-or-nothing game. In most cases, you're either going to wind up incredibly rich or with nothing at all. That's just how the math works out once you start taking on venture capital. You will cross the finish line with a big win, or else the creditors and investors will gobble everything up. So, there's no point in being stingy. You should use your precious equity to attract the very best talent in the business and never look back. That's what your equity is for.

※

Use your precious equity to attract the very best talent in the business . . . and never look back.

The same is true when it comes to funding in Silicon Valley. If a top-tier venture capitalist with an incredible track record is offering you a lower valuation than a novice investor, go with the best. Yes, there are limits to what you should accept in terms of valuation, but don't be cheap. This person will most likely be on your board of directors and help determine the fate of your company. The wrong person can lead to big mistakes and missed opportunities that far outweigh the dilution you will take.

When it comes to advisors, the same is true. At every stage of your growth, recruiting top advisors is essential. The more valuable they are, the more you should compensate them. It's not uncommon to give an advisor anywhere from 0.25 percent to 1 percent of the company at the early stages. If you are worried about giving away so much of the company, put down in writing what you expect from them and tie it directly to the equity disbursements. You can have the shares vest over time, so if they don't deliver, you don't lose out.

Once you raise a larger funding round, start paying your team, advisors, and even board members. Yes, it might up your burn rate, but it's the right thing to do, and your team will realize how much you value them.

You aren't just using them. You are looking out for them. Again, don't be cheap. Pay higher than the industry average. You want everyone to stick with you all the way to the end. Money speaks volumes. Remember, the cost of an employee jumping ship is so much higher than the difference between an average and above average salary. Err on the generous side, and you won't be sorry.

7

Should You Copy Competitors?

YES. COPY, COPY, COPY! THE most brilliant people in the world copy. Jack Ma copied eBay when he first launched Alibaba, which is now the most successful retailer in China. Pony Ma copied ICQ and launched QQ, the precursor to WeChat. Mark Zuckerberg copied Friendster and MySpace when he launched Facebook. Larry Page and Sergey Brin used Alta Vista as their inspiration for Google. Steve Jobs copied Xerox PARC when he created the Mac. You wouldn't believe how many breakthrough products began as copycats. That's because copying is the best business model in the world—bar none.

Nothing beats copying for lowering risk. If you can be the first to enter a brand-new market with an idea that's proven to work, there's a lot of money to be made. Rocket Internet used this strategy to build the world's largest copycat factory. They launched Lazada (an Amazon clone) in Southeast Asia, BillPay (a PayPal clone) in Germany, Kaymu (an eBay clone) in Nigeria, EasyTaxi (an Uber clone) in Latin America, StudiVZ (a Facebook clone) in Germany, Payleven (a Square clone) in Europe, and the list goes on. They were extremely successful for a while with more than seventy-five companies spread across more than fifty countries, but then the market caught up with them. Everyone else started copying Silicon Valley, too, and there was simply too much competition and a lack of innovation.

What you must remember is that copying should only be your starting point. You need to innovate beyond the existing model to ensure long-term success. If you look at Alibaba and Tencent today, they are nothing like their first incarnations. Alibaba is investing $15 billion into quantum computing, connected devices, fintech, human-machine interaction, AI, and big data, while WeChat has pioneered mobile commerce with a revolutionary payment system that makes Facebook look antiquated.

Copying is a great place to start, but if you stop there, you will lose. My rule of thumb is to copy everything your competitors do right, and then begin innovating on top of this. No one starts from scratch. Every innovation and invention that exists is based on what came before it. So, don't dismiss copycats. It's what all of us do, and if you aren't copying what your competitors do best, you aren't being smart. Your competitors have invested countless hours and large sums of money to get where they are. You would be foolish not to take advantage of everything they've learned.

※

Copy everything your competitors do right.
Then innovate on top of this.

When I sit down with a startup, I always ask the founders about their competitors. I want to see how much time they've spent with those products. Do they truly understand what makes their competitors great? If they don't know much about their competition and haven't copied their best ideas, I get nervous. What's wrong with this startup? Smart entrepreneurs venture deep into enemy territory, scouting out everything they can. If they're going to win the battle, they need as much intelligence on the enemy as possible. They must analyze every last feature, function, and facet of the competitive landscape. Knowledge is the key to victory.

If you haven't done it already, you should prioritize using your competitors' products daily. You need to become one of their power users. This is the only way to understand everything they're doing. It's not only important to look at the current crop of competitors, but also to look at past competitors. They can teach you even more. I was mentoring a startup about to launch a location-based social network. Their idea was that you could see where all your friends were on a map and interact with them. The first thing I told them was the honest truth: "You are going to fail if you head down this path. Do you know how many people have tried this and failed before you? Facebook even added this feature, and it wasn't popular. What makes you think you can succeed now?"

This wasn't the only startup I met who failed to do adequate market research. It's one of the most common mistakes founders make. Everyone wants to believe their idea is original, so they hop onto Google, do a few quick searches, and then declare victory. That's not enough. I know because I failed to do this for my own startup, and it was embarrassing. We'd spent months working on a product we thought was revolutionary, only to discover someone had launched exactly the same product several years earlier and not succeeded. They were bankrupt, and we were heading down the same path. That was a shocker. Even the dead can teach you a lot. Don't make the same mistake.

8

Where Do Great Ideas Come From?

HOW DO YOU COME UP with a brilliant idea? Where do you look for inspiration? Try starting with yourself. Many of the most successful entrepreneurs begin by building something they desperately want or need but can't find in the marketplace. Then they leverage everything and everybody around them. The reason this strategy works well is because these entrepreneurs know what the customer wants, since they are that customer. There's no guesswork involved.

That's what Patagonia founder Yvon Chouinard did. He couldn't find any high-quality pitons for mountain climbing, so he went into his parents' backyard, converted the chicken coop into a little blacksmith's shop, and built them himself. That was the start of his multibillion-dollar, outdoor gear and clothing empire. He kept doing it over and over. He couldn't find a good climbing shirt, so he made one. Then came climbing shorts. Eventually, he expanded into other outdoor segments. "If you want to understand entrepreneurs," says Chouinard, "study the juvenile delinquent because they're saying: 'You know, this sucks. I'm going to do it my own way.' And that's what the entrepreneur does."[1]

Another entrepreneur who solved her own problem is Sara Blakely. While selling fax machines door-to-door in the Florida heat, she often wore pantyhose. Blakely hated the appearance of the seamed foot while wearing open-toed shoes but liked the way that the control top model eliminated panty lines and made her body appear firmer. That's when she experimented with the idea of cutting off the feet of her pantyhose while wearing them under a new pair of slacks. It worked, except that the pantyhose rolled up her legs. With $5,000, she set out to fix this problem, launching Spanx. It became a hit with women across the country and made her a billionaire.

When Chieh Huang launched his startup, Boxed, he was trying to solve a problem he had. He was used to shopping at Costco, but when he moved to the city, he gave up his car, which made it a real hassle to get the bulk-sized packages to his apartment. That's when the light bulb went off. He would launch a startup that gave millennials a way to save on bulk-sized orders, combined with the conveniences of ordering through a mobile app and door-to-door delivery.

"I was basically trying to solve a problem that I myself have,"[2] says Huang. Apparently, a lot of other people had the same problem. In just three years, Boxed went from $40,000 in sales out of his parents' garage to more than $100 million in revenue and more than $160 million in VC (venture capital) funding.

At Founders Space, I'm always looking for entrepreneurs who are solving their own worst problems. I remember when Richard Lin came to me with his startup Thryve. He told me the story of how he took an antibiotic and wound up extremely sick, to the point of being hospitalized. This prompted him to research the microbiome, which is composed of the bacteria, yeast, and viruses that reside in our bodies and help determine our health. Surprisingly, the bacteria cells in our body outnumber human cells ten to one. This led him to come up with the idea for launching the most comprehensive way to gather, test, and analyze the microbiome and provide the results to consumers online.

The great thing about tackling a problem you have is that you are the customer. You don't have to interview anyone or take wild guesses. You know exactly what you want and understand the issues involved. This clarity is why so many entrepreneurs find success when focusing on their own problems, rather than the problems of others. If you can't think of what to do, look at your own life and the things that annoy you. Then work backward.

9

Defining the Problem

IT HELPS TO BEGIN BY clearly defining a problem to be solved and who will benefit from the solution. Below are five questions every entrepreneur should answer:

1. What is the problem?
2. What is the solution?
3. Who is the customer?
4. What are the benefits?
5. How large is the market?

Try answering each of these five questions in three sentences or less. You should take your time to write this as concisely as possible, then read it aloud to friends who know nothing about your business and see if they get it. If they don't, rewrite it until they do.

Creating an Elevator Pitch

THE NEXT STEP IS CRAFTING your elevator pitch. When you bump into a friendly investor in an elevator, at a cocktail party, or on the golf course, it helps to have your pitch ready to go. Here's a template that works. Keep each answer to one sentence, if possible. Remember, it's an elevator pitch, meaning you have to be able to say it before the doors open, which means in thirty seconds or less.

- Hello, I'm _____ (insert your name).
- Founder of _____ (insert your company).
- We make _____ (describe your product).
- For _____ (describe your customers).
- We solve _____ (explain the problem).
- By doing _____ (describe your solution).
- Our secret sauce is _____ (what makes you special).

Now test it out on people who have never heard of your startup. Spend five hours in an elevator accosting people. See if they actually grasp what you're saying. If they get a confused look on their faces, you know you've failed. By the time you're done, your elevator pitch should be so simple that even your great aunt Agnes gets it without asking a single follow-up question.

11

Should You Be Careful?

WE ALL KNOW THAT DOING a startup is risky, but is it wise to take big chances? Shouldn't you mitigate risk, play it safe, and stick with something you know will work?

It depends on what you want. For a slow-growth, traditional business, limiting risk is a fine strategy. However, if you want to break new ground, leapfrog the competition, and experience hypergrowth, risk is built into the equation. You cannot eliminate risk and come out on top in a winner-take-all market.

Let's say you take the safe path and focus on an idea you know will work because you've seen others do it before and make a lot of money. While this will reduce your risk because you know there's a market, it also limits your upside. Without blazing new ground, you cannot change your industry. Without innovating beyond what's already been successful, you cannot gain a significant competitive advantage. By definition, innovation means trying something new that hasn't been done before. The greater the innovative leap, the greater the risk, but also the greater the chance of achieving exponential gains.

In other words, safe startups aren't venture fundable. If a safe bet is making money now, you can be sure everyone is rushing to get a piece of the action. The market will be crowded in no time, and profit margins will get squeezed. It's extremely hard to build a billion-dollar business on a safe bet.

*The greater the innovative leap, the greater the risk,
the greater the chance of achieving exponential gains.*

When I see startup founders taking big risks, I'm thrilled. But when I see them get scared and stop taking chances, that's when I worry they won't win big in the end. The truly great entrepreneurs are always doubling down on their bets. They can't help but push it further. In the early days of Nike, Phil Knight, the founder and CEO, was constantly on the verge of bankruptcy. During Nike's explosive growth phase, he continually bet everything on the next month's receipts. He didn't know if he'd make payroll, but somehow, he pulled it off each time. And that led to Nike becoming the fastest growing shoe company in the world.

If you are not a risk taker and do not have this fire in your belly, you might want to consider another profession.

12

Keeping It Secret?

NO, PLEASE DON'T KEEP IT secret! That's a huge mistake. As I said before, there's a high probability that your idea, as it stands now, isn't startup-worthy. The only way you're going to find out is by sharing it with other people: customers, advisors, investors, strategic partners, friends, and family. If you keep your idea secret, you won't get the feedback and data you need to even know if it works or not, until it's too late.

I'm not saying you should go and announce your idea at a conference in front of a room full of competitors. That would be foolish. But don't let your fear of someone stealing your idea keep you from engaging the outside world. Let me put it this way. The chance of someone you know stealing your idea is probably less than one-tenth of one percent, while the chance of you failing because you haven't exposed your idea to the right people early on, when you have the time and resources to make a change, is upward of 80 percent. So, which risk do you want to take? Keeping your idea to yourself is irrational at best and the quickest way to failure at worst.

I can tell you from personal experience that far more startups fail because of excessive secrecy than exorbitant openness. Let me give you one example. There was a company in Los Angeles that had an amazing idea for a product no one was developing. Instead of keeping it secret, the founder did the opposite. He created a video that showed off the full potential of his idea, and he put this video up on Kickstarter for the world to see. The founder didn't even have any technology to back up the idea. In fact, he had nothing more than a vague notion about how to build the final product, but that didn't stop him. He was fearless. He didn't worry that others would steal his concept. He was more concerned with making it happen.

Sure enough, the world reacted. When people saw his idea, they started preordering the product. He vastly exceeded his Kickstarter goal. This caught the attention of tech bloggers who wrote about his amazing vision. When the mainstream press heard about it, the story went viral. In no time, everyone was talking about his idea. It was the furthest thing from a secret.

Word got around to Silicon Valley investors, and they couldn't resist. They began competing to fund his company. Remember, he didn't even have a product yet, and his idea was based on open-source software that anyone could use. Despite this, he raised tens of millions of dollars, and his idea spread around the world. That's when Facebook took notice and stepped in to buy his startup for $2 billion. This startup hadn't even released its product yet. It was years away from launch. What company was this? You know the name. It was Oculus VR, and its product was the Oculus Rift, which didn't actually launch until four years after that first video.

This is the power of sharing your idea. Oculus named and claimed virtual reality as its own. It built a brand even before it brought a product to market, and that brand, along with the promise of leading the virtual reality wave, was worth $2 billion to Mark Zuckerberg. Do you know what would have happened if Oculus VR hadn't shared its idea for fear someone else would steal it? Nothing. That's right. Virtual reality wasn't a secret. There were researchers all over the world who were working on it. The founder, Palmer Lucky, tapped into an open-source project at the University of Southern California. He didn't develop the technology, but the difference was he made it a reality by showing the world the full potential, riding the tsunami of excitement it generated all the way to the bank. All of those other folks, some of whom probably had much more advanced technology in their labs, ended up with nothing.

This is an extreme example of sharing an idea. Palmer Lucky truly got lucky. But I see the same thing play out over and over. The first-mover advantage is huge. If you can catch the wave by generating excitement, you can shoot ahead of everyone else. Being out there early with your vision makes you the thought leader, and that can translate into market leadership if you play your cards right.

There's also a more important reason to share your idea with the world. It gives you the feedback you need to test your assumptions. You may think there's a demand for your product, but until you put it in front of your customers and gauge their reaction, you have no idea what the demand really is. This is especially true for concepts that are breaking new ground. The newer and more radical your vision, the more you need early feedback.

✳

The newer and more radical your vision,
the more you need early feedback.

The goal of every startup should be to get as much feedback as early as possible, so it can course correct, and if necessary, pivot before it runs out of time and money. The clock is your real enemy. If you don't move fast, you will lose out to competitors. Remember, any idea you have is probably not new. There are close to eight billion people in the world. Some other entrepreneur is bound to be thinking the same thing. Do you want that person to get all the credit for pioneering the way? If not, don't keep your idea a secret. Get it in front of as many smart people as possible as early as possible, and don't stop until you sell your company or go public.

When Do You Quit?

ENTREPRENEURS COME UP TO ME all the time and ask if they should quit. They've usually invested years of their time and all of their money into the business. It's their life, but it hasn't taken off. They need to know how much longer they should keep pursuing the idea.

Each time I get this question, I answer the same way: "Yes, yes, yes. You should quit right now."

Why would I say this when I know the poor entrepreneurs have invested their reputation, life's savings, time, and dreams into this project? How could I be so callous? I will tell you how. The entrepreneurs wouldn't be asking me this question if they didn't already know the answer. No one wants to give up on their baby. No one wants to lose money. No one wants to fail. They are coming to me asking for permission to move on with their lives. They know the business isn't working, or we wouldn't be having this conversation. No one asks you if they should quit when things are progressing. In this case, it's clear all hope is gone, and it's just a matter of time before it fails. It's far better to cut the losses now than waste another six months or a year. That's just too painful.

This is why I tell them to quit. I'm not saying give up being an entrepreneur. I'm telling them to give up on this idea. They've tried everything, exhausted all possibilities, and they must move on. Great entrepreneurs quit often, but they never give up. They try one idea, and if it doesn't work, they cut their losses, swallow their pride, and move on to the next one. More entrepreneurs fail because they are afraid of quitting and hang on too long.

＊

Great entrepreneurs quit often, but they never give up.

It's hard to give up on something you believe in, but as soon as the data disproves your thesis, you need to drop it. Otherwise, you wind up like Sisyphus, rolling the same boulder up the hill, only to have it roll back down on you. I tell entrepreneurs, if you can't get an overwhelmingly positive reaction from your target customers after six months of introducing the product, it's time to move on. Otherwise, you will become Sisyphus.

14

Killing Your Baby

ENTREPRENEURS LIKE TO BELIEVE IT'S their duty to show the world how great their idea is. Despite all odds and legions of doubters, they must convince investors, employees, customers, bloggers, and everyone else that their vision will succeed no matter what. They must do everything possible to prove their concept works, even if the world is against them. I'm sorry, but this is a myth. Reality couldn't be further from the truth. When launching a startup, the entrepreneur's goal should be the opposite.

Your mission is not to prove your idea is right. It's to prove your idea is dead wrong. You must demonstrate that your grand vision cannot possibly succeed. Most ideas suck. An idea without any data to back it up is worthless. It's just make-believe. Your goal is not to convince everyone that you have all the answers. It's to uncover every reason your plan cannot possibly turn into a real business. Ask yourself which experiments you can run that will poke gaping holes in your project. How can you undermine your assumptions? What is the weakest point in your designs?

※

Your mission is not to prove your idea is right.
It's to prove your idea is dead wrong.

This may sound easy, but it's not. There will come a time in your life when you love your baby so much that you never want to let it go. It's your dream. You've invested your hopes, money, and life into it. That's the moment you have to remember these words: It's time to kill your baby.

It's never easy to let go of something you love, but sometimes there's no choice. I have a rule: If everyone tells you your baby is ugly, believe them. It's ugly. Fortunately, ideas are not human beings. You may have given birth to this creature, but it won't cry when it's tossed in the trash. You may cry, but it won't feel a thing.

If you're going to come up with that killer idea, you need to get used to killing. Your job is to slay as many babies as quickly as possible. I know this is a gruesome metaphor, but I need to make a point. You must prove to yourself and the world that your beloved vision is complete nonsense. The sooner you can do that, the sooner you can move on to the next idea. Only when you've exhausted all possible ways to shatter your vision should you start to believe in it. That's when your baby becomes real. Before that, your baby only exists inside your head.

15

Speed and Experimentation

THE FASTER YOU LEARN TO slay your babies, the better entrepreneur you'll become. This is what we call failing fast. Ironically, the faster you fail, the quicker you'll succeed. It's all about speed, iteration, and experimentation.

※

The faster you fail, the quicker you'll succeed.

It goes like this. Try something. Sorry, doesn't work. Try something else. Doesn't work. Try something else. Yes, it's working. It's working! It doesn't work. Start over.

Great entrepreneurs keep doing this again and again until they hit pay dirt. Each time, they are learning a bit more about the market and their customers. The faster they can learn, the bigger their competitive advantage. It's a race for knowledge. The entrepreneur needs to figure something out that the competition doesn't know, use it to gain a significant advantage, and then steal the market. That's what entrepreneurs do best. That's how they catapult past established players.

It's not only a race against your opponents but also against yourself. You need to cross the finish line before you burn through all your cash, family relationships, goodwill, and, most important, hope. The clock is constantly ticking. You can't waste a single day on something that won't move you a step closer.

This race is never in a straight line. It's more like a spiral. It's made of iterative cycles that lead you down a path. Each twist and turn in the path is another spiral. We call this process the *innovation loop*.

1. Come up with an idea.
2. Break down your idea into testable hypotheses.
3. Begin with your most critical hypothesis.
4. Devise an experiment to disprove it.
5. Gather data from the experiment.
6. Analyze and learn from the data.
7. If the data is positive, iterate, and test the next assumption (go to #2).
8. If the data is negative, pivot to the next idea (go to #1).

These eight steps define your track. Coming up with the idea is just the first step. The hard part is devising smart, quick, low-cost experiments. Each successful experiment means you're that much closer to your goal of validating your idea. The best entrepreneurs run around and around this track as fast as possible, and in the process, they learn more and go deeper than anyone else. That's how they win.

You need to place this process at the core of your startup. Think of your idea as a pointer, indicating the direction you're interested in exploring. The idea itself isn't the answer. It's only a compass. Head off in that direction but remain flexible. You will have to change lanes many times as you iterate. If you hit a dead end, it's time to start over, taking everything that you've learned and plowing it back into the next race—over and over, until you figure it out.

16

Why Do Startups Fail?

I SPEND A LOT OF time talking about failure because it's every entrepreneur's worst nightmare. There's no way to eliminate the risk. But there is a way to increase your odds of success, and that's by learning what others did wrong and staying vigilant so that you don't follow in their footsteps.

We'll focus on a study by CB Insights, where they analyzed more than a hundred startup postmortems and came up with the twenty most common reasons startups go belly-up. Many companies cited multiple reasons, so the percentages don't add up to 100 percent. Also, keep in mind that this is a self-analysis from the startup founders' point of view, so it's far from perfect. Even with this inherent bias, it provides valuable insights into why failures happen and how to avoid them.

- Forty-two percent can't find a product-market fit—This simply means their target customers didn't need or want the startup's product. This is the number one reason for startup failure. It's all too common for entrepreneurs to launch an innovative, groundbreaking product only to discover nobody actually cares.
- Twenty-nine percent run out of cash—Many startups build a business but then hit a rough patch where they are short on cash but have to make payroll or pay back creditors. If they

can't get a cash infusion in time, it can sink them—even though their long-term prospects might be excellent.

- Twenty-three percent don't have the right team—The quality of the team can make or break a startup. Entrepreneurs often fail because their team can't execute. Sometimes it's the lack of key skill sets or an inability to adapt to changing circumstances. This is a solvable problem, but many entrepreneurs don't spend enough time teambuilding up front and pay the price down the road, wasting precious resources and time.

- Nineteen percent get outcompeted—The world is hypercompetitive. One day a startup can be way ahead, and the next it's surrounded by cutthroats. These can be big corporations with unlimited resources or low-margin copycats dumping cheap products on the market. Either way, it can spell the end of a startup that doesn't have something defensible.

- Eighteen percent experience pricing and cost issues—A lot of entrepreneurs set prices based on how they feel. They go with their emotions instead of relying on data and experienced experts to determine the optimal price point. It's easy to underprice a product, then fall prey to cost overruns, quality control issues, and manufacturing delays. Other times, founders overprice their products, only to discover that their customers aren't willing to pay more. The more research and market testing a startup can do up front, the better.

- Seventeen percent have poor products—It's not easy to build great products, but that's what it takes to win. In technology, it's usually a winner-take-all world, where only the very best survive.

- Seventeen percent have a bad business model—As we discussed, a startup needs to figure out its business model, and not all business models are created equal. Some make a lot of money, and others never work.

- Fourteen percent suffer from poor marketing—A startup can have the best product in the world, but if no one knows about it, it won't go anywhere. There are simply too many products,

and most people aren't even aware of half the choices—
especially those from smaller companies.

- Thirteen percent ignore customers—Startups ignore their customers at their own peril. Engaging customers, gathering feedback, and collecting and analyzing data are essential to growing a business. Without doing this, a startup is running blind, and it's only a matter of time before it smacks into a tree.

- Thirteen percent have bad timing—Timing is everything. If a startup's product is too early or too late, it can miss the window of opportunity.

- Thirteen percent lose focus—Trying to do too many things at once is more dangerous than doing too little. Staying laser focused on solving the most important customer problems is how startups succeed. I've seen many startups who try to do five different things at a time, and invariably, all of them fail. Only by focusing can a startup go deep enough to gain the subtle insights that enable it to outcompete everyone else. In the early days of Salesforce, a major telecom offered a multimillion-dollar deal for a custom solution. This would have been the biggest deal in its short history, but the offer was turned down because it would have distracted from Salesforce's main focus to build the best CRM (customer relationship management) platform possible.

- Thirteen percent feud with investors or the team—I've seen how disagreements between the founders can kill a startup. The same is true with investors. If communication isn't good, and everyone is working at cross purposes, it's not long before the company implodes.

- Ten percent try a failed pivot—Changing directions isn't easy for a startup. Most pivots fail. Often, it's like starting over, except the entrepreneurs lack the money, resources, and staying power to see it through.

- Nine percent lack passion—If the founders don't have a passion for their business, it's hard to keep going when they hit a low point.

- Nine percent have a bad location—You know what they say in real estate: location, location, location. It's what matters most for some businesses, especially retail.
- Eight percent lack financing or investor interest—It pays to know what investors are looking to fund. When a sector or technology falls out of favor, most VCs (venture capitalists) won't even bother taking a closer look. On the other hand, if the sector is hot and investors aren't biting, then there's usually something seriously wrong with the startup.
- Eight percent suffer legal challenges—It pays to know the law. Sometimes governments heavily regulate or outright ban certain businesses. Other times, it's patent litigation or employee lawsuits that can kill a startup. Retaining counsel from the best lawyers early on is important.
- Eight percent don't use networks or advisors—Most entrepreneurs don't fully leverage their networks. It's not enough to have a board of advisors and a deep network. Startups need to know how to use those relationships effectively to achieve their goals.
- Eight percent burn out—Getting exhausted and burned out is a constant problem. The right mental framework and a balanced life are key. Doing a startup is not a sprint; it's a marathon. Make sure to set aside time to go on walks, exercise, meditate, and spend time with friends and family. A good strategy is to designate one day a week for activities outside of your startup, and don't let any business obligations interfere. Without this time, you can't have a balanced life.
- Seven percent fail to pivot—Too many startups continue on the same path for too long, failing to recognize that what they're doing isn't working. Often, by the time they admit their mistake, it's too late. They are out of money, time, and the will to go on. Be prepared to change directions over and over. If it feels like time to pivot, it probably is.

If you can avoid these twenty missteps, you're in good shape, but as we all know, it's easier said than done. It's hard to recognize your own mistakes as they are happening and even harder to take decisive action. Sometimes you'll realize there's a problem but ignore it because you're just too busy, you feel overwhelmed, or you can't come up with a viable solution. That's why it's critical to get feedback from mentors on the outside. They can point out problems that you don't even want to admit to yourself. Checking in with these mentors on a regular basis and getting their honest feedback can help you avoid the myopia that kills many startups. This is your reality check. Use it.

17

Rewriting the Rules

FOR AN ENTREPRENEUR, IT PAYS to rewrite the rules. If you follow the existing rules, it's hard to win. Why? Because the big, established players wrote those rules. It's like starting a game of Monopoly where all your competitors have monopolies with hotels, and you don't own a single piece of property. How can you hope to compete?

Instead, you need to say to yourself, "How can I make their monopolies worthless?" Look at what the established players are doing and ask, "Can I do this differently?" If they are using retail distribution, then you should look for alternative channels, like web, mobile, and social. If they are locking their customers into long-term contracts, you should consider having no contracts. If they are selling products individually, you might want to sell in bulk. Take whatever they are doing and see if you can flip it on its head to gain an unfair advantage.

✕

Look at what the established players are doing
and ask, "Can I do this differently?"

Chouinard, founder of Patagonia, sums this up beautifully: "If you want to be successful in business, you don't go up against Coca-Cola and, you know, these big companies. They'll kill you. You just do it differently. You figure out something that no one else has thought about and you do it in a totally different way. And so breaking the rules, you have to be creative. And that's the fun part of business, actually. I love breaking the rules."[1]

When breaking the rules, you may have to push into gray zones where you don't even know if it's legal. Uber didn't ask for permission to run a taxi service without taxi medallions. Airbnb ignored city zoning or administrative codes. Cryptocurrencies, like Bitcoin, didn't wait for governmental approval for their ICOs (initial coin offerings).

If you're going to launch a startup, rewriting the rules is the best way to come out on top. Sometimes you'll get your wrist slapped; other times you'll get shut down. It's a risk that startups have to take. The bigger risk is to play by other people's rules. If you aren't pushing the limits, taking chances, and rewriting the playbook, you probably won't be able to beat the competition at their own game.

18

Engaging the Customer

I HAD AN ENTREPRENEUR COME up to me and ask if his product was any good.

Do you know what I told him? I said: "I have no idea. Go ask your customers. Then come back and tell me what they say."

Being an enthusiastic chap, he ran around for the next few weeks asking potential customers what they thought of his product.

When he returned, he said that more than 90 percent of the potential customers he approached liked the product, and they wanted him to come back later when it was completed.

Do you know what I told this eager, young entrepreneur? I said that he had a serious problem. His product wasn't what they wanted, customers weren't going to buy it, and his company was going to fail if he continued down this path.

Why would I say this? Am I a sadistic dream crusher? No. I try to be kind to people, but I'm not going to lie to them either. This idea won't work because I didn't hear the one thing I needed to hear. Not a single customer said: "Oh, my God! This is amazing. I love this product. Can I get it tomorrow? How much do you charge? Can I order it in advance?" If you don't hear words like this, then you have nothing. No one will tell you your product stinks to your face. They don't want to be rude. They'll just smile politely, say it's nice, and ask you to come back later.

To get someone to pay for a product, they must love it. That means your product either has to be something they absolutely must have because it solves a critical problem, or it must provide a value they can't get anywhere else. If they don't really need or love your product, they will never take action. If you think about the last ten apps you downloaded on your phone, what happened to those apps that you thought were good but not great? Either they got buried in some folder, which you never open, or you deleted them.

There's a huge gulf between "must-have" and "nice-to-have" products. If you sell a nice-to-have product, no one, not even your best friends, will use it long term. We all focus on must-haves. Life is just too busy to bother with anything that doesn't provide extreme value. This means value has to be greater than the inertia of life. None of us likes to change. No one wants to learn a new piece of software for no good reason. We only move when compelled to do so. I like to tell my entrepreneurs, "Nice-to-have is the kiss of death for startups. God forbid you should fall into this category." If you find yourself in this position, you need to start over.

But how can you know if your product is a must-have? If you sell to businesses, it's fairly easy to tell. Just ask your customers what their top five priorities are, and if your product doesn't help them achieve one of these goals, you are dead on arrival. You have no business with that customer. Being priority number six, seven, or eight doesn't cut it. No one cares. Nobody ever has time for those. They might not even know what priority number eight is. It's best if you're in the top three priorities. Then you're in business.

The same is true with consumers. If you have an idea for a new consumer product, you can run a secret ad campaign where you create a video, throw up a landing page, and see how many people click on a buy button—even if that buy button leads to a page where they simply sign up to be notified when the product launches.

If it's software, build out a minimum viable product and run a beta test. Get potential customers actively using it at the earliest date possible. Analyze how they react. Do they come back? How often do they use it? Do they refer it to friends? Solicit their feedback. Is your app a nice-to-have or a must-have?

Stewart Butterfield, the CEO of Slack, got his enterprise messaging app into the hands of customers long before it was completed. In just seven months, he had the alpha version ready. "We begged and cajoled our friends at other companies to try it out and give us feedback," recalls Butterfield. "We had maybe six to ten companies to start with that we found this way." With each new company added, his team learned something and made critical changes to the product. "The pattern was to share Slack with progressively larger groups," says Butterfield. "We would say, 'Oh, that great idea isn't so great after all.' We amplified the feedback we got at each stage by adding more [beta testers]."[1]

At this point, I always get asked: "What about Steve Jobs? He never market tested his products. He didn't believe in that."

I reply, "That's because he didn't have to." Jobs already knew there was a market for personal computers when he launched the Apple I. It was the hobbyist market pioneered by MITS Altair 8800, which was available more than a year earlier. The same was true when Jobs launched the iPod. There were already numerous MP3 players on the market, and they were selling like hotcakes. He just made a vastly superior product. The same thing happened again with the iPhone. Palm Pilot launched in 1997, a full ten years ahead of the iPhone. Palm Pilot and Treo paved the way and validated demand. Jobs didn't have to ask anyone. He just had to look at the growing sales numbers, extrapolate into the future, and then build a much better product.

If you don't have this data, then you'd better get it, and the only way to do it, short of a crystal ball, is to engage your customers. Pull them in as early as possible and have them interact with your product. Pump them for information and analyze it. Don't get me wrong. I'm not telling you to have your customers design your products. That's up to you. Your customers often don't even know what they want until they see it. All you need from your customers is to know if they must have what you're offering. If they can't wait to get their hands on it, you're onto something.

19

Manufacturing Demand

ANYONE WHO EXPECTS TO MANUFACTURE demand for a product is living a pipe dream. No one creates demand out of nothing. It's a myth. Demand always exists independent of the product itself. Just because a product sounds cool, uses the latest technology, and has a bunch of bells and whistles doesn't mean it will succeed. It has to address some fundamental customer need.

I've seen this over and over again. I can't tell you how many times startup founders with failed products passionately try to convince me they have the next big thing. I hear them say, "This product is the future. We haven't sold many, but that's because people don't understand. If only I had a bigger marketing budget, this thing would take off."

I'm sorry, but it doesn't work that way. Even the most talented marketing person in the world cannot make people buy a product they don't need or want right now. If you're too early, it's too bad. You have to try something else. You cannot get ahead of the market and expect the market to catch up. It never happens.

Another kiss of death is when entrepreneurs tell me, "We just need to educate the market." It pains me to hear this, because I was in the same position when I ran an interactive TV startup. We had to literally explain to Hollywood what interactive TV was to get a sale. It made the sales cycles interminably long and painful.

Educating the market never works. You can't educate anyone into wanting your product. Either they want it or they don't. It's that simple. I agree that your product might be complex, but that's not the reason customers aren't buying it. There are plenty of complex products that sell like crazy because they fill a strong need. The products that take off are the ones where you show it to customers, and they instantly recognize the value.

As an entrepreneur, you only have one job, and that is to identify an unmet demand and create a product that fills that need. Savvy entrepreneurs don't focus on developing new, unproven products. Instead, they focus on discovering demand. This sounds simple, but you would be surprised at how much time entrepreneurs spend building products nobody wants, instead of using that time to find out what's really needed.

From the first day you launch your startup, your mission should be to hunt for demand. Forget designing, coding, marketing, and raising capital. Those come later. Undiscovered demand is the fuel that powers startups. When you find it, it's like hitting an oil gusher. Everything just starts flowing. Customers line up for the product. Investors line up to give you money. Journalists line up to write about it. The bigger the demand, the bigger your business.

※

*Undiscovered demand is the fuel that powers
startups—it's like hitting an oil gusher.*

If there's one thing I want you to remember, it's that demand is king. It makes the rules, and you must obey them.

2

Raising Venture Capital

Show Me the Money!

Journalists love to mythologize about venture-funded startups and unicorns. Tens of thousands of eager, starry-eyed entrepreneurs flock to Silicon Valley from all over the world in hopes of achieving the Silicon Dream. It's an invitation to a very special club, a badge of honor—a sign that you're ready for the big leagues. It gives your company the fuel it needs to rocket past everyone else. Who doesn't want to have a real office, marketing budget, employees who aren't holding two or three jobs, and laptops from this century?

Hold on. Enough dreaming. Life isn't always like a movie. It's not so easy to convince investors to hand over their cash. Despite the stories you have heard, you can't simply show up on Sand Hill Road with a duffel bag and expect the VCs to load you up. More often than not, fundraising can be downright excruciating—especially when you don't know what you're doing.

I've spent more than a decade helping startups raise capital. I see entrepreneurs all around the world squandering huge amounts of time and money talking to investors in entirely the wrong way. They don't grasp what VCs actually need to know or how they think. Understanding the perspective of the investor is critical to closing financing. It's not only the data a startup presents but how that information is delivered that makes the difference.

I'll go into all the elements entrepreneurs must grapple with, including how to determine the company's valuation, what makes a great lawyer, why social capital matters, and how to structure the perfect pitch. I'll also address difficult questions, like: How does an entrepreneur qualify investors? When is it important to walk away from a deal? What can a startup do to stand out? And what are the best strategies for managing an investor pipeline?

I hope this will save you from some of the pain, cut your fundraising time down, and enable you to negotiate smarter terms. At the very least, it will enlighten you to a few of the secrets venture capitalists rarely share.

20

Inside Venture Capital

LET'S BEGIN WITH AN INSIDE look at venture capital. There are several stages to venture investing in Silicon Valley. First come the angel investors. These tend to be successful businesspeople, many of whom have been entrepreneurs themselves. Angels supposedly earn their wings by helping startups in their time of greatest need. In the early stages, when money is tight, angels are crucial, not just for their investment dollars, but for their experience, guidance, and business network.

According to the National Bureau of Economic Research, startups that have angel backing are 14 percent more likely to survive for eighteen months or more after funding. Angel-backed companies hire an average of 40 percent more employees, and angel backing increases the probability of a successful exit by at least 10 percent. Angel-funded firms are also more likely to attract follow-on financing. All this means that angel funding isn't something you should thumb your nose at in favor of other types of financing.

Angels invest for multiple reasons. Some want to make big money, while others enjoy helping startups and want to give back. There are also the angels who crave the ego boost of bragging about getting in early on the next big thing, or those who want to live vicariously through the startup, without the burden of doing the heavy lifting. Sometimes it's all of the above.

The majority of angels in Silicon Valley are interested in startups that have the potential to become big businesses. They typically don't care about investing in a neighborhood laundromat, hair salon, or restaurant. They want the same type of startups that later-stage venture capitalists target, and their criteria roughly align. The one big difference is that most of them don't mind an early exit. This is because their business model is different. They invest smaller sums at an earlier stage, and they don't need to put more money to work. So, growing a startup into a billion-dollar business is not necessarily their priority. Angels usually invest anywhere from a few thousand to a few hundred thousand dollars. It's all over the map, depending on the size of their pocketbooks and their appetite for risk.

Next come the seed investors. They help bridge the gap between angels and larger VCs. Seed investors usually have smaller funds. Sometimes angels invest in the seed round, especially super angels, who have larger pools of capital. Seed funds tend to focus on early-stage startups that are primed for venture capital. The startups have something solid, but they need more time and money to prove it out. The amounts invested typically range from a few hundred thousand to a few million dollars.

After the seed round comes what is commonly called the pre–Series A round. This is a new term that came into vogue in 2013 when the larger VC firms began demanding more traction before investing in the Series A. At the same time, super angels, seed funds, and sprout stage VCs moved to fill the gap, investing anywhere from half a million to a few million dollars as a bridge between the seed and Series A rounds.

Keep in mind that the size and nature of these rounds is somewhat arbitrary. A lot depends on the sector, the capital required, the startup founders, competition for the deal, and a host of other variables. What I'm giving you are rules of thumb. In reality, there are no rules. I've seen companies, like Magic Leap, raise a billion dollars with no traction—just a sexy idea, a cool video, and perfect timing.

The Series A round is where the top-tier VCs usually step in. It's the sweet spot. Valuations aren't sky-high yet, but a lot of the risk has been taken out of the equation. Famous names like Sequoia, Kleiner Perkins, Accel, Graylock, and Andreessen Horowitz routinely invest in Series A rounds ranging from several million dollars to tens of millions. There is a lot of competition at this stage for the hottest deals. Because of this, some top-tier VCs have begun investing in promising seed stage rounds and even earlier. They want to get in early, if only to secure a seat at the table if it turns out to be the next Palantir or Square.

The problem many startups face is that if you bring in a big name, like Sequoia or Accel, early in the game, and they choose not to participate in later rounds, it can scare off other investors. Angel and seed investors aren't expected to follow on, but when a deep-pocketed VC refuses to participate in the next round, it can spell trouble for the startup. After all, if the company has real potential, why aren't the current investors all over this deal? By not participating, they are signaling to other investors that there's something wrong with the startup. The risk of negative signals is one reason I tell startups to avoid the bigger guys until they are ready.

Investor syndicates are another source of capital. Syndicates are groups of angel investors that join together to form a larger pool of capital. Often, a well-known individual or company will manage the syndicate, acting as the lead investor and taking a percentage of the profits. A lot of them use the site AngelList (angel.co) to organize and invest in startups. The syndicates used to be focused on early-stage startups, but the larger ones now act more like traditional VCs. In fact, many of them won't invest unless an established VC is leading the round, which places them outside the angel and seed stages. They do this primarily to lower risk.

Startups can also raise money from incubators and accelerators. People always ask me what the difference is between the two, and I say that depends on where you're from. In most cases, the terms are used interchangeably, but the technical definition is that an incubator helps startups at a very early stage, typically when they just have an idea. This has been true of incubators like Idealab, Betaworks, and Rocket Internet. Sometimes the incubator will come up with the concept, bring in the team, fund the entire thing, and take the majority of the equity. That said, in China and most other places, incubators are more like coworking spaces. Most don't invest any capital. They just provide a space and community for the startups.

Accelerators tend to focus on existing startups with fully formed teams and products, either in development or already launched. Their mission is to accelerate the growth of these companies. They often provide funding, education, community, and space for startups to work. Founders Space, Y-Combinator, 500 Startups, Plug and Play, and Techstars are all accelerators. Accelerators not only invest but also provide access to networks of angel investors and venture capitalists, as well as mentors, advisors, and strategic partners.

Another option is corporate investors. In the past, corporate venture capital tended to come late to the game, following the lead of established VCs. However, lately, many larger companies are leading the rounds themselves and investing at much earlier stages. Some also provide incubation and acceleration. The thing to be aware of is that corporates have their own agenda. They like to invest for strategic reasons over financial returns. There also may be conflicts of interest between what they want from a startup and the startup's best interests.

For the most part, corporate investors are worth engaging, especially if they can offer valuable resources, like software platforms, technology, distribution, engineering, and manufacturing. As long as the corporation doesn't impose onerous restrictions on the startup, it can be a win-win situation. The one thing startups want to pay close attention to is conflicts of interest. If a startup aligns with one corporation, it may be harder to do business with its competitors down the road. Money from angels and VCs doesn't have this downside. I have a rule when it comes to corporate investors: Never take money from a corporation that is a competitor to your other customers. This can severely limit your business.

※

Never take money from a corporation
that is a competitor to your other customers—
this can severely limit your business.

Another important thing to understand when raising venture capital is what investors want from a startup. The bigger VCs tend to raise money from institutional investors, which can include university endowments, banks, labor unions, pension funds, and insurance companies.

These institutions are called *limited partners*, and they invest large sums of money in the funds, expecting market-beating returns. This is good for the venture capitalists running the funds because they typically get a 2 percent annual management fee and 20 percent of the profits when the fund reaches maturity. The management fees alone can add up to $20 million a year on a billion-dollar fund, regardless of whether the fund ever turns a profit. Now you know why some VCs are so wealthy. They can't lose.

This structure incentivizes VCs to raise as much money as possible. In Silicon Valley, the top-tier VCs regularly close funds of a billion dollars and up. The problem is that the more money the VCs raise, the larger exits they require. This is because a VC firm with a billion-dollar fund needs to put this money to work. It's not easy to invest a billion dollars in startups, and most VCs must place this money within the first three years of the fund's life.

This means the larger funds are under pressure to invest huge sums of capital quickly. If a startup sells for $20 million, it means nothing to a larger venture fund, even if the return is ten times or more. Just do the math. Let's say the fund invests $1 million and gets a return of ten times. This seems respectable, but $10 million doesn't do much for a billion-dollar fund. It's just a rounding error. In other words, it was a waste of the VC's time. For this reason alone, the larger funds are looking for startups that exit at half a billion and up. That's the only way they can put enough money to work to meet their investors' expectations.

The thing VCs value most is their time. Their money might seem unlimited, but their time is not. Performing due diligence on startups takes a lot of time. So does filling board seats. The VCs can only sit on so many boards and be effective. So, they naturally limit the number of deals they do. This means they filter out all startups that won't need a lot of money. In other words, they want companies that grow large and fast enough so that they can literally feed millions of dollars to them over their lifetime; hence the explosion of unicorns.

VCs know that most of their investments will fail to deliver the necessary returns, but they also know that all it takes is one or two big winners to pay for all the losers and make a tidy profit. They want the next

Xiaomi, DocuSign, Spotify, or Dropbox. These are called *fund makers* because a single startup can return the entire fund.

Over the years, the larger funds have become laser focused on these types of deals to the exclusion of all else. Your startup may have an incredibly good chance of becoming a profitable business, but that doesn't matter to VCs. A small or medium-sized business isn't interesting to them. If your company doesn't have the potential to grow into a billion-dollar business, it doesn't work with their business model. This means that all of Silicon Valley is tied into a hit-driven system where everyone is looking for the next billion-dollar blockbuster.

There are always exceptions to the rule, but if you're coming to Silicon Valley, there's no use in bucking the trend. It's going to make it hard, if not impossible, to get funded. I'm telling you this now because not every business is suited for venture capital. In fact, very few businesses are right for VC funding. The majority of companies are simply better off without venture capital funding.

I spend a lot of time with entrepreneurs at the early stages trying to figure out whether their businesses are a good fit for Silicon Valley. More often than not, they aren't a perfect match, and the startup needs to either pivot or adjust its expectations. Unless a startup can show that it's in a position to grow exponentially over the next three years, meaning it will hit at least $50 million in revenue by year three, there's really no point in approaching venture capital. It's just a waste of time. Many startups complain about this, but that's how the world works. If your model isn't right for VCs, wishful thinking and lots of grumbling won't help.

21

Know Your Valuation

INVESTORS LOVE TO ASK STARTUPS, "What's your valuation?" It's sort of an unfair question because most startup founders, especially in the early stages, are clueless. In fact, the investors have a far better idea than the entrepreneurs. So, why do they bother asking? It's because investors don't want to bid against themselves. They want to see if the startup's valuation is in line with their own estimation. If the entrepreneur comes out with a lower valuation than expected, the investor is happy. If it's higher, then it's time to begin negotiating. The answer also tells the investor how knowledgeable the entrepreneur is. Savvy CEOs have a good sense for what the market will bear.

So, how do you know your true valuation? The answer is simple: You don't. You can never know your actual valuation except immediately after closing a priced round. Your value at that time is whatever investors are willing to pay for the shares. This is true of any company, whether public or private. However, stocks that are public are constantly being traded, so everyone has a clearer idea of the value. With a startup, it's another story.

I like to compare values of private companies to that of real estate. How much is a particular home worth? The size and features of the house itself aren't always the best indicators. Exactly the same house in a rich neighborhood will have more value than in a poorer part of town. The only way to know the value is to look at what other homes in the same neighborhood are selling for, and then approximate the value based on recent sales data.

In the old days, you'd have to ask a real estate agent for this information, but today you can simply look it up online. Unfortunately, with startups, it's not so simple. There are many types of startups, covering a huge range of industries. To complicate matters, much of the funding data is private, so it's not easily accessed. In most cases, the only people to turn to are the investors themselves.

Investors who place money in enough startups can get a pretty good idea of what companies are worth in a particular market. The greater the deal flow, the better the data. Investors form a model in their minds, which approximates what startups at different stages in various sectors are worth. When a new startup walks in the door, they automatically get mapped to this mental model. If the price is too high, the investor will balk.

I had a startup come to Founders Space and tell me his company was worth $15 million pre-money. I assured him this was too high. He'd be lucky to get half that. He didn't even have a product yet. It was just an idea. Yes, his team was excellent, but they were too early for that type of valuation. But the entrepreneur was insistent. He truly believed he was right. To break the impasse, I introduced him to some investors so that he could get a better feel for the market.

As I predicted, the investors loved the startup but couldn't get over the price. Even with this feedback, the entrepreneur persisted, refusing to lower his valuation. It was frustrating to watch. The entrepreneur went on for another year trying to raise money. Eventually, he came back to me with the original valuation I had quoted—only the market had moved on, and it was much harder to raise money in that sector. Two years from our initial meeting, the startup wound up closing funding at exactly the valuation I had estimated.

The lesson here is to get lots of feedback on your valuation early and adjust your expectation accordingly. It doesn't matter what you think your startup is worth. It's only worth what the market will pay for it. If you want to raise money, you have to be in line with the market. I recommend that every startup founder meet with as many people inside the venture capital business as possible right before fundraising. Don't ask them for money. Just ask them for a quick estimate of your company's value.

At the same time, go to other startup founders and ask what they are seeing in the market. I repeat: The more data you can gather, the better. There are also sites, like TechCrunch's Crunchbase, that will show you what deals are closing at. On AngelList (angel.co) and other funding sites, investors can see what all the startups on the site are listing as their valuations. If you have access, you can quickly get a sense for the market.

Once you've assimilated all this data, you'll have a pretty good idea of what your startup is worth in Silicon Valley, but you still won't have any clue how much it's worth in Beijing or Berlin. Just as with homes, valuations differ based on location. A home in New York is worth far more than the exact same home in Detroit. The valuation of a startup changes depending on where it is raising capital. Sometimes it's higher, like in China, where valuations are still sky-high, and sometimes it's significantly lower, like in most European countries. It all depends on the supply of venture capital and the demand for startups.

I advise startup founders to pick a valuation right in the middle of the range. If you go too low, you're leaving money on the table, but if you go too high, it will just slow down the fundraising process. It's better to price your startup in the middle of the bell curve. If you're really hot, you'll probably wind up with multiple bidders and have your pick of investors. This is a great position to be in. Just like with real estate, if you can get a bidding war going, you not only can boost your valuation and get better terms but also shorten your funding-raising time.

22

Love Your Lawyer

LAWYERS, LAWYERS, LAWYERS. WE LOVE to hate them. Yes, you need a lawyer. I don't recommend raising venture capital in Silicon Valley without one. Other countries may be different, but in the United States, I assure you that it's a big mistake not to get legal representation. So, I'm going to tell you what to look for in a lawyer.

The first choice you have to make is whether to go with a big-name law firm or a boutique one. The big law firms have a number of advantages. They bring credibility to your company. They have a brand, top lawyers, global connections, and robust legal teams covering everything from corporate law to IP (internet protocol) and litigation. The most respected firms also offer a halo effect. No top firm would risk its reputation on a startup that it thought couldn't succeed. The top Silicon Valley firms act as filters for investors. They select the best startups and introduce them to venture capitalists on a routine basis. These firms include Wilson Sonsini, Fenwick & West, DLA Piper, Cooley, Goodwin, Perkins Coie, and many others. I won't name them all because it's a long list.

If you land with a top firm, you should leverage their relationships to get warm introductions to the venture community. Keep in mind the amount and quality of the introductions depend on the partners you are dealing with and how much they believe in your startup. Some partners will bend over backward to help you get funded, while others only want to handle your legal work. It's smart to figure out who you're dealing with right from the beginning.

A smart indicator of how hard the partners will work on your behalf is whether or not they're willing to defer all payments until after you close funding. This can be a lifesaver for a struggling startup. Typically, they cap the deferment. The cap can range from $5,000 to $50,000 or even more, depending on how much they believe in you. A large deferment means the firm is invested in your success, and they are more likely to make valuable introductions. They're motivated, because if you don't succeed, they don't get paid.

But don't fool yourself. They aren't doing this for free. You will pay for it on the back end. The more risk the firm takes, the more reward they expect, and big firms charge big fees. Top lawyers can run a thousand dollars an hour or more in the Valley. So, be prepared for some hefty legal bills down the road. One safety precaution is to try to get some sort of package deal where costs are spelled out in advance for everything from company formation to patents and closing the Series A round. It's hard, but sometimes they will do this. It can't hurt to ask.

The other option is to go with smaller firms or individual lawyers. They often don't have the reputation to connect you with top investors or the deep pockets to defer payment, but they can be a lot cheaper. I always tell startups to negotiate with all lawyers. The greatest leverage you have is right at the beginning. Once you sign with them, it's harder, but not impossible, to get a discount. If it's a small firm, you can usually get a package deal. Sometimes they'll include everything from incorporating your company to filing provisional patents and setting up a stock option plan in a single flat-fee structure. You will have to pay up front, but this is a wonderful way to save money. They are doing it to win your business away from the bigger firms, and it can pay off down the road.

A lot of the smaller firms and individuals lack the halo effect and global networks, but they are just as competent as the big guys. They can do very good work at a much lower hourly rate. The downside is that you almost always have to pay up front, and if you don't have money, that can be a deal breaker.

Money problems aside, the most important thing to look for in a firm is the actual partner you'll be working with. Nothing matters more than the quality of the lawyer. You can have the best firm in the world, but if you don't get along with the lawyer, it's a disaster.

＊

You can have the best firm in the world,
but if you don't get along with the lawyer,
it's a disaster.

Before you sign up, you need to ask some questions. Will the lawyer you're talking to be actively involved in negotiating the deals and finalizing the agreements, or will junior associates handle the work? In the larger firms, chances are junior people will do most of the heavy lifting. Who are these junior associates? Are they competent? You need to meet them because you'll probably be spending more time with them than with anyone else. Make sure to ask these questions right up front. Don't be shy. It's part of the process. Also, take the time to interview more than one law firm. You are hiring them and want to make sure their culture, personalities, and values mesh with your own.

Cost aside, what do you need to look for in good lawyers? The most important thing is the type of advice they will give you. Bad lawyers give you fuzzy advice. For instance, you may ask about a specific term in an agreement, only to have them respond with a series of options, and then begin explaining the subtle legal ramifications of each choice. Trust me. This isn't what you're paying them for. You don't need a legal education. You just need straightforward business advice. Usually by the time they are done explaining, you are no closer to understanding the real issues than when you started. Why do lawyers do this? Because they feel it's your job to make the tough decisions. They are only there to provide legal counsel. Sorry, but this is nonsense. That's not the job of a good lawyer.

The lawyers I appreciate are the ones like Allison Tilley at the law firm Pillsbury. She was my lawyer through some tough times with two different startups. She understands how to give clear, definitive business advice.

Whenever I asked her difficult questions, she'd reply: "I suggest doing this. There's some risk, but it's your best option given the circumstances." She knows, because she's been through this many times with many start-ups. You need an attorney who understands how to think like a startup. Risk is inherent in everything a startup does. There's no way to eliminate risk. You just have to manage it the best you can. A great lawyer won't bury you in legalese. She will tell you clearly which risks are worth taking and which aren't.

⚒

*A great lawyer will tell you clearly which
risks are worth taking and which aren't.*

The next quality I look for in a lawyer is the dedication to be there when you need her. When I was negotiating deals for my startups, it was often do or die. I was down to my last penny, and I needed the deal to close or the company would go belly-up in a matter of weeks. Some lawyers simply aren't responsive enough. You'll be in the middle of negotiations, and they won't call you back for a day or two. That can kill the momentum. I want my lawyer on the phone the same day, helping push through the changes, so we can make the deal happen. Allison was always there for us when we needed her most, but not all lawyers are like this.

I've seen the damage slow responses can cause. I worked with one startup whose lawyer took weeks to respond to every request. The CEO was going nuts because every little thing took forever. I told the CEO bluntly, "Fire that lawyer." He didn't take my advice, saying they were too far along. For the next six months, I had to listen to endless complaints. Remember, lawyers are hired guns. You can let them go anytime. Legal documents are easy to hand off to a new lawyer. They're 98 percent boilerplate. Any halfway decent lawyer can pick up where another left off. In fact, it's much easier to replace your lawyer than your lead engineer.

Always do your homework. Don't just interview the lawyer; interview the clients. Find out which startups worked with the lawyer, take them out to lunch, and grill them. Find out if the lawyer is super responsive, provides clear-cut answers, knows the law inside and out, and does not pad the legal bills. The last one is the hardest. How the heck do you know?

In the end, the lawyer is a crucial part of your team, and you need someone who can back you up. I've learned so much from my lawyers. The good ones will actually teach you how to negotiate an agreement, making clear what terms are worth fighting over and what to give in on. I owe a huge debt to Billy Schwartz at Morrison & Foerster, who helped me out with my first startup. For a flat fee, he spent days teaching me and my partner all the intricacies of negotiating licensing agreements. This type of lawyer is rare, but they do exist. My partner and I have learned so much over the years that we now handle most of our smaller deals without involving our lawyers. Attorneys we negotiate with often think my partner is a lawyer because of the way she drafts or revises contracts. You just need to know when it's worth hiring someone, and when the risk is so small you can manage it yourself.

A lot of the top firms, like Orrick, have put a huge number of legal templates online. You can download them for free by searching for Orrick Tool Kit. If you're a cash-strapped startup, cannot get a deferred payment, and are comfortable with legalese, this may be your best option. I'm not saying don't use a lawyer, but if you can't afford one, do whatever you have to do to move forward. I use these templates when appropriate. They're pretty solid. They've been thoroughly reviewed by some of the top lawyers in the world. As long as you stick closely to the template and understand the terms you are committing to, you should be fine.

If you're a bootstrapped startup, I wouldn't hesitate to go to the websites of every major Silicon Valley law firm and download whatever free legal forms are available, and then use them whenever it makes sense. To save money, a good strategy is to open negotiations yourself, use a proven template, and then bring in the lawyer at the very end for a final run-through. This can cut the legal bill down by as much as 90 percent. Heck, I've even downloaded end-user license agreements from Microsoft and Google, then modified them to my needs. I figured that if it was good enough for the largest corporations in the world, it should be just fine for my startup. Any self-respecting lawyer would advise against this. But seriously, what bootstrapped startup can afford to spend thousands of dollars on legal agreements when it hasn't even proven out its idea? If it's the choice between having no end-user licensing agreement or creating one inspired by Microsoft or Google, why not go for it? You can always bring a lawyer in to update and customize your terms and conditions after you land funding.

Keep in mind that templates work great for simple things, like NDAs (nondisclosure agreements), authorization and release forms, independent contractor agreements, and so on. However, it starts to get tricky on more complex transactions, like negotiating a priced round. In this case, it's wise to bring in the best lawyers you can afford. You can't see the pitfalls, and if you screw up, there can be a high price to pay down the road. Things like liquidation preferences and board control are critical to your company's future, and you don't want to risk losing everything. Don't be pennywise and pound foolish. Like I said, it's all about managing risk. In the end, use your best judgment and don't stress too much. Everything you do has risk. Legal is just another one.

23

Your Investor Pitch Deck

CREATING THE PITCH DECK THAT you use when making a presentation to investors is different from creating the full investor deck. The pitch deck is the PowerPoint presentation you'll show to investors in person, while the full deck is the PowerPoint presentation you send to investors for them to review on their own. The presentation pitch deck must be concise and visual with as few words as possible on each slide, while the full deck is longer and more complete. It's meant to be read when you're not in the room.

Here is a template for the presentation pitch deck that I give to all my startups. This is designed for a three-minute pitch. It's short and to the point. I kept the slides to a minimum. You can add more slides for a longer presentation.

Slide 1—Title Page

- Show your company name and logo in big, clear, bold typeface.
- Taglines should only be a few words long.
- Include a beautiful picture that captures the essence of your business.
- Add your name, phone number, and email in the lower right corner.

Slide 2—Problem

- What problem are you solving for your customers?
- Make the slide as visual as possible with only a few words.

Slide 3—Big Vision (Solution)

- What is the big opportunity here?
- How will you change your industry?

Slide 4—Your Product

- What does your product do?
- How does it work?
- What benefits does your product offer your customers?
- If you have a short, powerful product video, show it here.
- Keep your video under thirty seconds.
- If your video isn't great, do not show it.

Slide 5—Addressable Market

- How large is the addressable market in dollars?
- How many customers need your product or service?
- How much are they willing to pay?

Slide 6—Competition

- Who are your competitors?
- What is your secret sauce?
- What makes you different?

Slide 7—Business Model

- How will you make money?
- What is your pricing strategy?
- What are your estimated profit margins?

Slide 8—Revenue Forecast and Milestones

- What's your expected revenue growth?
- What are your current and future burn rates?
- What are your key milestones?

Slide 9—Traction

- What's your traction?
- Include customers, revenue, strategic partners, and signed deals.
- Include metrics, like customer growth and engagement.
- Also include any validation, such as press, surveys, and letters of intent.

Slide 10—Team

- Show your team—include big, friendly photos of each team member.
- Below each photo, have their names and titles.
- Include one or two accomplishments for each member, such as a prestigious award, most recent job, or university degree.
- Do not use more than ten words total to describe each team member, including name, title, and accomplishments.
- Only include the top three to six team members. Be sure to mention the total number of employees in the company at the bottom.

Slide 11—The Ask

- How much have you raised to date?
- How much money are you raising now and at what valuation?
- How far will this money take you?
- What milestones will you hit?
- Include your company name and contact info.

If you follow the above advice, you should be in good shape to pitch investors, but keep in mind this is only a template. Feel free to modify it to your startup's particular needs. Every business is unique, and you may want to add and remove slides.

The one thing you should keep in mind is that less is often more. You should design each slide so that the investors can grasp the key points within a few seconds of seeing it. Then they can focus on you and what you're saying. The worst presentations are ones that are crammed full of text. I can't tell you how exhausted investors feel when they look at a screen with nothing but writing. Instead of thinking of your pitch deck as a written document, think of it as visual stimuli. It's the background, while you are the star of the show. Good luck!

※

Instead of thinking of your pitch deck as a written document, think of it as visual stimuli.

24

Selling Your Story

WHEN I SIT IN MEETINGS with the top venture capitalists, they often brag about how data-driven they are. They went to Harvard or MIT, and they like to say all that matters are the numbers. But then I've watched them after an entrepreneur tells a powerful story, and everything they said goes out the window. Like all people, investors distill facts down to feelings. Every fact is only as important as someone feels it is. No matter how logical investors might believe they are, they always wind up going with how they feel at the end of the day.

This is why the story matters more than anything else in your pitch, and you shouldn't be telling a story just about your product. If you can make it personal, it gives you an edge over the competition. Investors want to know who you are. They want to understand you as a person. After all, they are investing in the team, first and foremost. They need to see what drives you and get a feel for what brought your team together. In the end, they have to trust you. There's no better way to build trust in a short time than through a story that reveals your values and motives.

You might believe you don't have any personal stories to tell, but that's not true. Everyone has a story to tell. I don't care how boring you are. Even if you've been living in a cave your whole life, there's a story buried somewhere in your past that you can dig out. If you're going to capture the attention of investors, you need to find this story.

Great stories come from the heart. They tell who you are, why you're doing what you're doing, and what it means to the world. In order to come up with the best story possible, begin by answering these four questions:

1. Why did you start this company?
2. What makes you so passionate about this?
3. How will it upend and disrupt your industry?
4. What impact will it have on the lives of your customers?

Great stories combine your personal story, your product story, and your company's mission.

✳

Great stories combine your personal story,
your product story, and your company's mission.

Now let me tell you a story that illustrates the power of narrative. When Verizon launched a multimillion-dollar contest to award the top innovators around the world, one of the categories for the competition was education. Since my first startup was a game company that published business-learning games, like *Gazillionaire* and *Zapitalism*, I thought we were a good fit. However, because there were thousands of applicants, I knew it was a long shot. I filled out the application as quickly as possible and forgot about it.

A month later, to my surprise, I learned we'd made the first cut. With each new round, I became more confident of our chances. By the time we reached the finals, I was determined to win the grand prize. At this point, I had to craft my story and perfect my pitch. I knew that the in-person presentation to the panel of judges was the most important part of the process. When the day came to present to the judges, I made sure to include three main points. First, I told my personal story, emphasizing how I'd been creating nonviolent, learning games ever since high school, because I believed it was the best way to educate young people.

Second, I tied my games into the biggest problem our nation was facing at the time. This was right after the subprime mortgage crisis, when people all across the country were losing their homes because they didn't understand basic finances. Hundreds of thousands of hardworking Americans had signed up for adjustable-rate loans they could not repay.

Third, I explained how our young people could go from kindergarten through high school without ever taking a single class on financial literacy. Even the majority of college graduates know little to nothing about loans, compound interest, and financial planning. This is why so many Americans are in debt and can't get out. Families are not only losing their homes, but also their life savings, money set aside for retirement, and their children's college funds—all because they lack a proper education. I reiterated how we cannot afford to let this continue.

I went on to tell several stories of how players of our games had learned the dangers of high interest rates and thanked us for helping them cut up their credit cards and pay off their debts. I also highlighted how schools and colleges were using our software to teach business, math, and economics all around the world. I wrapped up my speech by stating we were going to use the prize money to bring our game *Zapitalism* to mobile phones. At the end of my speech, when I looked into the judges' eyes, I knew that I'd captured them. I could taste victory.

Over the next several weeks, Verizon sent a crew to film us and kept hinting that we were one of their very top picks. As you can imagine, we were excited. The grand prize was $1 million, and we didn't have to give up any equity in our company. It was too good to be true.

The day of the awards ceremony finally came around. My partner and I sat in the audience waiting to hear if we'd be called onstage. They started with fifth place and worked their way up the list. I was sure that our name would be the last one called. However, when they came to second place, I heard the host shout out *Zapitalism*!

I couldn't believe it. We hadn't won first prize. Given the vibe I'd felt, I was certain we would come out on top. I should mention that second prize was $850,000, so I shouldn't have been disappointed, but my expectations were set high. How could someone have a better story than the financial crisis and educating young people?

When the first-place winner was announced, an Israeli guy came on-stage. As he began to talk, I realized why he'd won. He had a better story. He passionately described how he'd developed his learning software to help his father who suffered from a debilitative brain disease. It was a heart-wrenching story, and I couldn't help but feel for him. His product was not only good for society, but he had done it for his dying father. Now millions of kids around the world could use the same software to improve their lives.

The best story always wins. Why? It's because human beings under-stand the world through stories. Ever since our prehistoric ancestors were living in caves, we would gather around campfires and tell one another stories of our lives and exploits. For generation upon generation, we have passed down knowledge and culture through storytelling. It's not a fluke that every major religion in the world is filled with parables. Just think of the Bible. It's much easier to remember and understand the stories than the other parts.

The same is true with the news. It's all stories. You don't open up the *Wall Street Journal* and get a list of facts and numbers on the front page. You get interesting stories about people and events. Knowledge is pack-aged into stories because that's how we best assimilate and process infor-mation. Without the story, it's hard for most people to remember a string of facts. But once an emotional story is attached, it sticks.

So, when you're talking about your startup, remember, it's the story that counts. That's what investors are going to walk away with. Most of the facts and figures will vanish from their memories as soon as they exit the room, but if your story makes an impact, it will remain with them. It's the startups with the best stories that get a call back the next day.

25

Qualifying Investors

JUST BECAUSE AN INVESTOR WANTS to meet with you, it doesn't mean it's a good thing. You need to be careful. Before you meet with any investors one-on-one, whether they heard your pitch at some event, found you on the web, or stumbled across an article about your startup, you need to thoroughly qualify them. Remember, your time is as valuable as theirs, if not more. They're usually rich, and you're struggling just to survive. You don't want to waste a precious day driving to a meeting only to find out the investor isn't serious.

I've had startups fly to another city to meet with a potential investor, only to find out that the angel doesn't have wings. The person just wanted to sell them something, like cloud hosting, advertising, or legal services. It's sad, but some unscrupulous people will pose as angel investors because they've found it's an easy way to get startups to meet with them. Often, they will offer to trade their services for equity, but if you don't want what they're offering, you've just wasted your time.

This is why I always tell every entrepreneur to qualify their leads. Whenever investors contact you out of the blue, not from a trusted source, there's one magic question you need to ask: "Can you tell me when you made your last three investments?" If they haven't invested in any startups in the past year, they probably are not a serious investor, and you'll be better off spending the time working on your business.

When engaging investors, make sure to ask what sectors they are focused on and what stage they invest in. If you're early stage, but they only focus on later stage, then it's a no-go. If you're doing mobile apps but they invest in biotech, it's a no-go. Now, if you just want to practice pitching, or if the investor is extremely well connected, it may still be worth taking the meeting, but don't expect to walk away with funding. It probably won't happen.

Always take the time to visit the investor's website in advance. Most VC firms will have the partners' bios listed on the site along with their portfolio of investments. It's good to read everything before you meet, especially the bios of the people with whom you'll be talking. They may have connections or experience that can be of value to you, but if you don't know about their pasts, you won't be able to ask the right questions.

You can also see what each partner in the firm focuses on. You might be meeting with the wrong person at that firm. On the website, pay special attention to the portfolio companies. Do you see any direct competitors? If you do, it's probably not a good fit. Keep in mind that the website is usually outdated and won't include many of the firm's recent investments, so it's a good idea to ask in advance if there are any conflicts of interest you should be aware of.

If it's an angel investor, search online. Most angels in Silicon Valley have a profile on AngelList that includes their bio and recent investments. You should also google the angel's name and see what comes up. I once found out that someone I was about to do business with had made his fortune through spamming. He had also been taken to court for illegal activities. This shocked me, to say the least, and I immediately cut off our relationship. But if I hadn't done my homework, I may have wound up taking his money, and that is not the type of person I would ever want involved in my business.

※

Most angels in Silicon Valley have an online profile on AngelList that includes their bio and recent investments.

How to Talk to Investors

AFTER QUALIFYING THE INVESTOR, IT'S time for the one-on-one meeting. If it's an angel investor, these usually take place at coffee shops. If it's VCs, they'll probably invite you to their offices. In either case, you'll most likely get anywhere from fifteen minutes to one hour to make your presentation. This isn't much time, so you need to use it efficiently.

My advice is to dispense with the small talk. I'm not saying don't be friendly, but don't launch into a twenty-minute discussion about your family or the latest basketball game. That's precious time taken away from presenting your business. You can say a few friendly words at the beginning, and that's enough. If the investor likes your company, there will be plenty of time to get to know each other later.

Investors are busy people. They'll want you to cut to the chase, so start with a short overview. I'm a big fan of brevity. Shorter is always better. If they've heard your pitch already, give them a two-minute refresher. If they haven't heard your pitch or have someone new in the room, give them a full five minutes but no longer. God forbid you should do a twenty-minute, nonstop presentation.

Remember, more than anything, investors want to talk to you about your business. They don't want a one-way conversation. They want an interactive dialogue. If they interrupt your presentation with questions, go with the flow. Don't brush them off with quick answers. Asking questions is a sign they're engaged.

According to a Harvard research study titled, "It Doesn't Hurt to Ask: Question-asking Increases Liking,"[1] people who ask more questions, particularly follow-up questions, are better liked by their conversation partners and perceived as more responsive. This may seem like common sense, but you'd be surprised at how few questions entrepreneurs ask during their pitch. Most founders think they're supposed to do all the talking, when the opposite is true.

Another trick is to avoid dominating the conversation. Don't feel compelled to be the authority on everything. I learned right after college during my first series of job interviews that the less I talked, the more likely I was to get an offer. Some people just love hearing themselves speak. If you're a good listener, they'll love you, too. If the investors want to contribute ideas and dole out the advice, just relax and soak up the feedback. You may find that they've sold themselves on the deal without you having to do much.

When talking to investors, avoid sales mode. No one wants to feel like they're being sold something. As soon as people feel like you're trying to sell them, their guard goes up, and they become suspicious. Think of how you feel when you walk into a store and a high-pressure salesperson pounces on you, hungry for a commission. It's off-putting. This is why I coach startups to take an entirely different approach. Think of yourself as an advisor, not a CEO. Your job is to help the investors understand your business as thoroughly as possible, and then if it's the right fit, they will decide to invest.

Rufus Griscom, the founder of online parenting magazine and blog network Babble, took this approach to an extreme. In his investor pitch, he went through the top five reasons investors should not put money into his company. This blatant honesty actually wound up working in his favor. By showing investors all the flaws, he not only won their trust, but he made them feel like trusted partners. Bringing on investors is like getting married. Nothing is more important than open, honest communication. Investors know this, and they are looking for entrepreneurs with whom they can collaborate.

Griscom did the same thing two years later when it came time to sell his company. He was meeting with Disney executives, and instead of trying to convince them his startup was perfect in every way, he talked about how Babble's back end was outdated and engagement was lower than anticipated. This put the Disney execs at ease. They felt like he wasn't trying to pull one over on them. In fact, he was the type of person they wanted in their organization. Disney wound up acquiring Babble for $40 million.

At some point in your conversations with investors, they're bound to ask a question you don't know the answer to. Instead of making up something, simply tell them you don't know and you'll get back to them with the answer. You may appear ignorant, but you're being honest, which will earn you more points in the end.

Occasionally, you'll be asked a question you don't want to answer—not because you don't know the answer or are hiding something, but because it will send you down a path that leads nowhere. I've had investors spend the entire time nitpicking my revenue forecast when we hadn't even launched our product. This is a waste of precious time during a pitch meeting, so I learned that instead of whipping out the spreadsheet upon request, which would only encourage a long, convoluted discussion, it was better to say, "Is it okay if I send it to you in a follow-up email?" Then I'd move on to more important things.

Last, you need to know if this investor is the right fit. As I said before, taking money from a VC is like getting married. The last thing you want is to get divorced, which usually means the CEO getting kicked out of the home. Trust me when I say there are certain investors out there who will make your life miserable. I've seen investors who caused so much trouble that the startups bought back their shares. It was better than continuing in a dysfunctional relationship.

Your goal should be to find out as much about the individual partner and the firm as possible. What is their philosophy? Are they hands on or hands off? What value can they bring? How do they work with startups? Who will actually take a seat on the board? Sometimes, you'll be surprised to learn that it's not the partner you're talking to. Most important, you should get a list of references you can contact. It's vital before handing over a board seat that you talk to other entrepreneurs who have worked with this investor.

✳

*Your goal: Find out as much about the
individual partner and the firm as possible.*

When they give you references, you don't want the entrepreneurs who were wildly successful. They will almost always say nice things. What you want are the founders who failed. It's when the going gets tough that investors can get rough. They're often best pals when the startup is a rising star, but when it's crashing, some investors turn from Dr. Jekyll into Mr. Hyde.

Keep in mind when you meet with entrepreneurs, they most likely won't want to bad-mouth the investor. Silicon Valley is a small community, so you have to become adept at reading between the lines. Beware if they say something like, "Oh, that investor was okay." It usually means the investor was a jerk or didn't offer much help. What you want to hear is that the investor was absolutely amazing. When the company was near collapse, the investor did everything possible to help the situation, and the entrepreneur would work with the same investor again in a heartbeat.

In the end, you can never know if you're making the right choice. But if your gut says no, then you better listen. Don't become so desperate that you'll take anyone's money. You will regret that decision. Even if your company dies, it's far better than living with a dysfunctional board of directors. You need to be able to count on your board. You need to be able to trust them. They are your partners and will help determine the fate of your startup.

Spend as much time as possible with your investors up front. Hang out on the weekends. Meet their families. The more you do together, the better you'll get to know who they really are. This isn't a waste. It's a wise down payment on the future. As I've said, the CEO's number one job is to build the team, and the investors are part of that team. Invest the effort in advance, and you'll reap the rewards on the back end.

Using Fear and Greed

"CAPTAIN HOFF, HOW DO I close a deal? I've met with dozens of investors. They all seem interested, but no one will fund my company. What am I doing wrong?"

Whenever I hear this, I nod my head in sympathy. I was once in their shoes. I wasted huge amounts of time using the wrong approach on the wrong investors. So, let me give you the benefit of my learning. What I'm about to teach you not only applies to closing investment deals but any other deal as well. If you want to sell something, whether it's your company, products, or services, this strategy works. I went from being one of the worst salespeople on the planet to consistently closing deals with investors, large corporations, strategic partners, and governments all over the world. The core techniques work across all categories, but for the sake of this book, I'm going to focus on raising venture capital.

The first thing you have to understand is that you need a clearly defined sales path. You need to write down every step required to close the deal. Only when the money is in your bank account is the deal done. Anything short of this is wishful thinking. It's like making it to third base. It's nice, but you don't score until you reach home plate. Here are the ten basic steps:

1. Meet with the investor.
2. Present your business plan.

3. Discuss and answer questions.
4. Cement the relationship.
5. Sign the term sheet.
6. Negotiate the agreement.
7. Go through due diligence.
8. Sign the final agreement.
9. Wait for the money.
10. Bingo!

The hardest part is getting to number five. Once you get the term sheet signed, you're over the hump. If the investor is reliable and you have no skeletons in your closet, you should be able to push the process through to completion.

Where most startups get hung up is cementing the relationship. They will meet with the same investors over and over, but the investors always seem to be sitting on the fence. They can't decide. They like what the startup is doing, but they're afraid of losing their money, reputation, or job. If you're meeting with angel investors, they're usually more afraid of losing their money. VCs tend to care more about their reputations, and corporate investors worry about their jobs.

Whatever the case, you need to get them over the wall of fear, and the best way to do that is with greed. They must come to believe your startup is a big win. If it's a small or medium-sized opportunity, that's not enough. Even if it's a safer bet, the small wins aren't that interesting to investors, because those don't do much for them—either financially or emotionally. To understand this, you need to take into account human psychology.

If it's a small deal, who cares? The investors cannot brag about it. It won't propel their career forward, and it definitely won't make their reputation. Yes, they might make some money, but it's small money. What they want is big money because big deals get talked about. Our society places a huge emphasis on how successful people are, and unicorn-sized deals make headlines. Everything else gets buried. In their world, success equates with finding the next WhatsApp, Cloudera, MuleSoft, or TripAdvisor ahead of everyone else. That's what will earn them street cred, take them to the next level, and open doors.

Greed is a powerful motivator, but greed alone is not enough. You still need to overcome their fears. I spent nearly a year running my startup from offices on Sand Hill Road. I was embedded in a tier-one VC firm, and I saw from the inside how it worked. The Silicon Valley venture community is an exclusive club. That's why top VC firms pay a small fortune for office space on famed Sand Hill Road. Fear and greed rule their lives. VCs are under tremendous pressure to bring in the next big deal. They need fund makers. But they're equally afraid of screwing up. If they champion a rotten deal and word gets around, their careers can take a nosedive. This is what you're up against.

Most VCs mitigate this risk by having all-partner meetings. This means every partner in the firm gets together and hears the final pitch. Then it's a thumbs-up or thumbs-down vote. Often, if a single partner nixes the deal, the firm passes. On the other hand, if the deal gets approved but the startup winds up performing poorly down the road, the fact that the entire partnership gave its seal of approval prevents anyone from saying, "I told you so!"

As you can imagine, partner meetings take on special significance. No VC wants to risk presenting a silly deal to the other partners. What if the flaws are so obvious that the VC winds up looking like a fool in front of everyone? Think back to your high school days. It's the same thing.

For this reason, many VCs are cautious. But once you understand the dynamics inside a venture firm, you realize not all of them act the same way. There are three types of VCs you can approach: full partners, associates, and top dogs. Most entrepreneurs like to approach full partners, but often these are the worst ones to champion your business. It's because they have the most to lose. They are in midcareer, rising up the ladder of success, and don't want to take any risks that could knock them down a rung.

A good strategy is to get an associate as your primary champion in the firm. Don't think that because the partner pushed you off to a lowly associate, you won't get funded. The opposite is often true. Partners like to have their associates do the dirty work. That way, when they invite the startup to make the full pitch at an all-partners meeting, if things go wrong, it's the associate who will take the fall.

Associates are usually fresh out of college and hungry to make their mark. They are on the bottom rung of the ladder, so there's nowhere to go but up. They're also new to the culture and don't mind taking risks. If they believe in your startup, they'll go all out lobbying for you. Surprisingly, they also have a tremendous amount of sway inside most firms because they are young, and Silicon Valley worships youth. The older partners often look to the associates as barometers of what's hot. It's incredible how much faith a venture capitalist with a twenty-year track record will put in a young Harvard MBA with no business experience.

The other champions worth having are top dogs. The top dogs have already proven themselves. They are industry icons, and they no longer worry about their reputation. They are more likely to go out on a limb for you because, even if the deal implodes, it won't affect them.

Of course, there are exceptions to every rule. For instance, if the firm is smaller, a lot of these dynamics don't play out. Or if the partner is simply impervious to what others think, that individual will take more risks. My point is that you have to be strategic about how you approach VC firms. The more you understand the dynamics of a particular firm and psychology of your champion, the better you can navigate the treacherous path. What you need to understand is who wins and who loses by pushing your deal forward, what risks your champion is willing to take, and each person's mental state.

I've felt the pain of navigating these firms. I remember how hard it was to raise capital. Often, I'd spend months nurturing relationships with specific partners in a firm and finally get them to invite me to the all-partners meeting. It was my big chance to close, and then one person in the meeting would give the deal a thumbs-down, and it was dead. Back to square one. All my efforts were for naught.

I learned the hard way that you can't let it drag on for months. You need to orchestrate it right from the start. You must let the investors know there's competition for the deal, and if they don't move fast to close, you won't be around. It always comes down to fear and greed. To get investors to bite, their fear of losing the deal has to be greater than their fear of losing their money.

28

Managing Your Investor Pipeline

WHEN RAISING CAPITAL, YOU'LL NEED to fill your pipeline with potential investors. If you don't have enough prospects, it's hard to gain momentum and close in a reasonable time. A good rule of thumb is to have approximately ten different investors in your pipeline at any one time. Some may be early in the process, while others are further along.

The reason ten is the ideal number is because your goal is to have at least two investors commit to the deal around the same time. This way you can run them in parallel and get the best terms possible. The only leverage a startup has is competition for the deal. If you only have one investor on the hook, this investor is in the catbird seat. He can slow down talks and negotiate every point. There's no pressure to close.

Conversely, if you're talking to more than ten investors at once, you get spread so thin it's hard to manage the process efficiently. That's why ten is the magic number.

Once you get multiple investors interested, you need to think about how to manage them. One strategy is to get a strong lead investor, and then keep piling on more investors. A strong lead will often leverage relationships to bring on additional investors. Lots of startups use this approach. The more investors you add to the mix, the more momentum builds toward closing. Keep in mind that this only works if you have a strong and fully committed lead investor. Adding more investors to a weak lead is a recipe for disaster. For my third startup, we brought together our two strongest investors, each of whom had fully committed to the deal but couldn't cover the entire round, and this was enough to push us across the finish line.

※

*Fill your pipeline with potential investors—
ten is the magic number.*

The other strategy that works is to keep the investors completely separate and have them compete against one another. They will ask you repeatedly who else you're talking to, but resist the temptation to tell them. I learned the hard way that investors don't always do what they say. A weak, undecided investor can poison the well. If you put a vacillating investor with a semi-committed one, it can sow the seeds of doubt and cause the deal to disintegrate. As a rule of thumb, if you aren't 100 percent sure that an investor is onboard and committed, never introduce this person into the mix.

If you use these principles when managing your investor pipeline, you should do fine. The more carefully you orchestrate the process, the more rewarding it becomes.

29

Keeping a Poker Face

PLEASE, NEVER, EVER ACT DESPERATE. VCs like to fund companies that don't need their money. Nothing is more attractive than a CEO who is so confident she can walk away from the deal. It's just like dating. Playing hard to get works. No one wants to date someone who's desperate.

I've actually had entrepreneurs come up to me at events and say, "Captain Hoff, you've got to help me find investors. If you don't, my company will be out of business next week. Please, please help me!"

I feel so sorry for them, but this type of pitch doesn't work. Even if I made an introduction, their desperation would be enough to scare off any potential suitors. After all, who wants to invest in a company where the CEO is days away from throwing in the towel?

An even worse scenario is when the company has real value. If the investors realize they have leverage, they'll begin to squeeze. I've known startups that had to accept cram-down rounds, where all the existing shareholders suffered massive dilutions. Meanwhile, the new investors took control of the company. Showing any sign of vulnerability is the surest way to screw up the negotiations.

I learned this lesson the first time I ever tried to raise venture capital. I made the mistake of letting our investors know how much we desperately needed the cash, and guess what happened? They cut our valuation in half. Furious, we walked away from the deal, even though we were al-most entirely out of money.

✳

Showing any sign of vulnerability is the surest way to screw up negotiations with VCs.

It was two painful months later before we had another VC willing to invest. Even though we were then on the verge of bankruptcy and our employees were about to quit because we hadn't paid them, I told our investors that I'd have to find other VCs if they couldn't commit to the deal. It worked. This may sound too good to be true, but we closed the round and had the money in our bank account within a few weeks.

Whenever pitching investors, no matter how you feel inside, keep an inscrutable poker face on the outside. You have to act like you don't need their money, even when you desperately do.

30

Three Strikes, You're Out!

FROM MY FIRST STARTUP ONWARD, I steadily improved my sales techniques. I honed my approach over time, testing what worked and what didn't. I would try something, fail, analyze the results, and tweak what I was doing, then try again. I became adept enough at this process to cut my Series A fundraising time down from one year to two months for my third startup.

I draw inspiration from baseball. You give each investor three swings, and if they fail to connect with the ball, they are out. You have to be ruthless in this approach for it to work. The first swing is the first time they hear you pitch, whether it's at a pitch event, demo day, coffee shop, or conference room. Be aware that it's extremely hard to get a term sheet on the first pitch. It can happen, but don't expect it. Just make your best presentation and prepare for a follow-up meeting.

※

Give each investor three swings.
If they fail to connect, they are out.

The day after the presentation, send the investor an email. Keep it short. You should say something like: "It was great meeting with you.

Please let me know if you're interested in moving forward. I'd be happy to send you any materials you need to make your decision."

Then sit back and wait for a response. Some investors appear enthusiastic when you meet them in person, but they never respond to your follow-up emails. I've watched as entrepreneurs email them over and over again, but nothing ever comes back. I've had entrepreneurs become so annoyed, they explode in vitriolic rants about how disgusting the investor is. Don't waste your breath. It's not worth it. This happens all the time. Some people like to be friendly in person, whether or not they are really interested. Often, this is passive-aggressive behavior. They don't even realize how impolite it is. They simply don't feel comfortable giving anyone bad news, so they ignore the emails.

Remember, this type of behavior has nothing to do with you. You don't want to spend an ounce of your precious mental energy obsessing about it. Instead, dispassionately follow these steps:

1. Send a follow-up email the day after meeting them.
2. Wait one week for a reply.
3. If no reply, send a second follow-up email.
4. Wait one more week for a reply.
5. If no reply, send the final follow-up email.
6. Wait one more week for a reply.
7. If no reply, strike three! They're out.

Remember, sometimes investors get distracted by a problem with one of their portfolio companies. Other times it's a family issue. More often than not, they've simply moved on, and they are not interested. What's important is to focus your energy on moving forward, not looking back.

The same approach applies to meeting with investors. Each investor gets three strikes, and then they are out. When you pitch an investor the first time, always bring along a term sheet or convertible note. This way, if they're interested, you can close a deal. It's unlikely, but it's always good to be prepared. Assuming nothing happens, follow up and push for a second meeting.

The second meeting is where you should be mentally prepared to close. When you schedule this meeting, actively set expectations. Ask the investors to bring along anyone they will need to help them come to a decision. This is important. Most investors hate to commit their money alone. They usually want confirmation from a third party. Asking for the presence of everyone necessary also sets the tone that this meeting will be about making a decision, not just talking.

If it's a larger VC firm or corporation, not just an individual investor, then sealing the deal at meeting number two probably won't materialize, unless you happen to be meeting the top dog, and this alpha animal has the habit of acting independently. You need to know the process for closing, and there's no better time to ask than on the first meeting, so you're prepared. If they require an all-partners meeting or approval of the chairman, instead of pushing for a close, which won't happen, you should push for a meeting with the decision makers. In either case, your goal in the second meeting is to move the process forward as quickly as possible.

In your own head, you need to believe your time is more precious than their money. It's your job to run your company and grow your business. It's their job to find good investments. You are doing them a favor by presenting your startup. If you internalize this fact, it will put you in the right mental state. You want to go into each meeting believing they need you more than you need them.

But don't let this go to your head. When you meet, always be polite. Don't act arrogant. That won't win you any points. But at the same time, be firm and know what you want. Whenever you kick off a meeting, present your company again, even if they've heard it before. Refreshers are key. Then start asking questions. Find out what's keeping them from moving forward to a close. During the discussion, make it clear that you're meeting with other investors, and there's interest in your company. Don't overemphasize this fact. Just subtly slip it into the conversation, as if it's an afterthought. This is your hook, and you want them to bite.

If they ask you to introduce them to the other investors, don't do it. This is a trap. They will collude on pricing, and it won't help you close. It may even kill the deal if one party isn't as interested as the other. It's better to keep all your investors running in parallel until you're 100 percent sure two or more are going to close at the same time. If they try to pressure you into revealing the competition, tell them politely that you'll make the introduction if the other parties are interested in having co-investors. This will incite their competitive natures. No one likes to be left out.

What's important here is to position yourself midstream in the fundraising process. If it seems like you're about to close with someone else, many VCs will back out because they don't want to waste their time. No one wants to be too late. You need to make clear that it's still early in the process with other parties, and you're trying to decide who will be the best fit. This gives them room to move forward, while you're still applying pressure to act fast.

From my experience, the probability of closing rises exponentially with each meeting. With the first meeting, it's small. Then it doubles with the second meeting and triples with the third meeting. Once you get all the decision makers in the room, it's at its peak. In this meeting, you have to ask the right questions, get them to articulate your model, and set a firm deadline. If they don't commit, your odds of ever closing will begin to plummet. Several meetings later, the probability will be asymptotically approaching zero.

When raising capital for my third venture-funded startup, I got all the way to the partner meeting with a top-tier venture firm. At the meeting, I told a room full of VCs that they must close within the next two weeks. It was the start of summer vacation, and I knew everyone would be leaving town soon. They pushed back, telling me it was impossible. So, I walked away from that deal. It was hard, but I don't think I lost anything. I stuck to my rules. It was three strikes, and they were out.

I used to feel awkward being tough and demanding action from people. It wasn't in my nature, but I learned that people will have far more respect for you if you are up front, unhesitating, and iron-willed than if you try to please them all the time. After the third strike, you aren't going to gain anything by continuing to pitch. If those investors truly want the deal, they will act. If they don't, it's time for you to get someone else up to bat.

31

Push for a No!

AS MY SALES MENTOR TOLD me: "Push for a no! Stop trying to get them to say yes." This seems counterintuitive, but once I understood what he meant, it made complete sense. In the end, the investors either want what you have to sell or they don't. If they don't want it, you need to know why as soon as possible. If you have this information, you can often turn a no into a yes.

People are fundamentally emotional beings. Feelings override logic every time—not the other way around. Human beings feel first and rationalize later. The important thing is to understand the investors' feelings and use them to achieve your goals. Nobody likes to be pressured into making a decision. Once you push for a no, you give the investors the chance to gain control and decide what they want for themselves. By pulling back, you can actually draw them in. Most investors are hyper-competitive and hate to lose out on a deal, so if you pull away, they will instinctively fight to keep their options open. In essence, you are swapping positions. They now have to sell you. By pushing for a no, you can compel investors to justify why they should be included in the deal. It's a subtle but powerful psychological shift.

This is what your second investor meeting is all about. It's not about selling. It's about flipping the dynamics. You must figure out if this deal is the right fit for everyone, and if it's not, why not. So, push for a no while keeping in mind that there are many different types of no, and each one can shed light on the situation.

※

By pulling back from buyers, you can actually
draw them in—they now have to sell you.

For example, an investor may say, "No, I'm not interested," while thinking something more specific:

- No, your valuation is too high.
- No, your market is too small.
- No, you don't have a strong enough team.
- No, unless you get a strong lead investor.
- No, I don't understand your technology.

You need to discover what's blocking investors from saying yes. Sometimes they don't even know, but your questions can help them sort it out. I can't stress this enough. Most people don't know exactly what they want. They have a mixture of emotions ranging from hidden fears to lofty aspirations. You need to allow them to clarify their thoughts and construct a coherent narrative that they can buy into. If you can help them create a story they believe in, you can close the deal.

The next step is to ask the right questions. Only by asking detailed questions in a carefully structured manner can you successfully uncover what investors are really thinking and guide them to the right conclusions.

- What makes you interested in this deal?
- How do you feel about my startup?
- What are the steps necessary for closing?
- What concerns do you have about the business?
- Is there anyone else you need involved?
- How do you go about making a final decision?

- Is there anything preventing you from moving forward?
- What would you like to see in the term sheet?

You see the tone I'm setting? Be respectful and inquisitive. Ask open-ended questions that get them talking. Listen carefully to each answer and calibrate your response. With each new question, the investors will be constructing a narrative in their heads. The story they envision is what will sell them on your company. The goal is to get investors to think through all aspects of the deal and come to a decision they can believe in.

For instance, let's say a startup is trying to raise capital to sell eyeglasses online. The CEO's primary hypothesis is that people want to buy eyeglasses online because it's cheaper and more convenient. How does the CEO get investors to believe this is true?

The founder can start by asking these questions:

- Do you like paying $400 for a pair of eyeglasses?
- If you could get the same glasses for half the price, would you?
- Wouldn't it be nice to have a much larger selection to choose from?
- What if we sent several samples to you to try on?
- What if we made it super simple to return them at no cost?
- Would this type of service be valuable?

This is basically the argument that Warby Parker made to its investors, posed as a series of questions. I'm not sure they pitched investors this way, but they should have. Nothing works better than having people convince themselves something is true. In other words, if you can get investors to articulate the core assumptions of your business and agree to them, you can orchestrate that "Aha!" moment when they tell themselves, "Yes, I want this!"

Everyone wants to get to a yes quickly, and you may be tempted to take shortcuts. But be careful. Not all yeses are equal. Some people say yes just to get you out of their hair, especially if you're being pushy. Other times, they are just affirming what they heard, but they don't necessarily agree. You need to be able to distinguish between the various types of responses. You'll know it's a true yes when you see the investor suddenly switch from inquiring and analyzing to actively trying to get you to close. Anything short of this, and you may be fooling yourself.

※

It's a true yes when the investor switches from inquiring and analyzing to actively trying to get you to close.

If things aren't going well, and you can't get the investor to commit, try asking questions like these:

- Have you given up on this investment?
- What makes you uncomfortable with this deal?
- Does this mean you cannot move forward?
- What is it about this business that doesn't work for you?
- If you could change one thing about my startup, what would it be?
- Let me clarify. It seems like you're saying _____.
- If we solve this problem, is there anything that would keep you from investing?

Notice how several of these questions allow investors to answer no while prompting them to move forward with the deal. They aren't being forced to commit to anything. Instead, they are being encouraged to articulate what's bothering them while justifying why they still want this deal. In the end, you need them to come up with why they feel your company is a good deal. They need to say it to themselves. You can't do it for them.

Once you've crossed this hurdle, it's either going to close fast or not at all. Believe me when I say that investors move with lightning speed on deals they want. They don't dawdle around. If the investor is making excuses, it means there's some problem you haven't uncovered. It may be a problem you can solve, or it may not. Either way, you need to know what it is, so you can address it.

32

Never Lie to Investors

I HAVE A RULE. NEVER lie to investors. It's important that you have integrity. You can stretch the truth a little, but don't cross the line. This topic deserves some discussion because there's a fine line between lying and good salesmanship. Some people will lie outright, but I never recommend it. First, lying will come back to burn you. It erodes trust and destroys relationships. This is a relationship business, and you don't want to tarnish your reputation. Second, it's not moral. You need to act like the type of person you respect. Your strength comes from who you are. If you lie to other people, you will wind up lying to yourself. No amount of money is worth your self-respect. Don't go down this path. This is my personal belief, and I hope it's yours, too.

That said, you still need to sell, and selling is an art. For my startups, whenever people asked if we could deliver the product on time, we always said, "Absolutely! No problem." We didn't know if we could do it. No one can ever know something like that, but if we hadn't been confident, we would never have won the contracts. No one wants to invest in a startup that can't deliver. Your job is to do the improbable—to make things happen. If you believe in your team and know in your heart that you can make it happen, then you can say so, even if you're afraid you may fail. Everyone is scared of failing, but you have to be bold and take chances.

When an investor asks if you can build a billion-dollar business, you will never know for sure if you can or can't do it. The only way to know is by trying. But you must believe it's possible; otherwise, why are you asking for their money? This is the fine line I'm talking about. You must drink your own Kool-Aid. You must believe so much in your vision that you can convince others around you that it's real. The odds of a startup failing are ten to one. Investors know this. Your strategic partners know this, but they are working with you because they believe you can buck those odds.

So, when you're in a meeting with investors, you need to think and act like you're going to make it happen, but you need to do it without lying or deceiving. Unfortunately, that means there's this gray area that you must wade into. This is the essence of life. If choices in life were always clear-cut, things would be boring. A robot could make those decisions. But most decisions in life fall into the murky zone. That's why it's important to check with your heart. If your heart tells you that you're crossing the line, pull back. You don't want to compromise your values. But if you know it's right, charge ahead. Sell them on your vision. Make them believe. And close the deal.

33

Artificial Deadlines

SOMETIMES YOU NEED TO MANUFACTURE your own dead-lines. If there's no deadline, investors tend to take a wait-and-see approach. Why should they commit to an investment if they aren't under any pressure? By waiting, they can gain more information and gauge your progress, and if a better deal happens to come along, they can jump on it.

Let me tell you a story. When raising money for my third venture-funded startup, I was meeting with Disney. My friend had just joined Steamboat Ventures, Disney's VC arm, and he wanted to invest. Because he was a friend, I broke my sacred three-strikes rule and kept meeting with him over and over and over. Every time he would say: "I'm really interested. I'm going to invest."

By the sixth time, I was getting fed up. I had other investors on the line, and they were interested. So, I told him: "Look, I have other investors ready to go. If you don't invest, I'm going with them."

Somehow, he thought I was bluffing, and he didn't follow up. So, I went back to the other investors. They were one of the largest hedge funds in the world. In a very short time, I had landed a meeting with the chairman and CEO. I knew this was the meeting where I had to close. By this time, I'd learned what I needed to do. I showed him our vision. Then, in a subtle way, I let it be known that one of the largest media companies in the world was interested in us. I didn't say Disney because I didn't want them colluding on the deal. I just left it vague. It could have been Viacom, Fox, or Time Warner.

Many people say you can't close a deal right before Christmas because everyone is thinking about their holidays, but I was determined to close this deal and disregarded conventional wisdom. After all, if I waited and didn't close before the holidays, everyone would go on vacation, and we'd lose momentum. Losing momentum is the death of most deals. All the excitement and pressure dissipate, and when you return, it's like starting over. Except, it's even harder. The sense of urgency is gone, and people have mentally moved on.

※

Losing momentum is the death of most deals.

With this hedge fund, I wasn't about to let this happen. So, I told them that if they wanted this deal, they had to close by Christmas. It was an insane request because it was already the first week of December, and we didn't even have a term sheet signed. But they understood that I wasn't joking. Now let me be clear. Disney was interested, but they weren't going to snatch up this deal before the end of the year. I knew this for a fact, but I had to push. So, I made it clear that I had a timeline, and if the hedge fund wanted to work with me, they had to move on my schedule. In other words, I created an artificial sense of urgency. I was driving the process. I set the deadline in stone, and this deadline became real because I made it real.

This is what you have to do when strategically closing. Otherwise, you're just relying on luck. The only leverage you really have is to be prepared to walk away if they don't act. I know it's hard, but that's the fine art of dealmaking. You have to be the one making the rules, not following them. If those rules are going to mean anything, you have to play by them. So, when meeting with the hedge fund CEO, I said, "If you don't close the deal now, it won't be around much longer." And I meant it. I was mentally prepared to cross them off my list and move on. It was three strikes and you're out, and they were up to bat. What happened? The hedge fund hit the ball out of the park, and the round closed days before Christmas, just in time to avoid the holiday exodus from Silicon Valley.

In the new year, I went back to my friend at Disney and told him. He was pissed. He couldn't believe I'd gone ahead without him. He thought I was just talking, but I had done exactly what I told him I'd do. Did I exaggerate when I told him I had another investor ready? Yes and no. I knew I could get them up to bat, but you never know if they'll hit the ball. This brings me back to creating your own reality. If you don't believe in your own deadlines, you can't make them real for everyone else. When you create a deadline, you have to be prepared to live or die by it. That's when everything clicks into place. That's when hard decisions get made.

In the end, because I valued Disney and the VC was a friend, I said that he could still come in on the deal as a follow-on investor. But I wanted to make sure he wasn't on the fence, so I told him the valuations. When he heard the terms, he balked. It was too rich for Disney. So, after all that, I found out he wasn't a good fit.

Only when investors actually come to the decision point will you know if they're really going to do what they say. Sometimes they don't even know themselves until they reach that point. That's why deadlines are so important. Without a deadline, there often is no reason to decide. And, ironically, it can take an imaginary deadline to reveal what's real and what's not.

34

Leveraging Social Capital

SOCIAL CAPITAL IS OFTEN AS important as actual money in the bank. If you don't know what social capital is, let me tell you. It's the endorsement of key industry influencers. The more influential the person, the more social capital you'll accrue. One positive tweet from Larry Page or Elon Musk can do more for your startup than a thousand no-name investors saying exactly the same thing. This is because Silicon Valley is a tight-knit community, and word spreads fast. It's follow the leader. If one of the top dogs blesses a startup with a nod, everyone else jumps onboard.

You should approach raising social capital in much the same way you raise real money. It's just a little harder, because getting lunch with the likes of Reid Hoffman, cofounder of LinkedIn; Brian Chesky, CEO of Airbnb; or Chris Sacca, early investor in Twitter, is no easy task. If you aren't lucky enough to have a cousin who happens to be best friends with Ashton Kutcher, the celebrity turned investor, or Michael Arrington, the founder of TechCrunch, how do you gain access to these influencers?

One way is to start at the bottom and work your way up. Begin with the people you know. Get them onboard as advisors and have them begin to introduce you to their networks. You might be surprised. If you've spent any time in Silicon Valley, you're probably only a few steps removed from some powerful influencers. Go to LinkedIn. You can see the connections. I've sat down with entrepreneurs and mapped out their networks, and they were shocked at some of the connections their friends had.

In reality, the chance of getting facetime with Jack Dorsey, the cofounder of Square and Twitter, or Ken Howery, the cofounder of PayPal and the Founders Fund, is pretty slim—let alone getting them to say something in public about your yet unproven business. Instead, what you need is the equivalent of these influencers, but in your specific industry. If your startup is developing BCI (brain-computer interface) technology, then make a list of all the top BCI researchers and thought leaders in this field. They might not be household names, like Ray Kurzweil, or even names known to most people in Silicon Valley, but they can be pretty influential inside BCI circles.

Do whatever it takes to get them onboard your startup. They are the next rung on your ladder. Landing the first big fish in your industry is always hard, but once you get one big kahuna onboard, the second is much easier. I've seen entrepreneurs who land in Silicon Valley knowing nobody, and within a matter of months, they seem to know everyone in their particular industry.

They do this by laser focusing on niche influencers. These are people with deep expertise and networks in a specific area. Don't ask for money. Don't ask for press. Instead, find out something they need and offer that to them. Can you show them a piece of new technology? Can you introduce them to someone valuable in your network? The bigger your network becomes, the more you'll have to offer. Or you can propose writing a story about them. Make it a guest post on a well-known site, like *Slashdot*, *Ars Technica*, *HuffPost*, or *Wired*. Or focus on a blog that caters to your specific vertical market. Most big shots in Silicon Valley love press. That's how they became so well known. Sitting down to interview them is your golden chance to get them onboard your startup.

※

Laser focus on niche influencers—people with deep expertise and networks in a specific area.

There are other ways to provide value to them. Read their blogs and try to figure out what they are interested in. It can be a hobby or a philanthropic endeavor. Whatever it is, see if you can provide something useful to them and, in exchange, get a chance to build a relationship. Only be careful not to make it phony. People can see right through it. If you're offering to help but you have no real interest in what they're doing, they'll realize you're just using them and wind up resentful. You should only offer to help if you truly believe in what they're doing and you're willing to do an excellent job. Otherwise, it will backfire on you.

It's not easy, but assuming you can come up with something real and you don't mind hustling, there's nothing that should stop you. Silicon Valley is a meritocracy at heart. Everyone likes to believe they are open to new ideas and new people. This is the beauty of the Valley. No one knows where the next big idea is coming from, and everyone wants to be part of it when it arrives. All it takes to raise social capital is your time and some street smarts.

35

Getting Warm Introductions

NOTHING BEATS A WARM INTRODUCTION. Many investors in Silicon Valley will only meet with a startup when it's recommended by someone they know and trust. Because I run Founders Space, startups are always asking, "Captain Hoff, can you introduce me to investors? Please!"

Unfortunately, it's not possible for me to personally introduce every startup I meet to the right investors in our network. There are too many startups asking for introductions. More important, the startup has to fit the investor's criteria. This type of intricate matchmaking takes time and effort. Even if I wanted to do this as my full-time job, there aren't enough hours in the day.

Sloppy introductions don't help anyone. The startups won't get funded, and the investors hate to have their time wasted. If I send the wrong startups to the wrong investors one too many times, the doors will close. Those investors wouldn't want any more introductions from me. Why should they? No one appreciates being spammed. So, if I'm not investing in the startup myself, either through our program or my angel fund, then I won't make the introduction. I will, however, invite startups to apply to pitch at our investor pitch events where my team can evaluate them and determine if there's a potential fit.

In addition, we recently launched a service where investors can reach out to our startups. It's called FoundersEdge.com, and it's designed so that investors can easily browse, analyze, and rate the startups on their own. We made sure to keep the investors' information confidential, since most investors don't want to receive business plans outside their focus. We also categorize all the startups by sector, customer type, country, and rating, making it easy to find the right startups. When investors find a good match, they can directly contact the startup founders. This has allowed us to connect more startups with investors than we could ever do manually.

That said, many startups coming to Silicon Valley still want personal introductions. The problem is, most people with extensive investor networks only recommend startups they know well, which makes it hard for newcomers to meet the right people. But that doesn't mean it's impossible. There is a way around every obstacle. First, I recommend every startup establish a board of advisors made of industry professionals. These are people who should have connections to investors, valuable business experience, or deep industry contacts and domain expertise. If someone agrees to join the board, that means he or she is committing to help the startup succeed and should be willing to leverage networks on behalf of the startup.

In addition to advisors, entrepreneurs should look to people with whom they are already doing business. This includes lawyers, public relations professionals, marketing consultants, advertising agencies, accounting firms, and so on. If these professionals have been working in Silicon Valley for any length of time, I guarantee they know investors. Everyone who has been here for a year or more knows at least one venture capitalist. Before the entrepreneur hires the firm, they should get a commitment that the firm will make a certain number of introductions. It might seem strange to ask an accounting firm for investor introductions, but it happens all the time. You'd be surprised at how many investors these accountants know, especially if they've been working with startups. In fact, they cultivate these relationships to drive their business.

The most overlooked source of warm introductions is fellow entrepreneurs. Nearly every startup in Silicon Valley is in fundraising mode. This means every entrepreneur knows at least a few investors. I'm always telling entrepreneurs to go out, network with other startup founders, and trade warm introductions. I know some founders who go to a single networking event, meet a dozen startups, and walk out with commitments for more than a dozen investor intros. It's simple. You scratch their backs, and they'll scratch yours.

✳

The most overlooked source of warm introductions is fellow entrepreneurs.

Last, there are professional organizations, accelerators, pitch events, meetup groups, conferences, private parties, and dozens of other ways to meet investors. Often, you don't even need an introduction. You just need to show up at the same place investors are and polish your gift of gab. That's how you get in the door. It's old-fashioned hustling. If you're friendly, outgoing, and interesting, doors tend to open. Always be expanding your network, and don't be afraid to use your relationships to help others. We call this *paying it forward*. If you help others today, they'll help you tomorrow.

36

Cold Emails That Work

IF ALL ELSE FAILS, THERE'S the cold calling or, in today's world, cold emailing or messaging. This is far from ideal, but it does work. Many investors will tell you they never respond to cold emails, but I know for a fact that plenty do. Many of the largest venture funds list the email addresses of the partners on their websites for precisely this reason. They never know where the next big investment opportunity is coming from, and they want to keep the lines of communication open.

Foreign-born entrepreneurs have helped cofound roughly half the venture-funded startups in Silicon Valley. The founders tend to have few, if any, contacts in Silicon Valley when they arrive. So, cold emails are one of their best options. The same is true for college students and recent graduates. They haven't had time to build up much in the way of networks, so cold emailing is a viable strategy.

When I launched my first startup, I'd never met a VC in my life, I had no rich friends, and my family had zero connections. At that time, incubators and accelerators didn't even exist in Silicon Valley, and there were far fewer networking opportunities. So, what did I do? I began cold emailing investors, and it worked. I began to get meetings. Not a lot, but enough to get me started.

I continued to use cold emails for my early startups. Why? Because it works. That's how I got into dozens of VC firms. I met with Doug Leone, managing partner of Sequoia Capital; Ann Winblad, the managing director of Hummer Winblad; Ken Howery, managing director of the Founders Fund; and dozens of other top VCs. I even cold emailed Steve Jobs and got a meeting at Apple. Unfortunately, Jobs wasn't in the meeting, but that's okay. It was a cold email, and I got to pitch his team.

Here's my formula for cold emails. Keep them simple. The ideal cold email will start with a single sentence describing your business. Without using any buzzwords, describe what your product does for the customer. Then list out three bullet points, each highlighting a key achievement. Insert a link to your video or a link to your investor deck. Sign your name, including your phone number, and that's it.

Here's a sample of what I just described:

Dear Tim,

My startup, _____, allows corporations to instantly screen, filter, and rank thousands of incoming résumés in a matter of minutes using artificial intelligence and big data, placing the best résumés on top.

- We just won first prize at TechCrunch Disrupt.
- Our team is from Stanford, Brown, and MIT.
- We've launched our prototype and signed IBM as our first customer.
- Here's a link to our video: _____.

That's the perfect cold email. It's short and to the point. I wish I received emails like this. Most people write me these long rambling essays that make *War and Peace* seem like a quick read. I get exhausted just looking at them. I usually skip to the end to find out what they want, and then forward it to the appropriate member of my staff. In other words, if you want a busy person to actually read your email, brevity is the key.

If you want a busy person to actually
read your email, brevity is the key.

Even if you can't find the email addresses of those you want to reach, there are a huge number of ways to harvest them. The easiest is LinkedIn, but you can also google the name, purchase email lists, ask friends, and, if all else fails, guess at the name. Trying a dozen combinations usually results in a hit.

Last, I want to warn you against trying to become friends over email. It seldom works and is more likely to result in the investor losing interest. On the same token, don't send more information than is absolutely necessary. Too much information only gives the investor a reason to say no before meeting you. When writing follow-up emails, you should be as concise as possible. Just ask, "When can we meet?" Getting the meeting is all that matters. Once you're with the investor, that's when you can elaborate.

That's all there is to cold emails. Even today, with all my connections, I'll often dash off a cold email to someone I really want to meet but don't have any relationship with. It works for me. It should for you.

37

How to Stand Out from the Crowd

THE WORST THING YOU CAN do during a pitch is to blend in with the crowd. I've seen it over and over again: The startup that does something different attracts all the attention. Remember, VCs are only human. They get bored. It seems like a glamorous job, but imagine getting pitched day in and day out for weeks on end. It can be mind-numbing. One pitch begins to sound like the next. I used to think being an investor was all fun and no work. After all, I would get to spend my days listening to incredible ideas from some of the smartest people on the planet. But that's not exactly how it works. Most of the ideas are me-too concepts. Most of the entrepreneurs aren't professional speakers and get lost in a sea of buzzwords. Most of the PowerPoint presentations wind up looking the same. It's rare that a startup offers something that makes you sit up in your seat.

I hate to say it, but investors are desperate for someone or something to break the monotony of their day. Give them just one thing to remember you by, and they'll be so grateful. This is why I coach entrepreneurs to do whatever they want except bore the audience. Don't be afraid to take some chances. Tell some jokes. Put on a show. A little pizzazz never hurts. If you run a food-tech startup, bring out the food! Let the investors have a bite. I guarantee they will remember you. If you're a robotics startup, get that robot on the floor dancing, doing backflips, or juggling. If you're a drone startup, show some of those amazing videos that make everyone's jaw drop. I don't care—just make it exciting.

I had a startup fly up from the University of Southern California to meet me. It was two recent grads who'd just launched a virtual reality company called Survios. This was shortly after Oculus VR launched on Kickstarter, and virtual reality was the hot new thing. The founders wanted me to help them with their business plan, but I insisted on first playing their VR games. These were only prototypes, but they blew me away. These guys had something real. They understood VR.

They wanted me to help them with their presentation, but I told them to forget PowerPoint. What mattered was getting the VCs, most of whom had never seen virtual reality before, to play their games. I advised them not to spend time running through their pitch deck. Instead, they should go straight to the demonstration. I assured them that if the VCs tried it, they would get funded.

I immediately signed on as an advisor and made introductions to top-tier VCs that I knew would be a good fit. I told the Survios founders that it usually takes several months to get funded but not to worry. They had something special. Even with my optimism, I couldn't believe how quickly it went. In just a few weeks, they landed $5 million in funding. They went on to produce one of the top grossing VR games to date. It's called *Raw Data*.

Another startup I heard pitch recently did something even more unique. Instead of launching into a long-winded explanation of the product, the CEO stood onstage at a pitch event, held up an odd-shaped object the size of a walnut, and said, "This device is going to change how we think forever. No one will be able to live without one. If you want to try it, come to our booth, and I'll show you."

That was the entire pitch. It lasted less than thirty seconds. After that, the CEO walked offstage. It worked. The investors were hooked. At their booth, an eager crowd fought to get a glimpse of the future, while the other booths were all empty.

You don't need earth-shattering technology or dancing robots to captivate investors. You just need to do something different. One startup I met did it with a plain old app. I met this entrepreneur at a conference and heard his story. He used to be a popular VJ (video jockey). But when YouTube tightened the copyright rules around music, his show died, and he wound up living in a trailer park somewhere in the Midwest. Depressed and unable to find a decent job, he and his friends decided they would create a music app together. But they needed money, so they started cold emailing VCs in Silicon Valley.

※

You don't need earth-shattering technology or dancing robots—you just need to do something different.

One of his rambling emails landed on the desk of a famously eccentric investor and the founder of a top venture capital firm. After a short exchange, the VC invited the team to come make a pitch. The only problem was, the entrepreneur and his cofounders were flat broke. But like all good hustlers, they scraped together just enough money to buy plane tickets to the Golden State. That's when the blizzard hit. Their local airport shut down. Unable to bear the thought of missing their only chance at a future, they drove through the night to a neighboring city and caught a flight to San Francisco.

The next day, they arrived at the VC's fancy offices on Sand Hill Road, the most expensive real estate in the Valley. Instead of playing it safe, they did the opposite. They dressed up in crazy outfits, got an oversized boom box, and blasted their favorite tunes as they waltzed into the staid offices. It was like something out of a movie. Everyone looked at them in shock and horror. What were they doing? They wound up dancing right into the VC's office and launched into an impassioned pitch.

According to the entrepreneur, they walked out with a check for $400,000. Why? Because the investor knew these guys had something. He wasn't sure what, but it had made his day. And he thought it was worth betting on. I lost track of this startup and have no idea if their app succeeded or not, but they certainly knew how to stand out.

38

Kissing Frogs

TO WRAP UP THIS SECTION, I'd like to compare courting investors to kissing frogs. I'm sure you've heard of the fairy tale about the princess who kissed the frog and it turned into her Prince Charming. That's what every entrepreneur dreams of when talking to VCs. They fantasize about the investor who will hand them gobs of money and carry them away to live happily ever after. When you're pitching VCs, think of them as frogs. Every time you meet with them, it's a kiss. If you've kissed the same investor three times and he hasn't turned into your Prince Charming, then I'm sorry, but that investor is just a frog.

3

Bootstrapping It

Guerrilla Marketing and Growth Hacking

ootstrapping is when you fund the company out of your own pocket. Even though this is how most companies start out, venture capital seems to receive the lion's share of attention in the media. But I can tell you, it's not as glorious as you think. Venture money seldom solves a company's problems, and often, it can be the cause of them. I've seen entrepreneurs literally break down under pressure from their investors. I've watched others battle it out, tearing apart their companies in the process and then walking away with nothing at all to show for it.

Before you run after the big bucks, take a moment to think about foregoing venture capital—at least for the first year. Just because you lack capital doesn't necessarily mean you're at a disadvantage. Having less capital instills discipline in a startup. You can't just spend your way forward. You have to be incredibly creative and resourceful to break through. Ironically, many successful entrepreneurs look back at these days as the happiest times in their lives, when they felt most connected to their companies and the people around them. It's often an intense fight for survival, and with that can come a powerful bonding with your teammates that's impossible to re-create once your company grows larger and more stable.

Having less capital instills discipline in a startup.

My goal is to help you navigate these treacherous but thrilling rapids. I'll give you the tools and advice you need to keep your head above water. I'll cover everything from growth hacking and guerrilla marketing to content generation and public relations. By the end, you'll know what it takes to bootstrap a startup without breaking your piggybank.

39

When to Raise Money

PRACTICALLY EVERY STARTUP I MEET is obsessed with raising money from VCs. It's almost like that's the end goal. Building a business comes second. Many entrepreneurs expect to raise millions on nothing but their PowerPoint presentations. This has become a sickness in Silicon Valley. We have entrepreneurs who believe that success equates to getting funded. Nothing could be further from the truth. Funding means nothing if you haven't proven out your business. The millions should come after you've validated your model, not before.

Getting too much money too early can be the worst curse of all. It can send you down the wrong path. It can distract you, even blind you to reality. I've witnessed companies with hundreds of millions in venture capital spend their way into oblivion without addressing any of the underlying issues. They simply masked the problems with greenbacks until it was too late. Upping the burn rate without any proven way to make money is like accelerating as you're approaching a cliff. There are so many stories of startups with great potential that raised too much, too early, and drove right off that cliff.

The most famous one is Fab.com, a flash sales site with a snazzy mobile app, which raised a whopping $310 million. At one point, they were burning $14 million a month but couldn't figure out how to retain customers. The money only served to obscure the problem. In the end, they wound up squandering everything and selling the company in a fire sale.

Too much funding too early can also kill innovation. Entrepreneurs who are handed huge checks tend to switch from discovery mode to expansion mode. A big infusion of cash means the startup begins hiring people, building out the business, and focusing on growth over experimentation. The problem comes when they haven't figured out their product-market fit. Scaling your business without understanding what your customer really needs is a death sentence.

※

Scaling your business without understanding
what your customer really needs is a death sentence.

The Startup Genome Report found that premature scaling is the most common reason that startups perform poorly. Their data shows that 70 percent of startups scaled prematurely along at least one dimension, including hiring up too fast, overbuilding the product, or overspending on marketing and customer acquisition.

If you don't want this to happen to you, instead of devoting months to raising capital, put that time into engaging your customers. Keep expenses to a minimum and spend as much time as it takes to run experiments that will prove or disprove your business hypotheses. If you disprove your core assumptions, you'll need to pivot. If you prove your model, investors will line up to get in the door. VCs love it when you've done the hard work. Venture capital is really good at scaling businesses that work but very poor at fixing ones that don't.

Most VCs don't even want to step into a deal unless they're convinced you have the next big thing. The term "venture capital" is a misnomer. Most VCs are not adventurous and don't want to take risks. They say they're hands-on and like to add value, but don't count on them to help you figure anything out. They usually don't know how and don't have time. Be prepared to do all the heavy lifting yourself.

The problem is that when entrepreneurs land large checks, they often believe they've made it. After all, why would a big-name VC invest in anything short of brilliant? Sadly, this isn't the case. VCs invest in losers all the time. Most startups in a typical VC portfolio will return little to nothing. It's only a few that become the big wins touted in the media.

There are also many ideas VCs simply won't fund because they aren't big enough, but these businesses can be a big win for the entrepreneurs. There's nothing wrong with building a business that grosses several million dollars a year and is profitable. VCs call these *lifestyle businesses* because they stop growing at a certain point, which makes it difficult to exit. Most entrepreneurs I know would be happy pocketing a million or more a year, which you can't do if investors want you to plow all your money back into the company to accelerate growth.

The startup Little Passports is a great example of this. They tried to raise capital, and it's a lucky thing they couldn't. Back in 2009, the founders, Amy Norman and Stella Ma, pitched their startup to seventy-five investors and got turned down seventy-five times. All they wanted was $500,000, and their business model was simple. Little Passports would deliver geography-themed activity kits via snail mail to kids ranging from six to ten years old. Parents would pay $10.95 a month for this service. But no one would take a chance on them.

They learned that at least one investor passed, saying, "One of the founders is pregnant with a second child, and the other has a child already." The investor failed to realize that these mothers might know kids better than they do. Eight years later, Little Passports has $30 million in annual revenue. Even though they managed to raise $5 million in angel money along the way, they never attracted a major VC firm. This quirk of fate actually helped. It forced them to be frugal and focus on small, inexpensive experiments. "We had to stand on our own two feet early on," Norman says. "We've had to use a lot of financial discipline."

Like all startup stories, it sounds easy, but it wasn't. Norman and Ma had to fund the company with $25,000 of their own money. They created the first kits themselves and tested them on fifty families they found on Craigslist. Then, days before the launch, everything went wrong. Norman found out that she was pregnant with her second child. At the same time, her marriage fell apart. After giving birth, she came down with Bell's palsy. "It was an absolutely horrific time in my life," says Norman.

Two months later, her father was diagnosed with cancer. She was told he had only four months to live. Her friends encouraged her to stop and look for a job with a steady income, but Norman refused. She believed in their business and didn't want to let it go.

By this time, they'd raised a little angel money, but it was still tough going. Norman admitted that she wanted VC money but not for the right reasons. "I have my Wharton degree and my McKinsey pedigree. Having venture capital [would be] another bragging right." But that right didn't come.

Taking a gamble, they spent $30,000 on Facebook Lookalike Audience ads. This approach worked, and sales began to rise. Norman concedes that if they'd had VC money, they probably would have tried expensive TV and print ads. Without the cash, they were much more careful. There were no lavish launch parties, free lunches, or trendy Silicon Valley offices. "If you rely on venture capital, it's almost like being on drugs," Norman says. "You're waiting for your next fix to come."[1]

I've seen a lot of startups get hooked on VC funding. Once you start raising VC money, it's hard to stop. Your company and your mindset change. I recommend you pass on pitching VCs at the beginning. Fundraising is hard and time-consuming, especially when you have nothing but an idea. Your time is better spent in the trenches with your customers than in the cushy offices of venture capitalists. I realize that it takes money to get started. I'm not saying you shouldn't raise an angel round early on. That's what angels are for, but when it comes time for the big bucks, you need to have solid proof your business will fly. Otherwise, your idea will never get off the ground.

40

What's the Right Business?

IT'S EASY TO TELL YOU not to take money from VCs, friends, family, loan sharks, and credit card companies, but then how can you possibly start a new company? Businesses require money. I have two answers to that, and they are simple: Get a job and save up the money, or pick a business that doesn't require a large up-front investment. Seriously, not all businesses require big bucks to get started. The right business is often the one you can grow to profitability with nothing but your time and savings. I did this with my first bootstrapped startup, and I see other entrepreneurs go down this path all the time and reap the rewards.

If you have a dream project that needs millions to get out of the gate, you'd be wise to shelve that idea until you have a success or two under your belt. There are countless ideas waiting to be discovered, many of which require little or no up-front capital to launch. Microsoft, Dell, and Facebook all started in dorm rooms. They didn't need any funding at first. They just got friends to pitch in and help. In my opinion, the right idea is always the idea you can develop with the cash in your bank account. The further along you can get on your own dollar, the better off you'll be.

I will tell you that there's nothing like validating an idea before you bring it to investors. Once you take someone's money, especially large sums of money, you are under pressure. They want you to show progress. They want you to move fast. They want to see growth. However, discovering a new opportunity is often a painfully slow, meandering process. Nothing is clear at first, and you need time. This puts you at odds with your investors from day one.

The worst thing about taking money from investors is when you have to go back and explain that the idea they funded simply doesn't work. At this point, investors can lose faith in you, and it's no fun. Once investors believe they must intervene in your business to save it, they can become your nightmare. I've seen it happen, and it's a mess. It's far better to have the freedom to try whatever comes into your head, jump from one idea to another, and run a variety of experiments until your business clicks into place.

The right idea is the one you don't have to make yourself believe in. It's the idea that shows you the path forward. When something is working, there's no need to convince anyone. It just takes off, and you're running to keep up.

41

Part-Timing It

IF YOU DON'T HAVE ENOUGH money in your bank account to cover the costs of your startup, one way to fund your company is to work part-time, or even full-time, while launching your business. This may require a lot of late nights and weekends, but it is possible. Just ask Phil Knight, the cofounder of Nike. In the early years, Knight worked full-time as an accountant while growing his business on the side. This was the only way he could fund the company. Knight isn't alone. Many startups begin as side projects, and some stay that way for years before they blossom.

Bill Drayton worked for McKinsey part-time for four years while growing Ashoka, his nonprofit organization. Ashoka is now the largest social entrepreneurship network in the world. Yoshiko Shinohara started Temp Holdings, a staffing company, while teaching English part-time. Her company now has $4.8 billion in revenue.

The founders of GitHub scrounged together a few hundred bucks to launch their company. They spent the next four years working on their online version control platform before raising a single dollar of capital. "The real cost was supporting ourselves as we grew the site and the business," says Chris Wanstrath, CEO and cofounder. "P. J. [Hyett] and I did consulting to pay the bills, while Tom [Preston-Werner] worked a full-time job."[1] As their business grew, they gradually began to pay themselves a salary. Things got even better when they landed venture funding and were able to scale up. Then Microsoft stepped in and acquired the startup for $7.5 billion. Not bad for what began as a part-time gig.

Daymond John didn't have it so easy. He had to wait tables from 10:00 a.m. to 10:00 p.m. at Red Lobster while launching his startup FUBU, a fashion brand. "I was working at Red Lobster for five years as a waiter as I was running this business," says John. "It was forty hours at Red Lobster and six hours at FUBU. Then it was thirty hours at Red Lobster and twenty hours at FUBU because money started to come in."[2] After a lot of late nights, he grew FUBU into a $6 billion fashion brand and is now a celebrity judge on the TV series *Shark Tank*.

If you can't handle working nights and weekends, you might consider talking to your boss and asking for some time off. Ryan Hoover negotiated a six-month transition period with his employer, Playhaven, so he could keep getting a paycheck while launching his startup. After exploring several business ideas, he settled on Product Hunt, a platform for geeks who wanted to learn about new gadgets. After a couple of years, he sold the company to AngelList. Jack Dorsey took it one step further and actually partnered with his employer, Odeo, to pursue his idea, which turned out to be Twitter. The cofounder of Odeo, Evan Williams, wound up not only funding Twitter but becoming the CEO.

If you can't handle the stress of a full-time or part-time job, you can always take a sabbatical. That's what Marc Benioff did when he came up with the idea for Salesforce. He had been at Oracle for a decade and was feeling burned out, so he got approval to go on a six-month leave of absence. During this break, he traveled the world and thought about how the software industry would change in the coming years. This sparked the idea for cloud computing and Salesforce. After he returned to work, he shared his concept with Larry Ellison, Oracle's CEO, who wound up investing $2 million.

Whatever your path, there are probably more options than you imagine. Sometimes you just need to get creative or juggle more than one job at a time to get over the bootstrapping hump.

Courting the Press

WHEN DOING A BOOTSTRAP, GETTING the attention of the press at launch can make all the difference. PR is how a lot of startups, especially consumer-focused ones, gain momentum. The problem is, hiring a PR firm isn't cheap. In Silicon Valley, the best public relations firms charge a hefty retainer, which most bootstrapped startups can't afford. However, having a top-notch PR agency isn't a requirement if you know what you're doing. This is because most bloggers and journalists prefer to hear directly from the founder than a PR firm. You just need to know how to approach them and what to say.

Hiring a top-notch PR agency isn't a requirement . . . if you know what you're doing.

When reaching out to the media, start with the headline. The job of almost every journalist is to capture the attention of more readers. Reporters are always on the lookout for eye-catching stories. A well-crafted headline will grab their attention. When designing your headline, it pays to look at the kings of viral content and see what they're doing that works so well. Buzzfeed, Upworthy, and other viral news sites have perfected the art of creating clickbait. It's no accident their stories get a huge number of shares on social media. Analyze what they do and how they do it.

Surprisingly, the headlines that journalists often like the most perform poorly when tested on readers. Intuition is outdated. It's the old-fashioned way of judging a headline. Data analytics is what the pros use now. Upworthy, for instance, A/B tests all of its headlines. It's more science than art. The process goes something like this:

1. Crank out twenty-five possible headlines for every article.
2. Select the top four candidates.
3. Post them to Twitter (or other social networks) and measure the clicks.
4. Pick the top performer, regardless of whether it's your favorite.

As for the types of headlines that work, here's what Upworthy recommends:

1. Be descriptive and clear.
2. Write in a conversational tone.
3. Fear is your friend. For example: fear of missing out, fear of disaster, fear of crime, and so on.
4. Readers love listicles. For example: "10 Best Ways to . . ."
5. Don't give it all away in the headline.
6. Don't express a strong opinion. Let the reader decide.
7. Don't sexualize the headline.
8. Don't overthink the headline.
9. Don't try to be too clever. Puns don't get clicks.
10. Don't bum people out. No one likes depressing stories.

The most viral stories aren't necessarily the most informative, relevant, newsworthy, or insightful. They are the ones that make the readers say, "Oh, my God. I can't believe it!" or, "I have to know that!" In other words, something out of the ordinary that gets readers to stop whatever they're doing because they have to find out more.

Once you have some great headlines, the next thing is to reach out to bloggers and journalists. Keep in mind that the respectable ones are overwhelmed with inquiries. They get bombarded day and night by people pitching their stories. Contacting them cold usually doesn't work. You'll have more of a chance with warm introductions, but even these often fall flat. It's better to meet journalists in person at events and conferences. At least then you can strike up a conversation, and if you have something interesting to say or can find out what they're looking for, that's a good first step.

Whether you contact a journalist online or offline, the key to getting a positive response is being prepared in advance with what you want to say and how to say it. Here are a few basic tips. First, put yourself in the journalists' shoes. What publications are they writing for? What types of stories do their readers expect? Why would your story matter to them? You will need to pitch different stories for different publications. If you're targeting *Wired* magazine, the type of story it accepts will be different from what you'd send to the *Wall Street Journal* or your local newspaper. Never just spam everyone with the same story. You need to take the time to figure out what each journalist wants to hear and tailor your pitch accordingly.

Take the time to figure out what each journalist wants to hear and tailor your pitch accordingly.

Once you learn the ropes, courting the press isn't that hard. You just have to put in the time and effort to understand their psychology and how they operate. Most journalists are underpaid and overworked. You can often start by simply feeding them useful data. Do you have access to information that can help them with their job? Can you come up with facts they might be able to use in their next article? If you help them, they'll want to help you. It's not uncommon for journalists to have a shortlist of people they call whenever they need quotes and data. You want to be on this list.

Many startup founders I know cultivate relationships with journalists and position themselves as experts on specific topics related to their business. Get your team together and find out who is a domain expert on what areas. You may be surprised that certain members of your team have a wealth of knowledge that can be valuable to reporters. Think of your company as the research arm of the journalist. If you do this, you'll be first to come to mind whenever they're writing a story related to the topic.

Another strategy that works is to write guest posts for prominent blogs. This can get your name out as an expert. It can also provide visibility to your company. I know a lot of authors, CEOs, and investors who spend a good chunk of every week writing. Many of them have built up large audiences and developed ongoing relationships with top publications. The only downside is that writing a good article is time consuming. If you do it regularly, which is important if you want to build a following, it's almost like having a second job. You have to ask yourself whether this is the best use of your time. If it is, then go for it.

There are many ways to spin a story, but it's up to you to figure out what works best for your business. If you take the time, you can do this, and it will pay off. I like to say that a great story is worth a thousand ads. Figuring out for yourself what goes viral and how to execute it is a smart investment for a startup without much of a budget, and it will do more to attract journalists than most six-figure marketing executives and costly PR firms.

※

A great story is worth a thousand ads.

The Rules of Guerrilla Marketing

GUERRILLA MARKETING IS ALL ABOUT being resourceful. It's about building your brand and acquiring customers through alternative means. There are as many types of guerrilla marketing as there are creative ideas. The only rule is you have to be different. You have to stand out. What you lack in money, you have to make up for in originality. That's the one way to get people to pay attention. Here are fifteen examples of guerrilla tactics to get your creative juices flowing.

1. Let's start with Casper's clever marketing ploy. They wanted consumers to think of them as more than a mattress company, so they launched a chatbot (a software application for online text conversations) called Insomnobot3000. This bot was especially designed for insomniacs. Whenever customers had trouble sleeping, they could strike up a conversation with Casper's AI, and it just might help them to relax.

2. How do you stand out at a crowded conference like SXSW did? Right in front of the convention hall, Foursquare hosted a game of four square, like kids play in schoolyards. It only cost Foursquare some chalk and two rubber balls, and they increased average check-ins from 250,000 to 350,000.

3. Would you give your saliva to a flight comparison platform? What if they offered to find out your ancestry for free by

analyzing your DNA? And what if you could win a free trip to your country of origin? Momondo, a Denmark-based travel platform, partnered with AncestryDNA to run this contest, and it turned out to be a hit with people all over the world.

4. How do you sell a blender? This low-tech category was as stale as month-old bread until George Wight, the marketing manager at Blendtec, came up with a brilliant idea: Why not shoot a YouTube series called *Will It Blend*? The concept was to stick crazy things like a rake handle, can of Coke, Big Mac meal, or iPhone into a blender and see what would happen. Like all things YouTube, it found its audience. With millions of views, it's now a marketing legend.

5. How do you know if your coffee beans are as fresh as they can be? Maybe they've been sitting on the shelf for days or weeks. Well, Café Pelé guarantees freshness by wrapping their beans in the daily newspaper. You can't beat that marketing message, and it garnered its fair share of press. What did it cost? Only the price of some newspapers.

6. What if you're just another ad agency? How do you stand out from the crowd? McCann Japan (formerly McCann Erickson) decided to build an ingenious robot, called AI-CD β, to work alongside its employees in developing new projects. AI-CD β provides its own creative input on print ads, TV commercials, and online marketing. "Our hope is for our AI creative director to work on many projects, gain experience, and grow into a world-class creative director that will leave a mark in the advertising industry,"[1] says Shun Matsuzaka, founder of McCann Millennials.

7. How do you know if you're coming down with the flu? One way is to walk past a billboard—but not just any billboard. Meet the Theraflu Thermoscanner advertisement, which measures the temperature of passersby and alerts them if they're sick. Now, that's a viral billboard.

8. What's another way to get people to pay attention to your billboard, especially exhausted people? How about you make

the billboard double as an advertisement for a rest stop, where tired drivers can take a nap. That's what Sodimac Homecenter did in Peru, where one in every three road accidents on the Pan-American Highway is due to fatigue. Each resting spot has a single-car garage decorated to resemble the interior of a bedroom. There's free Wi-Fi, eye-masks, and hot drinks. Now it's safe to fall asleep behind the wheel.

9. If you're flying instead of driving, how about taking a rest in Iceland? Have you ever been to this marvelous country? I've flown past dozens of times but never stopped. Icelandair wants to change that by offering its passengers a layover of up to seven nights at no extra cost. Icelandair will even provide a layover buddy who will give you a free tour of the country.

10. Who likes to get a parking ticket? Fixed is an app that fights unfair parking tickets. To promote its launch in San Francisco, the startup hired a group of volunteers, called *ticket heroes*, who searched the streets for cars with tickets on their windshields. Whenever they found one, they left a note telling the owner how to download the app and avoid paying the ticket.

11. For the movie *King Kong 3D*, the marketing team left monster-sized gorilla footprints on the beach, as well as a crushed lifeguard vehicle. The next morning, unknowing people began snapping photos and sharing the experience on social media, which drew in even more people and more photos.

12. Gold Toe launched a new underwear line by making a pair of briefs big enough to fit on one of New York City's best-known landmarks: the *Wall Street Bull*. The photograph of the bull in undies went viral.

13. To show how much he believed in Lifelock, an identity-theft prevention service, the CEO ran an audacious series of TV commercials in which he announced his actual Social Security number and dared identity thieves to go at him. The marketing campaign worked incredibly well. He received a huge amount of free publicity. However, he wound up the victim of identity theft, and so paid for it in another way.

14. Grasshopper, a startup that provides virtual phone solutions, sent chocolate-covered grasshoppers to five thousand business leaders, journalists, and bloggers. They included a link to a video that encouraged everyone to take unconventional risks.

15. The Ice Bucket Challenge raised a huge amount of money for preventing ALS, also known as Lou Gehrig's disease. The concept was simple: Video someone dumping a bucket of ice and water over the head to raise awareness of the disease. The result was more than 2.5 million tagged videos circulating on Facebook, leading to a surge in donations.

As you can see, the best guerrilla-marketing campaigns don't have to cost a bundle of money. Instead, they tap into an idea that resonates with people. They inspire an emotional reaction, create a conversation, and motivate people to share. They go beyond simple publicity stunts and tap into elements of our culture and our understanding of the world. By piggybacking on emerging trends, they can spread across the country and around the world on their own, without big marketing budgets or celebrity endorsements.

Here are twelve rules for creating successful guerrilla-marketing campaigns:

1. Get creative.
2. Ask why it matters.
3. Dare your audience.
4. Make it fun and witty.
5. Keep your message simple.
6. Target the right communities.
7. Get influencers onboard early.
8. Be outrageous and cut through the noise.
9. Incorporate videos and photos that can go viral.
10. Allow the audience to participate and inspire them to share.
11. Leverage social platforms like Facebook, Instagram, and Snapchat.
12. Avoid doing what's been done before. Originality matters.

It's time to get your most imaginative cohorts into a room and begin brainstorming on the activities and ideas that embody the spirit of your company. The one essential ingredient in all successful campaigns is creativity. If you're the first to come up with something entirely new and captivating, the world will tune in.

Thinking Viral

WHEN YOU DON'T HAVE A lot of cash for marketing, which is the case with most startups when they launch, it pays to think viral. No one is better at this than Chris Lindland. I've known him since the early days when he first launched his startup, Betabrand, a direct-to-consumer clothing brand. He's grown the company through hilariously creative techniques that are tied directly to his clothing line.

Atop a skyscraper platform, an attractive young woman in Betabrand glittering shorts flings herself off the building, smiling the whole time. It's just another Betabrand publicity stunt, only this time Lindland's fans came up with it themselves. Lindland's brand is inextricably linked to his community. He is constantly asking his members for their feedback and fashion ideas. He features them as models in Betabrand's photoshoots and videos, and he is always organizing social events where they can participate.

"Our business is brand-new ideas nonstop," says Lindland. "[We] see what sells through and build a web community around that product." He always asks himself this simple question: Why would someone forward this when there are so many great cat videos to share? If it doesn't pass the cat video test, he doesn't release it.

To give you an idea of Lindland's marketing style, here are a few of his products:

Dress Pant Sweatpants—Formal sweatpants you can wear to a board meeting.

Disco Hoodies—Sparkling clothing made from doubloons salvaged from a sunken Spanish galleon, or so he claims.

Glutton Trousers—Slacks sporting three buttons appropriately labeled Piglet, Sow, and Boar to accommodate waistline expansion during feeding time.

"We are an imminently bloggable brand," says Lindland. "We really think hard about each product for the sake of getting bloggers to write about us because we don't have Ralph Lauren's marketing budget."[1] His approach has worked. Bloggers love his material, and so does the mainstream media. He's gotten millions of dollars' worth of free press and viral shares from his guerrilla tactics.

Another success story in viral marketing is *Cards Against Humanity*, a silly, raunchy card game that has caught on with hipsters. A group of eight friends launched their card game on Kickstarter, and it has since grown into a nationwide obsession. The founders like to call it "a party game for horrible people."[2] Imagine an adult-rated *Apples to Apples*.

"At some level, it's such a stupid product!" says Max Temkim, the ringleader of the bunch. "We had this moment of 'I can't believe so many people like this that some truck driver had to unload two thousand boxes of poop jokes.'"

Despite the inanity of it all, or because of it, *Cards Against Humanity* managed to rake in $12 million in sales its first year, and it keeps growing thanks to a series of viral marketing tactics that border on the absurd. On Black Friday, the company ran an anti-sale, stating, "Today only! *Cards Against Humanity* products are $5 more. Consume!" Inexplicably, sales shot up—not down. People willingly paid an extra $5 to buy them on Black Friday.

These pranksters continue to build their brand on a series of shrewd marketing stunts. These include cutting up a Picasso, selling cow pies, offering a *Holiday Bullshit* expansion pack, and blatantly asking for money.

They also raised more than $2 million to buy a plot of vacant land on the Mexican border in an attempt to block Trump's wall.[3] This garnered a huge amount of press. Less political but even more inspired, they raised $100,000 to dig a giant Holiday Hole and put a video of it on their website along with the following FAQ:

Is this real?
Unfortunately, it is.

Where is the hole?
America. And in our hearts.

Is there some sort of deeper meaning or purpose to the hole?
No.

What do I get for contributing money to the hole?
A deeper hole. What else are you going to buy, an iPod?

Why aren't you giving all this money to charity?
Why aren't YOU giving all this money to charity? It's your money.

Whatever they do, it involves their unique sense of irreverent humor, and that catches people's attention, fueling the virality. If you want to take lessons on creating the kind of content that goes viral, just study these guys.

45

Strategies for Inbound Marketing

IN THE US MARKET, ANOTHER great way to make an outsized impact with very little cash is by using inbound marketing. This is where you create content that draws users to your brand. Many of the most successful companies in the world use creative content and sophisticated search engine optimization techniques to scale their businesses. The beauty of this method is that, if you have the necessary skills, it doesn't cost more than your time. That's why it's perfect for many startups.

Make sure the content is valuable to your customers. If it doesn't inform, educate, or entertain, it probably won't succeed. People seek out content for specific reasons, and you need to know exactly what your target customers are looking for and why they need it. The more personalized and targeted the content, the more effective it will be.

A good example is Bentley University, which wanted to recruit students for its MBA program. It created an informative articled titled "12 MBA Interview Questions You'll Be Asked." This article ranked number one on Google for the keyword phrase *MBA Interview Questions* and has been getting thousands of visits per month ever since.

When launching an inbound-marketing campaign, a good strategy is to focus on content that's performed exceptionally well in your industry. The more specific and targeted the content, the better. You need to identify what's missing in that content category and make something that fills this gap. This doesn't require a stroke of genius or a lot of money. It just requires you to figure out what's already out there and come up with your own variation that adds value. The goal here is utility over novelty.

Start by asking yourself these four questions:

1. What are people in your industry clicking on?
2. What information do they need that they aren't getting?
3. How can you deliver it to them in a more effective way?
4. What can you offer that no one else is providing?

Take special note of the content your competitors are putting out there and understand how it's performing. For example, let's say that you're launching a fitness app. You can go to a site like BuzzSumo and enter basic keywords, such as *weight loss, burn fat, dieting,* and *healthy habits.* BuzzSumo will then show you exactly which articles with those keywords are getting the most traffic. Make a list of everything you find particularly compelling and relevant to your customers.

Next, examine the titles of each article, and write down the keywords that come up. Then go to Google and mash those words up in various searches. Continue to add promising results to your list. Last, enter competitors' URLs and see what content they've developed that ranks highly. Add these to your list.

By now, you should have a robust set of articles that rank highly with your target customers. Your goal is to create your own content that is similar but much better. How do you do this?

- Take the time to research competitors' content. You can learn exactly what works and what doesn't from their trials and errors.
- Research what influencers are talking about and use this as the basis for your content. Influencers know how to communicate and have their fingers on the pulse of what people care about. You can learn a lot from them.
- Take a short article and rewrite it as a full blog post, with an introduction, body, and conclusion.
- Look for unanswered questions your readers may have and answer them. What do your readers need to know? What might

they be looking for that isn't easy to find? Is there anything missing from your competitors' articles that you can add?

- Fill your article with useful information. The fact is that people love to share helpful stuff. It works far better than clickbait. Add as much practical information as possible.

- Combine information from three or more different articles into one. Just putting everything in one place makes it so much easier to share. No one wants to share three articles. They'd rather share one complete article.

- Keep it simple. Don't expound upon things. People want to get to the meat quickly. If they don't, they will move on. Being clear, concise, and well organized are key to increasing virality (the potential to go viral).

- Structure it as a list. Lists are easier to scan and digest than paragraphs. Just like I'm doing now.

- Nothing beats using photos, videos, charts, and infographics to create an engaging visual experience that stands out from the clutter. People are visual, and by visualizing something complex, you can add a lot of value, turning a good article into a great one.

- Make the experience fun. Fill your site with personality. Develop a mascot that captures the attention of visitors. Endow your site with a personality that reflects your brand, values, and spirit. You'd be surprised at how much this matters.

- Make content that has nothing to do with your brand but everything to do with what your customers value. Don't try to sell your customers on your brand. Have them love you because you care about what they care about.

- Come up with an original title that's both descriptive and compelling. You want something users haven't seen before and can't resist clicking on.

- Link to other key sites with additional information.

- Encourage people to share it. Just reminding them can boost the virality significantly.

Once you've done all that, it's time to promote your content. Remember, there are millions of blog posts published every day, so you can't expect people to magically find your content. You need to actively push it out there. Here are some strategies:

1. Start building your email list from day one. It helps to give users something in return for signing up, like a valuable online course, white paper, e-book, audiobook, video, or discount coupon.

2. Create buyer personas. These are detailed descriptions of typical customers. Once you have clearly defined buyer personas, you'll waste less time focusing on leads that will never convert.

3. Get out of the office and participate in events that target your customers. You should be everywhere your customers are, and you should let them know that you have content created just for them.

4. Identify where your customers are hanging out. If they are on a particular community, social network, app, or website, you need to go there. These include Reddit, Quora, Facebook, Twitter, Instagram, Snapchat, LinkedIn, WeChat, and so on. Always obey the unspoken rules of the particular medium. You don't want to alienate your audience. You need to introduce your content in a manner that they feel is helpful, not intrusive or exploitative.

5. Analyze your data. If you're going to make inbound marketing work, you need to know exactly what customers are doing with the content, how they are sharing it, and what's the return on investment. Inbound-marketing platforms, like HubSpot, provide tools that enable you to gain insights on your visitors, convert them into paying customers, and tie them into your community.

6. Search engine optimization is at the heart of inbound marketing. It helps to have multiple pages focused on a single keyword or long-tail phrase (a key phrase that is more specific and usually longer). Your goal should be to capture as many top slots as possible on each of the most important keywords to your business.

7. Create a quiz to engage visitors. According to BuzzFeed, the majority of its users finish a quiz after starting one. This

high completion rate, combined with the ability to find out more about your visitors and what they want, makes quizzes a smart tool.

8. Ask everyone, including employees, friends, influencers, strategic partners, vendors, suppliers, and investors, to share your content on their social media channels. Also, encourage them to write reviews, submit articles for your site, and participate in your events.

9. Use dynamic forms to gather more information every time someone comes to your site or app. Most people will visit a site seven to thirteen times before becoming a sales qualified lead, so it pays to gather additional information with each visit, without asking the same question twice.

Most people will visit a site seven to thirteen times before becoming a sales qualified lead.

10. Real-time communication helps reduce the bounce rate. Try incorporating live chat, chatbots, or webinars into your site. Let users participate and provide feedback. The more personalized the experience, the higher the engagement levels and conversion rates.

11. Create feeder sites and apps that drive traffic to your main business by offering resources or value to your target customers.

12. Think across mediums. It pays to repurpose your top-performing written articles as podcasts, white papers, videos, e-books, infographics, audiobooks, and animated gifs. This will broaden your distribution and reach.

13. Make sure your website's FAQ (frequently asked questions) pages are well structured and useful. A site without a great FAQ is like a movie without a great plot. People will walk away frustrated. The FAQ is there to answer all your customers' most pressing questions. It's often the most sought-after content on a site.

14. If you have a marketing budget and high conversion rate, another option is to buy ads on search engines, apps, websites, and social networks, and then drive the traffic to your content. This gets expensive fast, so it doesn't work for most content.

15. Last, you may want to explore developing an app for voice commerce platforms, like Amazon Alexa, Google Assistant, Microsoft Cortana, and Apple Siri. They are evolving fast, and you could gain a competitive advantage by being the first to exploit them in your market.

46

Aligning Brands with Values

WE ALL KNOW THAT THE right name makes a huge difference in building a brand, especially for startups short on cash, but there's more to branding than a name. In today's world, it's about expressing the right values.

Soma, a water filter company, has gone out of its way to court younger consumers. Its tagline is to "hydrate the world." They aren't just selling customers a filter. They are on a mission to save humanity, one cup at a time. "We believe clean drinking water is a basic human right," says the Soma website. "That's why we're a proud sponsor of CharityWater.org and partner with them in their mission to bring safe drinking water to over 663 million people without access to it." This type of talk appeals to Gen X and Y consumers, who want to see their dollars and values aligned.

Bouqs is an online florist. This is nothing new, except for the fact that Bouqs takes flowers to a whole new level. They were founded "with the bold intention of bringing romance and delight back to what was once a noble exchange." They even offer a Happiness Guarantee. If you don't feel happy, you get your money back. To top it off, all their suppliers practice sustainable, eco-friendly farming. "We cut only what we sell," says the website, "so we don't waste one out of every three stems like others." Again, it's about social values above price, selection, and quality.

Ritual, a multivitamin startup, takes it one step further. Unlike the thousands of other vitamin providers, Ritual has made a mission out of transparency, right down to its clear pills and the snazzy slogan: "The future of vitamins is clear." They go on to say: "Ritual is a new kind of health brand. We believe in simplicity, traceability, and ingredients that work best in the body. You deserve to know exactly what you're getting and where it's coming from." To make it even more personal, they exclusively target women with the bold statement: "Created for and by women who wouldn't settle for less than the truth." Are they just another vitamin company? Or are they a brand that embodies the values of women?

The list wouldn't be complete without bkr, which sells water bottles. Only these aren't ordinary bottles. They are fashion statements. The company's mission is to prove that "beauty will change the world, with water bottles so beautiful that drinking from them becomes a joy." And if that's not enough, "Each bkr breathes new life into the maxim of eight glasses a day, inspiring sippers to drink water like it's a special treat and helping create the foundation for a gorgeous complexion so skincare and makeup can do their work." Can a bottle really do all this? Clearly, bkr wants you to believe it can.

It doesn't seem to matter that most of these products are produced in the same factories as their competitors. It's not about the product. It's about the feeling you get when you engage with them. They are turning ordinary consumables into a lifestyle choice. Your purchasing decisions define who you are and what you care about, and this is the crux of their branding strategy. This used to apply only to big purchases like cars, but now it's creeping into everything from toothbrushes to toilet paper. So, if you're going to compete in the age of experiential commerce, you need to take your game up a notch and speak to the heart, not the head.

※

It's not about the product. It's about
the feeling you get when you engage with them.

Investing in Images

THEY SAY A PICTURE IS worth a thousand words, but a video is worth a thousand pictures. One of the cheapest ways to capture the imagination of customers, investors, and the press is with video. No other medium can match video for its ability to communicate new ideas and activate emotions. It's also incredibly viral.

No other medium can match video for its ability to communicate new ideas and activate emotions.

Dollar Shave Club, the men's grooming startup, is the poster child for video done right. A single video literally made the billion-dollar brand. Michael Dubin spent just $4,500 on his first video and put it out on YouTube. In the video, he asks the question, "Are the blades any good?" and answers, "No. Our blades are f**king great."[1] The video instantly caught on because it was different, raw, and witty. With more than twenty-six million views, it launched the company and cemented the brand in the minds of millennials.

Dollar Shave Club isn't the only one to crack the code for viral videos. Studio M produced a video for WestJet airlines that sent its brand soaring. When boarding a flight, they asked passengers what they'd like for Christmas. When the plane arrived at its destination and everyone went to claim their baggage, out of the carousel appeared a stream of presents wrapped in colorful Christmas paper. The passengers were amazed to receive the exact gifts they'd wished for only hours earlier. This simple video has more than forty million views on YouTube, and it's made a lasting impression.

Whether you decide to create a viral video or a simple explainer video, it pays to get professionals to produce it. You need someone who has at least taken a videography course. If your video appears amateurish, it will impact your brand. Most investors I know today look at the video before the investor deck or any other material the entrepreneur sends. So, if your video is rubbish, they'll probably pass on your startup.

Consumers are the same way. If they go to your website and the video looks schlocky, don't expect them to buy your products. If you look at Indiegogo and Kickstarter, you can see a direct correlation between the amounts raised and the quality of the videos. Investing in video production isn't an option anymore. It's a ticket to play.

48

Why Stories Matter

WHETHER YOU'RE PRODUCING A PRODUCT video, talking to investors, or chatting up a journalist, telling stories matters. But you can't just tell any story. You have to understand on an intimate level what your audience wants and expects from your brand. If you don't have any idea, you can't communicate effectively.

Here is how Chris "Drama" Pfaff became a master storyteller. He had no MBA, not even a college education. He didn't seem like a likely candidate for an entrepreneur. He was just a skateboarder . . . until he had an accident. Pfaff fell off his skateboard and fractured his skull. He had a brain hemorrhage and was in a coma for four days. There was no long-term damage, but it made him rethink his priorities.

"I don't think this is what I should do," Pfaff told himself. So, he decided to move to Los Angeles, get a studio apartment, and work in a skate shop. But as life would have it, things turned out differently. His second cousin had landed a gig filming a pilot for MTV that was all about skateboarding. Pfaff became his assistant and would go around with him negotiating deals with DC Shoes and Monster energy drinks. This is when he got the idea for putting together his own business and clothing brand.

Pfaff named his startup Young & Reckless, and he set out to design shirts that would appeal to guys just like him: skateboard rats from middle America. He had a buddy who knew graphic design, and he had him sketch up the original logo. Then he leveraged his cousin's show on MTV to get partners and retailers onboard. He had a friend of a friend manufacture the shirts on a 50/50 revenue split, then went to the retailer PacSun and said: "This is going to be the next biggest clothing line in the world. You guys can have it exclusively for the next six months. But you have to take it for all your stores." They said okay, and Pfaff was in business.

When PacSun paid him for the shirts, he took the money and plowed it right back into the business. He paid $50,000 to a rapper he knew, Meek Mill, and had a photo shoot with him doing wheelies on a dirt bike. He had no way of knowing if this promotion would pay off or not, but he had to take the chance. "Part of me felt like I was the ultimate businessman," says Pfaff, "because I was writing checks now, but at the same time, I thought I could crumble and nobody would care."

His friends came up with the idea that if the brand is Young & Reckless, then Pfaff had to actually be young and reckless. So, they convinced him to film himself jumping out of a sixth-story window. They put a stunt man's airbag on the ground next to an abandoned warehouse, and Pfaff proceeded to launch himself from the window. This did the trick. His customers went wild, and sales at PacSun boomed.

He knew his audience, and he knew what they wanted. Young & Reckless was more than a brand. It was a lifestyle. Pfaff began telling stories about his heroes. One of them was Darius Glover, a kid with a passion for racing dirt bikes. He'd gotten in an accident and was paralyzed from the waist down. However, instead of giving up, Glover figured out how to strap himself onto a dirt bike and continue racing. Most racetracks didn't want to accept him because, if he fell, he couldn't get back up. But he fought the system, not only overcoming his paralysis but the rules that were stacked against him.

This video spoke directly to his audience, and when CNN featured it on the news, Young & Reckless was off to the races. Sales soared. Pfaff wound up amassing 3.5 million followers on Facebook, Instagram, and YouTube, but these weren't just passive viewers. The stories Pfaff told resonated with them, and they responded by buying the products.

Pfaff did make some mistakes and learned from them. He wound up paying a celebrity $150,000 to wear his clothes, but this turned out to be a big waste of money. "There was no story to tell," said Pfaff. "There was nothing reckless to tell. The campaign wasn't just a loss; it hurt the brand long term." Pfaff screwed up again when Tillys asked for baseball jerseys because baseball jerseys were huge. "We put our logo on a baseball jersey," says Pfaff, "and it just didn't work. We didn't have a story about why we were making baseball jerseys."[1]

In the end, the stories and the brand are integrally linked. Without the right story, there is no connection to the brand. Fortunately, Pfaff not only understands the brand deep down in his soul, but he's a master storyteller. He puts out hundreds of pieces of content each year. All of them are linked to his core theme of being young and reckless. The result is that Young & Reckless has grown into a nationwide brand, with distribution in more than three thousand Macy's, Dillard's, and PacSun stores. Eventually, its revenue reached $30 million. Pfaff went on to line up celebrity endorsements from Sean "Diddy" Combs to Justin Bieber, and none of it would have happened without the right story.

Just as Pfaff did, you need to experiment with different types of stories to figure out what works. The stories must fit with your brand, reinforce your core message, and speak directly to your viewers. If they don't accomplish all three of these, you won't activate your customers.

Your story must fit with your brand, reinforce your core message, and speak directly to your viewers.

49

Narrative Types

FOR EVERY BUSINESS, THERE ARE many different types of stories you can construct. I've composed a list of some of the most popular ones. Hopefully, these will spark your imagination.

Success Stories—We all love Horatio Alger stories, where the protagonist goes from rags to riches. Can this be your story?

Personal Stories—Did you start your company to solve a problem you personally faced? Or did you do it for someone in your family or a close friend? What did you go through to launch your business? What or who in your life inspired you to become an entrepreneur?

Cause Stories—Can you tie your story into a popular cause, like climate change, homelessness, disease prevention, or education?

Scary Stories—What are people afraid of? Robots stealing their jobs? Pedophiles praying upon their kids? The rash of gun violence sweeping America? Can your company help prevent any of these?

Data Stories—Some startups manufacture stories out of their own proprietary data. They look at what their users are doing on their site, and then come up with a story like, "Our data shows that 83 percent of females under thirty prefer men with lumberjack beards." It doesn't have to be that silly, but you get the idea.

Growth Stories—How fast is your company growing? Are you the next big thing? Think of Uber and Airbnb. There were a whole series of stories about how fast they were expanding and how much their valuation had soared.

Trend Stories—This includes social trends, business trends, and tech trends. Do you know what's trending online right now? It's easy to find out. There are hashtags on Twitter and keywords on Google. In a matter of minutes, you can see the current trends globally. Find out if any of these apply to your business, and if they do, incorporate them into your story.

Future Stories—What's coming next? How are you shaping the future? We're all curious about where the world is headed, especially when it affects our lives and jobs.

Underdog Stories—It's the old David vs. Goliath story. People gravitate toward tales of the little guy defeating the big, bad ogre.

Disaster Stories—Have you suffered a disaster? How did you deal with it? Did a hurricane flood your store? Did a fire destroy ten years of research? Did your dog eat your $100,000 prototype? How did you bounce back after this setback?

Wacky Stories—Things that are just plain bizarre can make good stories, like the kid who ate two hundred toothpicks for breakfast or the man who married his stuffed cat.

Dirty Stories—Yes, we all know that sex, drugs, and practically any type of vice sells. I'm not saying you should resort to this, but it is clickbait.

You aren't restricted to the stories mentioned above. The point is to be creative. Don't limit yourself. Experiment with different types of storytelling and see what takes off. The key is finding the best fit for you and your brand. The story must not only attract eyeballs but reinforce your key messaging, express your values, and drive awareness of what you have to offer.

How to Growth Hack

NO SECTION ON BOOTSTRAPPING A business would be complete without a chapter on growth hacking. It is the process of rapid experimentation across your marketing funnel, product development, sales segments, and other areas, with the goal of growing the business. Sean Ellis coined the term in 2010, and it literally means hacking your way to growth. The difference between growth hacking and traditional marketing is that it's much more inventive and creative. There are no rules. You have to figure things out that nobody else has.

The growth hacking funnel looks like this:

1. **Acquisition**—Optimize your online customer acquisition.
2. **Activation**—Engage your customers coming to your site.
3. **Revenue**—Increase first-time and repeat sales.
4. **Referral**—Get customers to share your products.
5. **Retention**—Create loyalty and increase frequency and length of visits.

To achieve these goals, growth hackers use a combination of creative marketing, software engineering, automation, testing, and data analytics. Let me give you some practical examples to nail down the concept.

1. **Acquisition**—Airbnb literally hacked Craigslist, a popular classifieds site, to drive traffic to its fledgling marketplace. It accomplished this by building a bot to scrape Craigslist and then spammed the users, with the goal of getting them to post on both sites. The key was getting a link from the Craigslist posting to Airbnb, thereby driving traffic to Airbnb. This strategy, although not exactly ethical, worked to generate the critical mass of users Airbnb needed to get off the ground.

2. **Activation**—Twitter employed data analytics to determine that new users who began with an empty feed were less likely to engage, while those who followed five or more people from the start were far more likely to return to the site. This knowledge led them to prompt new users to follow popular Twitter accounts, thereby filling their feed with interesting content.

3. **Revenue**—Ticketmaster, the largest site for selling tickets to concerts, found that by adding a simple countdown timer when users were at the point of buying a ticket dramatically increased sales. This timer made it seem like users were going to miss out if they didn't purchase immediately.

4. **Referral**—Dropbox, the cloud file-hosting service, discovered that it could increase virality by offering additional free cloud storage to users who succeeded in getting friends to sign up.

5. **Retention**—YouTube learned through experimentation that adding continuous play to its videos increased customer loyalty and time on site.

As you can see, growth hacking involves carefully analyzing what users are doing with the product, and then trying different creative hacks to increase the desired metrics. After each experiment, you tweak and re-engineer things until the optimal results are achieved. The advantage for startups is that growth hacking can be inexpensive, especially when it's focused on simple changes to the funnel. For this reason, growth hacking has become a powerful tool for startups to gain traction early on, when marketing budgets are tight.

Can Bootstrappers Compete?

IT'S NICE TO TALK ABOUT saving money, but can bootstrapped companies compete in today's winner-take-all world, where the supercharged startups dominate the headlines? Can they challenge venture-backed companies with billions in their war chests? What about standing up to the Amazons, Googles, and Facebooks of the world? Is it truly possible to build a big business by bootstrapping it?

Absolutely. Not only can you compete, you may do better than your well-funded cousins. Let me give you some examples of bootstrapped success stories. If this doesn't convince you that all the pain is worth the gain, nothing will.

MailChimp—Back in 2000, Ben Chestnut, the CEO, was running a small design consulting firm, and his clients kept asking him to create newsletters. This was fine, except for the fact that he hated designing them. It was so boring. His solution was to build a tool that would streamline the process, which he named MailChimp. Today, his startup has close to half a billion dollars in revenue and more than five hundred employees. The best part is that he did it all without a dime in venture funding.

Shopify—The founders of Shopify were looking for a shopping cart solution when setting up an e-commerce site for snowboarders.

Unable to find anything suitable, they decided to build it themselves. It turned out that lots of other startups needed the same solution, and it became their main business. The founders ran the business for six years without any venture funding. Today, they're a public company with a market of around $16 billion.

Braintree Payments—Exchanging money online without getting fleeced by fraudsters is what lots of businesses want. The founders of Braintree built a solution that helps companies accept and process payments. They survived on the proceeds for four years before raising venture capital. PayPal wound up acquiring them for $800 million.

SurveyMonkey—This scrappy startup took eleven years to raise venture capital. It's now the world's number one online survey software with more than sixteen million questions answered daily and $100 million in revenue. "I worked seven days a week, probably fourteen- or eighteen-hour days, and never took a day off," says Dave Goldberg, the CEO. "That's just what I had to do."[1]

Shutterstock—As a serial entrepreneur, Jon Oringer had a problem. When creating marketing literature and websites for his companies, he couldn't find enough high-quality art and photographs at a reasonable price. With little other choice, he took his digital camera and began creating his own photos. Amassing thirty thousand photos from his personal library, he built Shutterstock, one of the largest online stock photo sites in the world. Without ever raising venture capital, he took the company public. It's now worth close to $2 billion.

CoolMiniOrNot—You don't have to be a billionaire to be cool. The founders of CoolMiniOrNot found this out. They began life as a website where geeks showed off their ability to paint Dungeons & Dragons figurines. How nerdy is that? Eventually, they expanded into producing their own board games. To date, they've run more than twenty Kickstarter campaigns and raised $20 million from their customers. Who needs venture capital when fans will fund you?

Tuft & Needle—This feisty startup entered the online mattress space with just $6,000 in seed capital. Despite facing off against eight-hundred-pound poltergeists, like Casper, which raised hundreds of millions in venture funding, Tuft & Needle is doing just fine. They've kept costs down, focused on the bottom line, and grown their business to more than $100 million in sales, all while remaining profitable. Their venture-funded brethren might be bigger, but Tuft & Needle is in the black.

Tough Mudder—Will Dean, a former British counterterrorism officer, wanted to create the toughest and scariest athletic challenges in the world. These crazy races involve crawling in the mud on your belly under electrified wires, climbing over frighteningly tall obstacles, and pushing yourself beyond exhaustion. Who would want to endure this type of torture? Apparently, a lot of people. With just $7,000 in seed funding, he grew his business to more than $100 million in revenue. His secret was preselling registrations to races, and then using the money to build the insane obstacles courses. Do you know any VCs who would have taken a chance on this wild business plan in the early days?

AppLovin—This little startup set out to help app developers promote themselves. "I couldn't find anyone to give us an investment at what I thought was a reasonable starting point valuation (maybe $4 million or $5 million),"[2] says the founder and CEO, Adam Foroughi. A year later, it was profitable, and today it has hundreds of millions in revenue. A Chinese private equity firm just acquired a majority stake for $1.42 billion. Not bad for a company that raised only angel funding.

Wistia—Sometimes it pays to focus on the boring stuff no one else seems to care about. That's what the founders of Wistia did when they set out to host corporate training videos. It was the anti-YouTube. Nothing viral or even entertaining about it. Despite this, or because of it, they managed to build an eighty-person team that serves more than three hundred thousand customers, including big names like Starbucks, Cirque du Soleil, and Casper.

Grammarly—Another way to make money is to simply build a better mousetrap. That's what the founders of Grammarly did. They wanted to make a better spelling and grammar checker and managed to sign up more than eight hundred universities and hundreds of thousands of writers. After nearly ten years of bootstrapping it, the company finally raised $110 million in venture funding.

I could go on and on with more examples. There are so many boot-strapped startups that wound up doing incredibly well, but we seldom hear about them because the press loves overnight success stories and big money. As you can see, self-funding can move much more slowly, but it can be just as rewarding in the end.

The one thing all these companies have in common is that they addressed real problems, often ones that they encountered themselves. That's why they were able to survive the hard times. They had customers ready to pay for what they were offering. When in doubt, making something truly valuable is always the answer. The money will come if you address a pressing need. You just have to be prepared to put in the sweat, blood, tears, and time to get it off the ground.

4

Unicorn Hunters

Finding Your Mojo

In this section, I'm going to show you how the top investors in Silicon Valley deconstruct startups, evaluate business models, and separate the winners from the losers. Why do some investors consistently outperform others? What do the top dogs on Sand Hill Road use as their benchmarks when picking startups? And how can you know if your startup will make the cut?

It's easy to identify a great startup after it has traction. When a company has exponential growth, it's clear there's market demand. But how do VCs identify a unicorn before it grows its horn? What essential ingredients must be present for a newly hatched company to blossom into a full-fledged business? Are there early signals that indicate whether a startup will fly or die?

Sadly, most investors lose money investing in startups because they fail to comprehend the underlying factors and business fundamentals. It's incredibly hard to determine the future potential of a startup when it has little or no revenue and only a handful of users. We struggle with this at Founders Space every day. We receive thousands of business plans and listen to hundreds of pitches a year. Out of all the startups, how do we select the ones with the highest probability of success?

I'll share with you what I've learned working with incredibly smart investors. I'll explain which qualities matter most in the management team, how to tell if a business model scales, and when to spot a company that is truly ready for funding. By the time you're done, I hope you'll understand how investors analyze complex situations, the criteria they use to screen deals, and why some startups are worth exponentially more than others.

Investing in Teams

SMART INVESTORS ALWAYS START WITH the team. In Silicon Valley, VCs like to say they bet on teams—not on the idea or even the business. Why is this? Aren't the idea and business more important than the team?

The answer is no. You can have the best idea in the world. But if you have a crappy team, you will fail to execute on it, and the business will be worth nothing. It's important to remember that startups aren't mature companies. They are works in progress. If a startup has a winning team, even if it starts with the wrong idea and a broken business model, the team will eventually figure it out, change directions, and keep iterating until they find a way forward.

So, what makes a winning team? How do you know if you have one? The first thing to look at is the leader. The CEO is the most important person on the team. A weak chief executive means a dysfunctional team. A company without capable leadership will go nowhere fast. The person in charge is too important. But how can an investor tell if a CEO is up to the task? What qualities define a leader?

One of the most popular filters that investors rely on is the university that the startup's CEO attended. This is because many startup founders pitching to VCs are young and inexperienced. Their résumés are often less than one page. What work and life experience does a college student have? A job at the dorm cafeteria? An internship or two? The one thing that tends to stand out is the university itself, and this is why investors latch onto it. They believe that if the CEO went to Harvard, MIT, Stanford, or some other prestigious school, this entrepreneur must be CEO material. While this may be valid in some cases, it's not universally true. Getting into a top university is more about test scores, grades, and extracurricular activities than any innate ability to lead or run a company. Just because the founder is Harvard material does not mean he can inspire, motivate, and lead an organization.

I personally know many graduates of respected schools who should not be entrepreneurs. They are better suited to a career in academia, research, government, or some other profession. Putting too much weight on brand-name universities is a mistake—not only because it leads to false positives, but also because it arbitrarily filters out interesting personality types, like rebels, free spirits, and late bloomers—many of whom chose alternate paths in life. The data backs this up. The National Bureau of Economic Research found that there is no difference in lifetime income between students who graduated from elite universities and those with similar SAT scores who went to other colleges.

So, even if you haven't attended a brand-name university, do not be discouraged. You may even be surprised to learn how many successful entrepreneurs never went to top-tier colleges. This list includes Benjamin Franklin, Thomas Edison, Andrew Carnegie, John D. Rockefeller, Henry Ford, Milton Hershey, Ray Kroc, Colonel Sanders, Walt Disney, Barry Diller, Michael Dell, Richard Branson, Jack Ma, and Steve Jobs. Should an investor pass up the next Jack Ma or Steve Jobs because he didn't go to Brown or Yale?

※

If you haven't attended a brand-name university,
do not be discouraged—many successful
entrepreneurs never went to top-tier colleges.

I'm sorry to say that far too many investors fall into the Ivy League trap. They equate the name of the college with success, and it blinds them to what's most important: the qualities of the individual. Who is this CEO? What type of person is she? Why is she launching this startup? What does it mean to her? Did she accomplish anything noteworthy in the past? Is she the type of person who can step up and become a leader, build an organization, and inspire others? Has she overcome extreme difficulties and uncertainty? Does she have the maturity to lead a company and noteworthy mentors to guide her? These are the things that indicate whether an entrepreneur is capable of building a world-changing business.

Another mistake I see investors make is putting too much weight on résumé bling. They tend to choose entrepreneurs who come out of high-flying tech companies, like Google, Apple, Tencent, and Microsoft. It's great that the CEO worked for a world-class company, but that doesn't mean this person is going to make a brilliant startup founder. Google has more than 60,000 employees, and Microsoft has 125,000. Not all of them were born to run a company. Some are much better suited to working at Google or Microsoft.

On the same token, titles also don't matter as much as people think. Being a vice president is nice, but I know a lot of vice presidents who are great executives but not born risk takers. There are even some executives who do nothing but play corporate politics on the job. I'd rather choose a junior project manager who championed a new idea and brought it to market than a vice president who did little more than greenlight the project. Smart investors look beyond the résumé and dig into the type of decisions and responsibilities the individual had at previous jobs.

When vetting startups, my technique for evaluating the founders is to probe deeply and ask a lot of questions. I want to find out if the entrepreneur ever came up with any original ideas. If so, how did he get his coworkers and management to buy in? What roadblocks did he encounter along the way, and how did he get around them? Were there decisions he made in the past that led to failures? And what did he learn from these setbacks? Questions like these allow me to see if this CEO can handle difficult situations, persevere through hardships, and use creativity to solve seemingly intractable problems.

The other thing I look at is the founding team. Who did this CEO bring onboard to launch the startup? If the entire team is made up of equally incredible people, I know there's something special going on. I like to ask the CEO how he came to know his cofounders. Did he take whomever was available, or did he seek out the best possible people? Could his employees easily have gotten six-figure jobs but instead chose to work for nothing but equity? How did he persuade them that his startup was their best choice?

Exceptional leaders are magnets for talent. People want to work for them and are willing to take huge, even irrational, risks to do so. That's the type of person who can move employees to believe in the mission over money. That's how startups, with little or no resources, can outperform entrenched corporations and beat them at their own game. My philosophy is that no single person ever builds a billion-dollar business on her own. It's always the team that does it. The CEO is just the catalyst that kicks everyone into action. Jack Dorsey didn't build Square alone. Reid Hoffman didn't take LinkedIn public by himself. Pony Ma didn't grow Tencent without a lot of amazing people backing him up. If a CEO can't assemble an A-list team at the beginning, don't count on it happening down the road. It usually only gets worse.

This is why the team should be the first test of a CEO's leadership ability. If the CEO can assemble a winning team with nothing but words and equity, she has the magic to make it happen. In the end, being able to lead is the single most important quality a CEO can possess. A solid team with an extraordinary leader can figure its way out of almost any situation.

※

Being able to lead is the single most
important quality a CEO can possess.

When assessing a team, I don't just ask about their backgrounds. I like to understand their relationship to the CEO. What makes this CEO so special? Do they really believe in her? What is motivating them? Are they willing to stick around when everything goes wrong?

A strong team is one that's 100 percent committed and believes in the company's mission. It's not just a job. It's do or die for them. They will go down with the ship. That's the type of attitude that defines winning start-ups. Investors need to understand the team's psychology because how they think about the company and one another has more impact on the final outcome than anything else. I can't tell you how many teams appear excellent on the surface, but as soon as I peel back the layers, I can see they'll never make it past the first year. That's why I spend more time analyzing the team than anything else.

※

A strong team will go down with the ship—that's the type of attitude that defines winning startups.

Do you have a team of A+ players and true believers? If not, you have some work to do.

Sizing Up the Market

THE NEXT THING UNICORN HUNTERS look at is the market. If your market is too small, it will limit the growth of your startup. It's like trying to raise a whale in a fishbowl. The company can only grow as big as its market. This doesn't mean that companies that begin with a small niche market cannot expand beyond that, but it's important to see a clear path to the larger market. If there is no path, the startup will have to pivot at some point or stop growing, both of which can spell trouble.

There are a number of reasons why VCs avoid small markets. First, it's risk versus reward. A local bakery, no matter how tasty the croissants, can only make so much money. The risk may be low, but the rewards are limited. However, if the vision of the founders is to create a special chain of bakeries, utilizing secret recipes and an innovative business model, then it gets more interesting. It's high risk to launch a national chain, but the rewards are exponentially greater.

Another factor investors consider is the exit potential. Small, slow-growth businesses seldom, if ever, IPO, and acquisition offers are few and far between. Even if the niche company has an incredible new technology, the value of the technology almost never matches the value of a rapidly growing company targeting a big market. Major corporations, which have the money for large acquisitions, tend to focus on growth markets, not niches without the potential for expanding to larger markets.

Early-stage investors also need to consider follow-on investors. If they invest in a business with a small market, this automatically excludes later-stage venture capital. Institutional VCs are not interested in small exits. It's not their business model. They need supersized returns, and that means big markets and rapid growth. If a startup can't deliver this, tier-one VCs won't come in, and the startup will have trouble raising future rounds. Smart angels don't want to put money into a company knowing that few, if any, late-stage investors will follow suit.

Last, big markets mean more mindshare. Few people hear of smaller startups, but everyone knows the top unicorns. Those logos on every VC's website are usually names that most of us recognize, not some tiny startup that sold for $25 million, even if the return was 10x. So, all things being equal, bigger is not only better, it's often the only logical option. Remember this when your startup is raising funds. If the market isn't big enough, don't count on venture capital. They aren't coming to your party.

Who's Really Your Customer?

ONE OF THE FIRST QUESTIONS I ask when a startup approaches me is, "Who's your customer?"

I once had an entrepreneur answer, "Women."

I prompted him to say more, but all he said was that his startup targeted women, all women, and no more details followed.

I wound up telling him I wasn't interested in investing.

Why was I so quick to decide? Is it because I don't like women? No, I can assure you that I like women. My problem was that this CEO didn't know the customer at all. What did he mean by women? Elderly women? Teenage girls? Working mothers? Professional women? The customer is never just "women." A startup must know exactly whom it is trying to reach and exactly why the customer wants to buy the product. How can a CEO build and market a breakthrough product if he doesn't even know who his customers are?

It's critical for you to understand absolutely everything about your customers. What do they value most? Are they young, old, or middle age? How much money do they have? What type of cars do they drive? What type of movies do they watch? What are their goals and desires? The more you know, the greater your chances of success.

If you run a B2B (business-to-business) startup, the process is fairly straightforward. Spend a lot of time with your customers. Get to know them. Take them out to lunch. Find out about their lives, families, businesses, problems, and ambitions. Make note of everything. The more you know and the earlier you know it, the better. You shouldn't do this alone. You should get your entire team involved in the process of gathering, compiling, and analyzing customer data.

※

*Get your entire team involved in the process of
gathering, compiling, and analyzing customer data.*

Here are some questions to ask your customers:

- Why do you need this product?
- Why does your company need this product?
- Who needs to approve the purchase of this product?
- Who are all the stakeholders in your organization?
- How important is the product on a scale of 1 to 10?
- How does it compare to the competitors?
- If it didn't exist, what alternatives would you use?
- Are you willing to place your order now? If not, when?

These are just a few of the many questions you should be asking. Whenever possible, it's a good idea to record these interviews on video or audio. If they are overwhelmingly positive, you can show them to angels and VCs. They can act as early proof that there's a real need for your product.

If you have an online application, it's often better to rely on analytics tools than in-person interviews. This is because users will often say one thing and do another. What matters is what they do, and analytics software can show you precisely what's happening inside your app. Whether you put up a landing page with a video or release a minimum-viable product, you can mine data from users, gauge how they react, and use this to make sure you're on the right track.

Smart investors will always want to see this data before placing their money. When I'm vetting a startup, I like to gain full access to the analytics platform because it's important to review and verify everything firsthand. I pay special attention to the DAU (daily active users), MAU (monthly active users), retention rate, engagement patterns, virality, and growth.

If the startup hasn't launched yet or has no online component, there may not be any analytics. Without data, it's a blind bet. In this case, I often resort to asking a bunch of questions: How does the CEO know her business will be successful? What proof does she have? What experiments has she run? If the CEO hasn't attempted any experiments and has zero data, this is a red flag. It usually means the CEO is going completely on faith and doesn't understand how to validate a market. In this case, I'd be reluctant to recommend this startup to investors.

Even at a very early stage, your startup should be accumulating data, running experiments, and figuring out if there's a real product-market fit. If you aren't doing this, that's a problem. You should not be spending all your time building your product, fundraising, generating hype, and going to conferences. In the end, those won't matter half as much as understanding your customer. The reason most startups fail isn't because their product doesn't function as promised or because they didn't get enough money or press. It's because they haven't identified what their customers really want, and the only way to do this is to know your customer inside and out.

Tapping the Trends

I LIKE STARTUPS THAT TAP into trends. Nothing is more powerful than getting in at the beginning of an emerging wave and riding it all the way to the bank. A trend is like having a jet engine on your back. It can propel your tiny company forward with incredible speed and force. Most successful startups tap into some sort of trend, whether it's a tech trend, like AI, blockchain, or DNA editing, or a consumer trend, like yoga, extreme fitness, or health food.

Unicorn hunters are always on the lookout for companies that have identified a new trend ahead of everyone else and are positioned to exploit it. Take Shake Shack, the fast-food chain. They rode the gourmet burger trend all the way to an IPO. Stitch Fix is another trendsetting startup. Using fancy algorithms, big data, and hip stylists, they became experts at handpicking clothing that fit their customers' personal tastes and needs, and then shipping it directly to them every month. Stitch Fix led the hyper-personalized clothing trend to an IPO. Similarly, Pluralsight identified software training as the next big thing and turned it into an even bigger business. With more than six thousand courses on everything from C# to JavaScript, its IPO came in at nearly $2 billion, and Pluralsight's founders did all of this without a dime of venture funding.

If a startup can identify a trend ahead of everyone else and take on the market leadership role, it can leverage a growing customer base as well as become a press darling. The media is always on the lookout for the next hot thing, and if they spot a startup blazing the trail, it can become the poster child for the trend itself. This means an enormous amount of free marketing. For a cash-strapped startup, there's no better way to build a brand quickly.

Unicorn hunters are always on the lookout for companies that have identified a new trend and are positioned to exploit it.

Just look at RxBar, which piggybacked on the healthy protein bar craze. When the founder, Peter Rahal, asked his father for money, the reply he got was, "You need to shut up and sell one thousand bars." That advice proved to be pretty sagacious. With just $10,000 of their own money, Rahal and his partner, Jared Smith, launched the company and began making their health bars by hand. It was an entirely bootstrapped operation. "I'm not a designer, but Jared and I knew that we needed to get to market as soon as possible. So, we opened up PowerPoint and created the best packaging we could," Rahal says.

With their first protein bars in hand, they went around to local coffee shops and grocery stores and offered them for free. "We didn't care," says Rahal. "We just wanted people to start trying them out." Lack of designers, manufacturing, and a marketing budget didn't matter because they caught the wave. People just loved their product and started buying.

"We knew we were onto something pretty quickly," admits Rahal. It was the right thing at the right time. Instead of protein bars packed with sugars and other unhealthy and unknowable ingredients, RxBar kept it simple, putting all the ingredients in bold type on every bar. A typical bar would announce in big, bold print: "3 egg whites, 6 almonds, 2 cashews, 2 dates, no B.S." That resonated with their customers.

The demand was so powerful that they couldn't keep up with sales. The bars marketed themselves, word spread faster than they could scale, and the press loved them. They raised no venture capital or outside funding.

They just kept it going until Kellogg stepped in and acquired the company for $600 million. How's that for tapping a trend?

Trends also afford startups the opportunity to build a community. Trends happen because people are passionate and excited about something. "I even put my cell phone number on the package," says Rahal. "I wanted to make sure I was [as] accessible as possible. Feedback is how we grew."[1] You may not want to put your personal phone number on every product, but it shows how committed the founders of RxBar were toward engaging their community.

If a startup is early in the trend, it can become a de facto community hub. This puts it in the driver's seat. The startup can produce events, run conferences, create meaningful content, build a platform, engage customers, spark dialogue, and, in the process, grow the entire market. If the founders do these things well, they can create a bond between the customer, their brand, and the trend itself. This will put them in the market leadership position, while competitors late to the market will be seen as copycats.

Smart founders will make it their mission to completely own the trend. This means doing everything they can to take the helm and steer the trend in a positive direction. The trend's success becomes the startup's success. Smart startups actively seek to prevent scandals, protect customers, provide guidance, and build loyalty. The more the startup invests in the trend, the more it gives back in return. An investor can't ask for a better opportunity than this.

56

Good vs. Great

I WANT TO FIND OUT early on if a startup can be number one in its market. If I don't feel confident that the team has the potential to lead the market, my interest diminishes.

Why is this? Because it's a winner-take-all world. The more scalable the business, the easier it is for the company with the best products to dominate. This is because everyone gravitates toward greatness. If there are two competing products, and one is great while the other is good, which will you choose? Great usually wins. Who wants the second-best search engine, chat application, smartwatch, or painkiller? Why choose something that isn't as good? Just to be clear, if a lower quality product is half the price, then many people will settle for less. That's because the greatness of a product is the sum of all its attributes—including price. OnePlus phones are not as nice as iPhones, but for the price, they're a great value.

Great products are category killers. They eat everybody else's lunch. This is why Google dominates search and is worth exponentially more than its closest competitors. The same is true of Apple, Amazon, Facebook, PayPal, Netflix, and most other top performers. What's the value of Amazon's closest rival in the United States? Or the value in China of the next biggest social network after WeChat? In any highly scalable business, the number one player tends to capture the lion's share of customers.

Some investors may be tempted to avoid the market leaders because their valuations are so high and instead invest in laggards with heavily discounted valuations. Unicorn hunters know this is not a wise move. It may feel like a bargain at the time, but in the long run, the market leaders usually end up accelerating at a faster pace, leaving everyone else as tiny specks in the rearview mirror. This is especially true of platforms, which become more valuable the more people use them.

As a startup founder, if your goal is to be number three in the market, give up right now. If you aspire to be number three, it probably means you'll wind up number seven, eight, or nine—if you're lucky. Those start-ups may not even survive. If you don't honestly believe you can be number one in your market, then get out before you waste more time and money. Pick something you can win at.

※

If you don't believe you can be number one in your market, get out now before you waste more time and money.

When Snapchat launched, Facebook was already the dominant social network on the web, so going head-to-head wasn't a winning strategy. Instead, Snapchat focused on mobile communications. Back in 2010, Facebook wasn't yet a dominant player in this market. That meant the playing field was open. Snapchat targeted teens who wanted a free way to text and share photos. The disappearing messages made it even more attractive to this demographic. Snapchat also worked not only on phones but also over Wi-Fi, so teenagers without a data plan could still use it. The app turned out to be a winner for its investors. Snapchat wound up going public in 2017. On its first day of trading, the stock soared 44 percent, valuing the company at $28 billion.

If you look across product categories, you will always find one company that owns not only the space but also the name itself. For example, when most people think of CRM (customer relationship management), the first name that pops into their heads is Salesforce. For databases, it's Oracle. For marketing automation, it's Marketo. Inbound marketing is dominated by HubSpot. SurveyMonkey is the survey king. Zendesk leads customer support. DocuSign is equivalent to e-signatures. And Zuora owns subscription billing. You get the idea.

By owning the name, leaders in any market obtain a huge advantage. They have greater brand recognition. They garner the most media attention. They appear more trustworthy. And they can offer more value—especially if there's a network effect. All of these add up to enormous barriers to entry, making it virtually impossible for a competitor to catch up.

Another key factor is scalability. In highly scalable businesses, a small head start can rapidly expand into a huge lead. Once a market leader with a superior product moves ahead of its competitors, it will gain momentum. It has an easier time raising capital. It can take advantage of economies of scale. Its brand becomes ever more valuable, and it can fuel its growth by reinvesting more and more of its resources into sales and marketing.

We see this story being played out over and over again in Silicon Valley. Even if competitors come out with better products, it doesn't matter. Once a company is established as the market leader, it owns the space. The graveyard is littered with corpses of PC operating system companies that tried to displace Microsoft. Apple was nearly one of those. If it were not for Steve Jobs returning to the helm and pivoting the entire company into online music, Apple may have died. That radical move is what saved it and opened the way for the iPhone, which in turn boosted Mac sales. The fact is that customers hate switching and will stick with the leader whenever possible. That's why giants, like Alibaba and Amazon, just keep getting bigger, gobbling up market share, while their competitors struggle to survive. For a startup, good is never good enough. You need to be great. So, I want to ask you a question. Is your product truly great? If not, it's time to start over—just like Steve Jobs did.

57

What's Your Secret Sauce?

ONE QUESTION I ENJOY ASKING founders is, "What's your secret sauce?" I want to know what makes their startup special. If they reply, "Well, we're like Product X, but we have this amazing feature," my heart sinks. I don't care how amazing that feature is. I need to hear what makes their startup so incredible that it will redefine the product category. I want to see something unique that sets the company apart from everyone else. That's the only way for a new entrant to break through.

Listen carefully. I need you to understand this. There are only two ways for a startup to crack a market. If it doesn't do one of these two things, it will never rise above the noise. It must either be exponentially better than the competition, or else it must be radically different.

※

Be exponentially better or be radically different.

Let's start with exponentially better. To truly leapfrog competitors, a startup needs to innovate in a way that makes its product so much more valuable to its customers that they cannot afford to stick with what they are currently using. People don't enjoy switching products. No one wants to learn anything new. There's a huge amount of inertia in the market. The best way to get customers to abandon one product and try another is to make them feel like they can't live with the status quo.

Apple did this when it launched the iPhone. It was 10x better than any other phone on the market. The user experience blew the competition away, and that's why this company, which had never produced a hit phone, could steal market share from entrenched giants like Nokia, Motorola, and Blackberry.

Google is a similar case. Its search engine was significantly better than the closest competitor. It delivered the results that users wanted but weren't getting. This helped Google roar past the established players, leaving Yahoo!, Infoseek, Alta Vista, and others eating their dust. If Google had only been slightly better than the competition, it might not exist today.

※

If Google had only been slightly better than the competition, it might not exist today.

Skype is another example. It didn't invent VoIP (voice over internet protocol). The technology had been around for years, but the phone companies didn't see a need for it. They had monopolies and could charge their customers outrageous fees for long distance calls. Along comes Skype, offering calls that were inferior in quality, required specialized software, and didn't even work over a phone. People needed a PC. So, how did Skype win? It won by making the calls free. To many customers, especially those calling overseas, this was exponentially better. They were spending a small fortune on long distance calls to family and friends, and they'd jump through almost any hoop to save that money. As a result, Skype had no problem competing with the big players.

If a startup can't provide exponentially more value to its customers, then it needs to offer something radically different. By this, I mean offering value that customers cannot get from anywhere else. Let me give you a couple of examples. There were already a lot of instant messengers available when a startup called Slack launched its own service. Facebook Messenger, Snapchat, Instagram, and WhatsApp dominated the market, and competing instant messengers began dropping dead like flies. But that didn't stop Slack. It not only survived; it grew into one of the Valley's top unicorns.

How did this happen? Slack used the same technology as everyone else but offered a totally different value to its customers. Instead of being a personal instant messenger, it was designed from the ground up as a business collaboration tool targeted at enterprise customers. It's not Facebook Messenger, Instagram, or WhatsApp with an extra feature. It's a business tool. Most people use Slack right alongside their personal instant messengers. It doesn't compete with them because it offers a fundamentally different core value.

Another startup that won by being different is Affirm, a consumer finance company. When Max Levchin launched the company, there were already plenty of payment and financing options available for US consumers, including Visa, MasterCard, Discover, PayPal, eCheck, debit cards, and so on. Retailers didn't have any incentive to add yet another one to their growing list, and consumers weren't demanding one. So, how did Affirm break into the market? It did it by offering something none of the competitors had thought of: a simple, elegant way to make flat, monthly payments at the point of purchase online. It was a loan where the interest was built into an easy-to-grasp payment plan. This one innovation took off like wildfire, and Affirm grew into a healthy unicorn.

If you analyze enough tech startups, you will see a similar pattern. If the startup isn't exponentially better or radically different, it's extremely hard to crack a category and grow into a unicorn. That's why you should look at your startup and ask yourself, "What's our secret sauce?" If you don't have one, you'd better start cooking something up.

58

Business Models Made Simple

HERE'S MY TEN-MINUTE MBA COURSE on business models. There are really only two business models that work: 1) Either the customer pays you directly, or 2) an advertiser pays you. All other business models are subsets of these two.

Let's start with the customer paying you. For this model to work, the average amount customers pay over their lifetime using your product or service must be significantly more than the average customer acquisition costs plus cost of goods. The bigger the profit margin, the healthier your business. When investors see fat margins combined with a big market, they start lining up to get in on the deal. VCs don't care if the startup loses money in the short term as long as they can see a clear path to high profitability down the road. By giving the company money now, they are betting it will become the market leader and turn into a cash cow.

We all hear about viral growth, but in reality, very few products manage to grow virally. At some point, almost every startup must have a significant marketing budget to expand beyond the early adopters. Because customer acquisition is almost never cheap, a startup needs to extract a lot of money from each customer. There are two ways to do this: Either the startup charges a onetime fee up front and uses the profits to fuel growth, or the startup charges incremental fees over a longer period.

The problem with onetime purchases of non-consumable goods is that the customer only pays once, and then it's over. No more money. A good example of this is selling a couch, lawn mower, or hairdryer. The company gets paid upon purchase, then typically doesn't hear from the customer again unless there's a problem. This is a suboptimal business model for a startup. It costs a lot to acquire new customers, and the startup won't see another penny unless it can figure out something else to sell that customer. For startups, it's costly to develop and market a continual stream of new products. The onetime-purchase business model is better suited for established brands that have name recognition, strong distribution channels, long-term marketing partners, and economies of scale.

Even if the startup develops a new product that is radically different from anything on the market, it's usually not long before rivals copy it. They'll begin by undercutting the price to gain market share. We see this in consumer electronics. It's a brutal business as low-cost copycats drive down the price. This is why hardware startups have such a tough time. Unless they have proprietary technology that cannot be copied or some other significant barrier to entry, their margins quickly erode, leaving them little money to build their brand and grow the business.

To complicate matters, copycats are getting faster and smarter. In today's hyper-connected world, if a product is at all successful, in a matter of months, a wave of clones will appear on the market. I've seen this firsthand. A startup spends a year or more innovating and comes up with a cool new gadget, puts it on Kickstarter or Indiegogo to raise money and awareness, only to have copycats selling the same thing at a lower price in no time. For this reason, smart investors tend to shy away from companies with onetime-purchase models. It's a rough business.

※

Smart investors tend to shy away from companies with onetime-purchase models—it's a rough business.

Instead, unicorn hunters like to focus on startups with a strong, recurring revenue model. They don't care what the business is. It can be software, hardware, food, medicine, transportation, or anything else. What matters is whether the company can deeply monetize its customers. Let's go over four popular ways to monetize customers: subscriptions, consumable purchases, premium upgrades, and marketplaces.

1. **Subscriptions**—When the subscription model works, it provides a steady, predictable revenue stream. Investors love this because they can easily extrapolate from the past data and predict future growth. Most subscriptions have a monthly or annual fee. Unlike a onetime purchase, the initial cost is low or even free, meaning customers can try it out to see how they like it at little risk. The beauty of this model is that, over time, even a relatively cheap subscription can add up to far more than a large onetime purchase. Good examples of this model are Zendesk, GitHub, New Relic, and Domo. These are all enterprise SaaS (software as a service) unicorns with robust subscription models. It also works for consumer products and services. Just look at Verizon, Netflix, and Dollar Shave Club.

2. **Consumable Purchases**—Almost nothing beats selling consumables, because once you get customers hooked, they keep buying, sometimes for the rest of their life. Whether the consumable is a particular brand of deodorant, a favorite restaurant chain, or power-ups in a game, this model scales far better than a onetime purchase. Good examples are Pfizer's cholesterol-lowering drugs, Huggies diapers, and Centrum vitamins. I particularly like it when consumables are tied to a larger, onetime purchase. For example, games for Sony's PlayStation, K-Cups for Keurig's coffee makers, ink for HP printers, and replacement toothbrush heads for Braun's electric toothbrushes. Once customers invest in the initial purchase, they become psychologically locked into the brand's consumables.

3. **Premium Upgrades**—This is when a company sells add-on products or features. A good example is when you download an app and have to pay a onetime fee to unlock advanced

features. I'm not crazy about premium upgrades as a business model for most products. The problem is that there are only so many upgrades most products can offer, and then the revenue stops. However, for certain products, such as card games, it can work incredibly well. For instance, a card game, like *Magic: The Gathering*, can offer a virtually unlimited stream of premium upgrades, making it a cash cow.

4. **Marketplaces**—Creating a marketplace is arguably the most powerful business model of all because it scales so well. Marketplaces typically work by taking a small cut of every transaction. These small fees add up as the number of transactions increases over the lifetime of its customers. These businesses gradually turn into cash machines, netting sizable profits. Even better, marketplaces are highly defensible. Getting buyers and sellers to engage on a new platform is incredibly difficult, but once a company achieves critical mass, the network effect kicks in. This means the more buyers and sellers participating in the marketplace, the more valuable it becomes to everyone. Once a marketplace, like Amazon.com, Alibaba's Taobao, eBay, or Airbnb, achieves dominance, competitors find it almost impossible to catch up.

Now let's talk about the second primary business model: advertising. For advertising to work, it typically requires two things: lots of users and high engagement. Most online ads sell for tiny amounts of money, which means the startup will need millions of active users before the ad model begins to generate significant revenue. The second part of the equation is engagement. The more frequently users return and the more time they spend, the higher the revenue. Facebook and other social networks are good examples of companies ideally suited for the online ad model.

※

For advertising to work, it requires two things:
lots of users and high engagement.

The ad model breaks down when there aren't a lot of users or the users don't engage deeply. I had a startup founder come to me and say, "I'm going to use an ad model." But when I asked how often a typical user would engage with his app, the founder estimated it would be once every two weeks. I had to tell him this wasn't going to fly. If users aren't engaging multiple times a week, it's going to be pretty tough to grow a large business. The ad model is simple, but it only works for a small fraction of startups. These tend to be mass appeal media and social media startups. If a startup is not in that category, chances are the ad model isn't right.

To sum up my ten-minute course, let me say that there is no single best business model. It comes down to the business itself and the needs and desires of the customers. Many startups experiment with various business models before picking the right one for their product. For investors, it doesn't matter what the model is as long as the startup deeply monetizes customers, nets a sizable profit, and scales.

Business Model Emulation

WITHIN MONTHS OF UBER MAKING headlines with its innovative business model, Silicon Valley was Uberizing their business plans. There was the Uber of laundry, Uber of car washing, Uber of housecleaning, Uber of parking, Uber of body massages—even the Uber of ice cream. Each startup wanted to take Uber's secret sauce and use it in another line of business. Just press a button on your smartphone, and the service would magically appear. Unfortunately, most of these are out of business now.

Business model emulation looks great on paper, but it seldom works. The reason is that on the surface the two businesses may appear to be similar, but when you dig deep, you start to notice fundamental differences. It only takes one missing element to invalidate the model. In the case of Uber, it worked so well not only because it was convenient for the user but also because it had all of the following traits:

※

Business model emulation looks great on paper, but it seldom works—one missing element invalidates the model.

- Recurring revenue stream.
- Customers make frequent purchases and remain engaged.

- Lifetime value of customers is higher than customer-acquisition costs and cost of goods.
- Marketplace network effect created by matching drivers with customers.
- Difficult to circumvent Uber and go directly to the driver.
- Better service than traditional taxis.
- Easy for customers to provide feedback on drivers and service.
- Excellent user experience.

It's the combination of all of the above that makes Uber such a valuable company. Startups that transposed this model onto other services, like housecleaning and massages, found that leakage and retention were real problems. Startups that tried to deliver on-demand ice cream, perform car washes, or park cars using Uber's model discovered that the unit economics didn't work out. A lot of these startups raised substantial amounts of funding, only to fall flat on their faces.

The same thing happened with Warby Parker's direct-to-consumer model. Warby Parker has done extremely well selling eyeglasses directly to customers online. After this success, hundreds of copycats tried to apply the same model to selling suitcases, home furnishings, jewelry, toothbrushes, bras, socks, tampons, you name it. There was an entrepreneur for practically every consumer product category out there trying to build their online brand and steal customers away from more established brands.

Some of these were highly successful. Dollar Shave Club led the way with an online subscription for men's razors. This personal grooming company leveraged a hip image, viral videos, and low prices to grow rapidly, and wound up selling to Unilever for $1 billion. Other startups in different categories weren't so fortunate. They each launched trendy brands that appealed to millennials, designed cool products and packaging, and leveraged social media and viral videos. The majority of them are now struggling or out of business. What went wrong? Why did some succeed while others failed when all of these startups used similar tactics?

The reason is that not all product categories are equivalent. They each have their own economics. In the case of Warby Parker, the eyewear market has been dominated by Luxottica, which owns most of the top brands and retail chains. This pseudo-monopoly allowed Luxottica to charge a sizable premium. Warby Parker disrupted the market by slashing prices while offering equivalently stylish products. The lower prices encouraged consumers to refresh their look throughout the year, which meant buying more glasses and boosting Warby Parker's recurring revenue.

Dollar Shave Club took a similar approach. Gillette dominates the razor business and marks up its products accordingly. By offering their own branded blades at a discount, Dollar Shave Club was not only a hip alternative to Gillette but a good value as well. It was also convenient to never run out of blades. They just showed up in the mail each month. This subscription model enabled Dollar Shave Club to lock in customers, monetize them over a long period, and spend more on customer acquisition, thus creating a virtuous circle of growth.

Many of the other markets don't share these attributes, and that's why startups in those markets are struggling. If there are already dozens of products on the shelves in all price ranges, it's hard for a startup to enter the market and distinguish itself. For example, there is already a wide selection of underwear and dental floss on the market in all price ranges. Simply adding another option isn't always enough. It might have an appealing new aesthetic and maybe even a convenient subscription model, but that usually won't lure customers away from what they already know and trust.

This is why I caution entrepreneurs about simply appropriating a business model and running with it. If you run too fast without looking where you're going, you risk tripping and falling hard. You need to deeply analyze the market and all the factors that go into forming the business model before you conclude that emulation is the right path to go down. Sometimes it's easy to get funded by saying, "We're the Warby Parker of fountain pens!" But you have to be careful. Are you really the same?

Locking In Customers

ANOTHER COMMON CHARACTERISTIC OF UNICORNS is their ability to lock their customers into long-term relationships. The stronger the bond, the harder it is for competitors to steal away their customers, which results in higher profit margins and long-term growth.

Locking in a customer typically means getting customers to invest their time and resources into the product or service. A good example is a social network. The more deeply users engage, the more valuable it becomes. When users invite their friends, establish relationships, upload photos and videos, create pages, form groups, and conduct business on the social network, they are making an investment. If users choose to leave the social network, they stand to lose this investment. The result is a high switching cost, which can act as a huge barrier to entry for competitors.

This isn't just true for social networks. It's true of many successful unicorns. These companies have built entire ecosystems around their products that can make switching a painful process. Take Automattic, which runs WordPress.com, one of the most successful blogging platforms in the world. Once customers choose WordPress.com, they begin to upload their content and build their websites. This investment in time and creativity binds the user to the platform. In addition, customers can tap into the thousands of third-party plugins and themes. The more

WordPress add-ons they use, the harder it is to leave because these won't necessarily be available on other platforms.

One common attribute of locking in customers is the ability to get them to invest their time into the product or service. With software, users typically spend time learning it, customizing it, and integrating it into their workflows and lives. This makes it increasingly hard to cut ties down the road. Look at HubSpot. Once customers buy into HubSpot's ecosystem, they begin using it to deploy content, attract and engage customers, manage relationships, and grow their businesses. By the time companies are done integrating HubSpot into their workflows, it's hard to consider moving to another platform.

One common attribute of locking in customers:
the ability to get them to invest their time.

Locking in customers has been how most of the biggest software companies in the world became so profitable. Microsoft did it with the Windows operating system. SAP has done it with its enterprise resource planning and business services. Oracle did it with its database management system, and Zendesk did it with its integrated customer support solutions.

After adopting any of these platforms, it's tough to contemplate backing out. The software tentacles can reach so deep into a company's business processes and organization that the effort to unwind becomes greater than any benefit competitors can offer. This helps guarantee high profit margins over a long period, which investors love.

Hardware vs. Software

I AM OFTEN ASKED WHETHER investors prefer hardware or software startups. My answer is that software beats hardware almost every time. There are several reasons for this. First, hardware is hard. It's difficult to develop. Most first-time entrepreneurs don't realize how risky it is to bring new hardware to market. It's not like an app that you can continually tweak and improve. Once you begin manufacturing, costs can escalate, and one miscalculation can sink a cash-strapped startup. That's why we've seen so many Kickstarter and Indiegogo projects raising money but never shipping. The inexperienced founders often underestimate the time, money, and complexity.

Some of this risk can be mitigated if the company brings on expert help early in the process. Indiegogo has moved to this model by connecting entrepreneurs with partners who are experts in design engineering, manufacturing, and distribution. This is helpful, but it's only the first hurdle. Making a profit is the truly tough part.

Another reason I'm hesitant about hardware is that it's difficult to lock in a customer with hardware alone. After customers buy a gadget, they typically disappear. There's no ongoing relationship or investment customers have to make beyond the initial purchase. Without this relationship, the startup suffers. It can't monetize the customers deeply, upsell future products or add-ons, and get feedback. The best way around this is to connect hardware to the internet using software. That's why there was so much enthusiasm around IoT (Internet of Things). It was supposed to change everything, giving hardware the same power as software.

However, despite all the hype surrounding IoT, there have been relatively few success stories. This is because most startups are either good at hardware or software. I seldom find a startup proficient in both, and if the startup fails to execute well on either, the product won't live up to its promise. This invariably means longer development times, higher costs, and more moving parts that can get screwed up in the process.

Another reason why consumer IoT hasn't taken off like everyone predicted is that most people aren't interested in having an ongoing relationship with their toaster, microwave oven, or thermostat. In addition, many IoT devices are more difficult to use than what they're replacing. No one but a gadget freak wants to learn how to interact with a new device unless it provides significant value over existing solutions. If the device doesn't do something extraordinary, what's the point in learning to use it? Who wants to download new apps and figure out new interfaces? Often the best devices are the ones that don't require any learning curve. IoT still has some ways to go.

In the early days, everyone was raving about how Nest, the smart thermostat company, would provide the gateway into the connected household. That's why Google purchased the startup for $3.2 billion. After this acquisition, venture capital showered consumer IoT startups with money. They were the next goose that would lay the golden eggs. Unfortunately, most of the eggs ended up rotten. Even Nest hasn't turned out to be what Google imagined. It continues to underperform. The deep monetization and engagement with consumers never materialized.

The one smart home product that broke through was Amazon's Echo, which was originally supposed to be a voice-controlled music jukebox. It has now expanded into a voice platform for the home called Alexa, with an entire ecosystem of apps and developers. Alexa and its offspring offer significant value to users, including accessing almost everything on the web through voice controls. Alphabet, Alibaba, Microsoft, and countless other companies have piled on with their own competing products.

Even with the success of Alexa and its clones, it's still hard to monetize IoT. Getting people to pay for a subscription or consumables isn't easy. It can't be slapped on top of just any connected device. The model has to be intrinsic to the value it provides. If there isn't significant value accrued over time, a subscription makes no sense. Who really wants to pay a monthly subscription fee for using a smart vacuum, lock, or blow dryer, let alone a connected light bulb or toilet?

On the enterprise side, things look rosier. Industrial IoT, which combines hardware with software to solve critical business problems, can offer value to large and medium-sized enterprises. This is an area that will become increasingly promising as manufacturers, transportation companies, and other businesses adopt IoT. If startups can identify difficult business problems and provide solutions with a combination of hardware and software, they have the potential to create scalable models that justify venture funding.

Hardware is most valuable when it can enable a startup to enter a new market and capture the leadership position ahead of competitors. I consider hardware to be the Trojan horse. If it can get the customer to bring a product inside the gates while the software stealthily takes over, that's a winning combination that investors will back.

62

When Do Patents Matter?

I HAVE HAD HEATED ARGUMENTS over the value of patents with startup founders. Yes, I know that companies like Qualcomm, 3M, and Intel have built their market dominance on incredible patent portfolios, but for most startups, especially software startups, I believe the majority of patents filed are worthless. It's rare for patents to become extremely valuable. When I look at startups and dig into their patent portfolios, I'm often dismayed. Just because a startup has filed ten patents doesn't mean they are useful or effective. Anyone can file a provisional patent and get it approved, but what matters is how that patent gives the company a significant edge over competitors.

Just take a look at Jawbone, the startup that produced Bluetooth earpieces, wireless speakers, and fitness trackers. It raised $900 million from investors and had an extensive patent portfolio. Despite being an early entrant into the market and filing hundreds of patents, the startup failed because of quality control issues, production problems, and poor products. Jawbone tried to save the company by filing patent suits against Fitbit, but this Hail Mary didn't work. The fact is that patents are seldom enough to keep a sinking ship afloat.

When I analyze patents, I always ask myself:

- Does this patent provide a real barrier to entry?
- Is this patent essential to doing business in the space?

- Can this patent be used to block competitors or extract a licensing fee?
- How hard is it to work around this patent?

I need to know the answers to these questions before assigning any real value.

The second problem is that having a great patent portfolio is expensive. To develop a strong patent takes time, research, and money. Hiring patent lawyers is a significant expense. Most early-stage startups simply don't have the resources to cover these costs, and even if they do, the benefits tend to lie years down the road. Usually, by the time the patents kick in, the startup has already either succeeded or died, and the patents played little or no part in this.

Even if the patent is granted quickly, which typically isn't the case in the United States, most startups don't have the money to enforce the patents. Patent litigation is expensive and time consuming. Litigation can get tied up in court for years. Often the best a startup can do is trade patents with other companies to avoid lawsuits.

For all these reasons, I think it's wise for most early-stage startups to invest their time, money, and resources into building their businesses—not filing patents. The reason most startups fail isn't because they lack patents. It's because they never figured out the right business model in the first place. Even if a startup has solid patents, those patents often get sold in a fire sale or handed to creditors if the company goes belly-up.

That's why smart venture capital tends to avoid startups with lots of patents but no real business model. If a startup's only viable model is to license its patents, that typically is not a good investment because patent licensing seldom turns into a billion-dollar business. It's usually much smaller. Businesses that rely solely on patent licensing don't perform as well as companies with real products that solve real problems. If you look at why unicorns have such high valuations, it's almost never because of their patents. Their value is primarily predicated on their market leadership and growth potential.

WhatsApp is a good example of this. The instant messaging startup surprised everyone when it sold to Facebook for a whopping $19 billion.

This was the fourth largest technology acquisition of the decade, according to *USA Today*. Even more surprising was the fact that WhatsApp did not bring Facebook any patents. WhatsApp is a great example of a startup that put 100 percent of its energy into developing its product and chose not to pursue patent protection. This is because patents wouldn't have added much value. The value was in their rapid growth, and they didn't get distracted from this focus.

I'm not saying that filing patents is never a smart idea for startups. Some patents are extremely valuable. For startups developing capital-intensive businesses and new core technologies, such as semiconductors, new materials, medical devices, robotics, pharmaceuticals, agtech, space-tech, and biotech, patents can be critical and well worth the investment in time and money. A lot of these patents come out of universities, research centers, and large corporations because the cost is high and the research and development times are so long. These types of patents often have the potential to revolutionize entire industries, and filing them as soon as possible can make all the difference.

That said, a typical bootstrapped startup, with little or no money, seldom develops new core technologies, and therefore, filing patents early on doesn't always make sense. Even if the patent may generate sizable licensing fees down the road, that won't do much for a startup in the early stages. It all comes down to a careful cost-benefit analysis. My point is that startups shouldn't blindly file patents because they think that's what investors want to see. It may fool inexperienced investors, but not the type you really want to attract.

So, what do I believe would be the optimal patent strategy for most startups? I recommend that bootstrapped startups with no new core technologies focus on validating and building their business model first and file patents later. That's what matters in nine out of ten cases. Once the startup figures out its product-market fit and is in a position to scale, that's when it should begin thinking seriously about patents. This should be part of a long-term IP strategy. The larger the business grows, the more important the patents will become. After the startup's business scales up, then it's in a better position to begin diverting resources toward patents and defensible intellectual property development.

63

Shoehorning Technology

I SEE A LOT OF startups that grab the latest hot technology and paste it into their business plans. For example, as soon as AI became a buzzword, every startup with an algorithm and database was suddenly peddling its artificial intelligence to investors, customers, and even the press. In most cases, these startups didn't alter what they were doing; they just leveraged the latest lingo to give their startup a quick makeover. At the top of the hype cycle, plenty of unsophisticated investors went along for the ride without really understanding the technology or the startup's business fundamentals.

Even worse is when a startup attempts to shoehorn a technology into a business model that doesn't fit. This happened when the blockchain came into vogue. Everyone, including investors, was touting how the blockchain was bigger than the internet and would change every business on the planet. Hungry entrepreneurs jumped on the bandwagon and began using the blockchain to power every possible type of business: social networks, auctions, movies, e-commerce, search, and on and on. Their thesis was that just by using the blockchain, they could outcompete the established players. In most cases, this was wishful thinking.

Here's a conversation I had with a startup founder at the height of the blockchain madness.

"Should I use the blockchain to create our online rental marketplace?"

"Why? Will it give you a competitive advantage over Airbnb or HomeAway?"

"I don't know."

"Does it provide any additional value to the end customer?"

"Not really."

"Does it make implementation easier or provide additional functionality?"

"Well, it actually makes it harder."

You can see where this is headed. The entrepreneur is not thinking it through. He just wants to raise money from gullible investors regardless of the suitability of the technology to the task at hand. To me, this is not only bad business but unprincipled. Using new technology when there's no fit is not a strategy for success. The reason centralized databases power most of the internet right now is because they get the job done. Unless the decentralized blockchain can do a significantly better job at a particular task or enable an entirely new type of service, it doesn't make any sense to adopt it. It's like trying to pound a nail into the wall with an electric drill. Even if investors are infatuated with the idea, what's the point?

Unfortunately, this type of short-term thinking is rampant everywhere in the world. It's driven by greed and ignorance. Startups desperately want funding, investors want to get rich quick, and the media overhypes whatever is hot to attract eyeballs. The result is that startups choose a technology not because it's the best possible solution but because it's an easy way to get attention and raise capital. Whenever you're doing a startup, please don't shoehorn. It's unethical and unproductive, and you won't be creating anything of value for anyone, including yourself.

Design Thinking

UNICORN HUNTERS KNOW THAT DESIGN innovation is where much of the value lies. Design is often more important than technological innovation at the early stages. Why is this? It's because developing new core technologies tends to take a lot of time and money. It's not like investing in a newfangled coat hanger. Anyone can do that. It's low tech. But in the high-tech world, developing a core technology can take years and tens of millions of dollars. Most startups don't have the time or the money. They are bootstrapping it and must get to market as quickly as possible. The result is that design innovation tends to be at the heart of most successful startups around the world.

Design innovation tends to be at the heart of most successful startups around the world.

Dropbox became a unicorn by designing a superior way to share files; Facebook designed a new way to communicate with friends; WeWork remade the work space; Pinterest reimagined a social network based on a visual metaphor; Spotify reinvented how a generation consumes music; Hulu re-created the television experience online; and the list goes on.

Smart design allowed these unicorns and many more to break into the market and redefine their product categories.

What are the most important elements in good design? The first is simply how the product looks. Everyone likes to say, "Don't judge a book by its cover." But they say this precisely because that's what everyone does. We all judge books by their covers, so the book cover had better appear darn enticing or it probably won't make it off the shelves. If you want to sell your product to consumers, businesses, and investors, looks matter. This includes everything from your product design and packaging to your website, app, video content, and even business cards. They are all part of your book cover.

If you're developing a physical product, the materials, colors, ergonomics, form, functions, and packaging are all part of the design. For software, it's the UI (user interface) and UX (user experience). How do users navigate your app? Is the flow intuitive and streamlined? Is there an emotional component?

The best products create a remarkable connection with the customer. They are a joy to use—some bordering on addictive. They provide visual, auditory, and sensory feedback. Pressing a button can almost feel magical, like the product is alive and responding to your touch as much as a living organism would. This is what's called a great user experience.

For physical products, there are a number of factors, including how it feels to the touch. Does form follow function? Do the features seem to be a natural extension of the product itself? Does the product give the customer that remarkable feeling that only truly special products have? A product's ability to tap into the full range of emotions, from delighting the customer upon first touch to becoming an indispensable companion over time, is what separates hit products from mere wannabes.

I always look for products that enchant me. Does the product somehow appear as if it were designed specifically for me? Do I feel that desire to possess it? Does it radiate authenticity? Would I be proud to show it off to friends? People buy products, including cars, computers, phones, and homes, as much for what the product says about them as for what the product does. It's often more about self-actualization than anything else.

Think of how attached people become to their phones. It's not just an indispensable communications device. It speaks to their identities. It's something they take with them everywhere and use in all types of social situations. True design thinking transcends how beautiful something appears and taps into an innate understanding of the psychological and emotional needs of the people who use it.

Steve Jobs understood design at its deepest levels. "Most people make the mistake of thinking design is what it looks like," said Jobs. "People think it's this veneer—that the designers are handed this box and told, 'Make it look good!' That's not what we think design is. It's not just what it looks like and feels like. Design is how it works."[1]

Design thinking is an entire process that involves defining the problem, researching, forming ideas, prototyping, and testing. Great design teams often include more than just engineers and product designers. They also tap into experts on psychology, ethnography, cultural anthropology, ergonomics, cognition, and perception. Tom Kelley, the general manager at IDEO, one of Silicon Valley's top design firms, sums it up well when he says: "Cool technology alone is not enough. If it were, we'd all be riding Segways and playing with robotic dogs."[2]

Smart investors know this, and that's why design is a central consideration when hunting for unicorns. They know that design will ultimately play a pivotal role in almost every startup's success or failure. As a startup founder, hiring a top-notch designer is one of the best investments you can make. If your company doesn't have strong design DNA, it's time to go out and get some.

Building Superior Products

ONE PERSON WHO BELIEVES THE product matters more than anything else is James Dyson. After studying furniture design, then architecture and structural engineering, his first job was designing things for an engineering company. The owner, Jeremy Fry, was an inventor who liked to hire young people and see what they could do. Dyson was told to design a new type of flat-bottom boat, even though he had absolutely no experience whatsoever with watercraft.

As it happens, Fry also knew absolutely nothing about boats. This was just an idea he'd come up with. Fry, however, had a unique approach. He believed that you shouldn't think too much; you should just run with your ideas. He hated experts because they knew too much and wouldn't take chances. He wanted someone who was open to anything, no matter how outrageous. That's why he chose to hire young designers with little or no experience but a lot of talent.

Dyson accepted the job, even though he thought it was a bit crazy. Having no clue, he dove into learning everything he could about watercraft. When it was time to create a prototype, he encountered his first of many problems. He didn't know how to weld, and this was a necessary skill. He assumed Fry would hire a professional welder, but Fry refused. "Just go and try!" Fry retorted.

With no other choice, Dyson set about learning how to weld, as well as work with fiberglass and other materials. When he finally managed to build a boat that would float, Fry told him to take it to market. Again, Dyson was caught off guard. Wasn't Fry going to hire a professional sales and marketing team? Dyson was a designer, not a businessperson. He knew nothing about selling.

"Don't be ridiculous," says Fry. "You designed every square millimeter of it—every nut and bolt. You know everything about it, so go out and sell it!"[1]

So, Dyson put on his salesman's hat and went out to find customers. Within the first year, he'd sold a hundred boats at a healthy profit margin. He couldn't believe how successful it was. The British military, construction companies, and oil companies all became buyers.

Dyson went on to build other projects for Fry. He learned a tremendous amount on the job, and after seven years, he got the itch to start his own company. Fry offered to fund it, but Dyson wanted to see if he could do it entirely on his own. After a lot of contemplation, he decided to invent a new type of wheelbarrow. Instead of a wheel, it had a giant ball. He came up with the idea as he was fixing his house and noticed the deficiencies of wheelbarrows. The narrow wheels and legs sank into soft ground, especially when it was muddy. This made them hard to use. Wanting to solve this problem, he replaced the narrow wheels with a giant ball that was more maneuverable and wouldn't get stuck in soggy soil. Dyson called it the Ballbarrow.

The Ballbarrow worked incredibly well, but the difficult thing was selling it. Hardware stores didn't want it because they thought it looked strange, so Dyson resorted to placing little advertisements in the newspaper, right next to incontinence pants and baldness cures. Surprisingly, he wound up selling a decent number of Ballbarrows, but he never made much money. It turned out that there was no money in wheelbarrows. It was an important lesson to learn. No matter how good the product, the market also matters. Not many people buy wheelbarrows, and when they do, they don't want to spend much, so profit margins are slim. Dyson admits that he should have charged more for his innovative product instead of competing on price, but at the time, he didn't know better.

Dyson made another mistake. In order to grow his business, he took on outside investors. These investors weren't as open-minded as Fry.

When Dyson proposed the company launch a second product, his investors became annoyed. It didn't help that the second product was a new type of vacuum cleaner. Dyson became fascinated with the idea of having a vacuum that required no bags and created a massive amount of suction. His idea was inspired by industrial-sized cyclones that are used in factories to vacuum away particulate matter. Dyson figured that if he could miniaturize this technology, it would make the most powerful vacuum in the world, and that vacuum would have the added benefit of never needing any bags.

He thought his concept was solid, but his investors thought it was crazy. They insisted that if this was such an incredible idea, why didn't Hoover or Electrolux do it? These were giant companies that knew the industry inside and out. They'd been around for eighty years and had the resources to develop a consumer cyclone vacuum, if it were even possible. Since they hadn't done it, it clearly wasn't worth pursuing. When Dyson insisted on moving forward with his idea, the investors became so upset they kicked him out of his own company.

Dyson was left with no money and no prospects, but that didn't deter him. In fact, it motivated him to try harder. He realized that his invention was valuable because vacuums had a problem. The bags are not efficient. Long before the vacuum bag actually fills up, the tiny pores that allow airflow get clogged, making the vacuum less effective the more the bag is used. That's why people have to change the bags so often. With a cyclone, this wouldn't be a problem. Suction would never decrease because there are no tiny holes. The air flows right through, while the particulate matter sticks to the sides.

After completing more than five thousand prototypes, he finally managed to produce a fully functional cyclone vacuum cleaner. With the product in hand, he went around to the big vacuum and appliance companies and tried to license it. To his dismay, all of them rejected him. They weren't interested. They liked selling vacuum bags. It was lucrative having a recurring revenue stream.

With each passing day, Dyson's financial situation worsened. He now had a pile of debt, no income, and no customers. But instead of giving up, Dyson became more determined than ever to prove them wrong. His friends and family thought he was nuts to continue with this fruitless project, but Dyson knew the vacuum companies hadn't given him a good reason this wouldn't work. If they'd given him one good reason, he would have tried something else.

Without a reason to stop, he simply kept going even though things looked bleaker by the month. At the eleventh hour, he managed to secure a licensing deal from a small Japanese company. This deal, along with winning a patent infringement lawsuit in America, saved Dyson from bankruptcy. Putting up his home as collateral, Dyson took out a loan and began manufacturing vacuums. Then he went around trying to find distributors and retailers in the UK.

When the catalog manager asked why he should remove a Hoover or another top brand to make room for Dyson's strange, unproven invention, Dyson said, "Because your catalog is boring."[2] That proved to be enough of a reason. Within two years, Dyson had the top-selling vacuum cleaner in the United Kingdom.

Flush with victory, Dyson set his sights on the much more lucrative US market. In his now famous TV commercials, he appeared in the ads himself and explained why he'd invented this vacuum and how it was far superior to anything else on the market. Product sales exploded, transforming Dyson into one of the top vacuum brands in the world.

After ten years, Dyson stepped down as CEO to focus 100 percent of his energy on inventing new products, including an elegant bladeless fan, the first washing machine to feature two counter-rotating drums, an innovative hand dryer, and other breakthrough appliances. Dyson attributes his success to the mentality of a long-distance runner. He firmly believes that when you start to get tired, you should run faster because everyone else is tired, too. If you want to win, you cannot give up when it hurts. That's when everyone else stops, and only by pushing further can you break through.

✻

If you want to win, you cannot give up when it hurts—
that's when everyone else stops—you should run faster.

Back when Dyson was developing his first vacuum, he was forty years old and deeply in debt with no signs of success on the horizon. He's now worth around $6 billion, owns 100 percent of his company, and he did it all by taking a long-term approach focused around great design, with the faith that the best products always win out in the long run.

Unicorn hunters realize this, too, and that's why they pay special attention to well-designed products and creative teams. In the end, the products have to be exceptional or you're just running another copycat business.

Why Media Attention Matters

WHY IS MEDIA ATTENTION SO important? The first reason is because most startups are broke. At the beginning, they have nothing. No name recognition, no customers, and almost no money. Building a nationally recognized brand in the traditional way, through advertising, is prohibitively expensive and usually takes years. But if a startup can manage to catch the media's attention, all this can happen in a matter of months and cost practically nothing.

The media is excellent at spotting trends. After all, that's the job of most journalists. They are paid to predict what's coming next and make a headline out of it. Their senses are highly tuned to what stories will go viral, and when they see something special, they jump on it. If the story sticks, more journalists will pile on, propelling the story to new heights and further developing the narrative. With each subsequent retelling, the story becomes richer and more ingrained in the public's imagination, thus becoming more valuable. Piggybacking on top of this growing narrative is the startup's brand.

This is why smart investors pay special attention to media. It's a key barometer of a startup's potential to break through the clutter.

Startups are stories. Each company tells its story, but only certain stories resonate with the public and take off. If a story is trending, it's a good sign the company is onto something bigger—something that may turn out to be a game changer.

Riding a wave of press can do for a startup what almost no amount of funding can do. It can make the startup's product a part of popular culture and its brand part of the everyday vernacular. As much as we like to think of ourselves as individuals, human beings act as a herd. We tend to do what everyone else around us does. We tend to use the same apps, eat similar foods, buy similar clothing, and use similar expressions. A study at the University of Leeds confirms this, showing that just 5 percent of any group tends to influence where the other 95 percent go. This is how we've evolved to form cooperative societies. It's why millions of people spread across thousands of miles of land can feel they're part of a single nation and culture.

The combination of traditional media, new media, and social media sits at the center of this giant web of communication. Traditional and new media act as our filters. Editors, journalists, and bloggers capture and craft the stories, while social media acts as the viral engine, causing them to spread faster and farther. The combination of influential curators, compelling headlines, and user reactions validate ideas and raise them above the noise. In this way, the media acts as a virtual traffic cop continually directing the flow of the public's interests and opinions.

Public relations agencies know this, celebrities live and die by it, and politicians exploit it. As a startup founder, you should spend the time to understand how media works in the age of social networks and develop a strategy to take advantage of it. If you don't possess this knowledge, you need to bring someone onboard who can help you craft your approach. Launching a product today is as much about media adoption as it is about marketing, pricing, and distribution.

※

Launching a product today is as much about media adoption as it is about marketing, pricing, and distribution.

Despite all the trouble Uber and Facebook had with the press, in most cases, the old saying still holds true: No press is bad press. Even when the media is dissing Airbnb, Facebook, Snapchat, or YouTube for doing something stupid or corrupting our children, it's still press, and it's embedding those brands deeper into our psyche.

Most startups, especially in the early stages of their development, garner uncritical, positive exposure. The media tends to embrace entrepreneurs, and this is why investors who see a startup gain traction in the press often leap on it. This happened with both Oculus VR and Nest, two media darlings, which made out nicely riding a tsunami of positive press to multibillion-dollar exits.

Slack, the instant messaging platform for enterprises, grew from nothing into a billion-dollar company in just two years, and it didn't run any large marketing campaigns. It didn't have an elaborate email strategy or spend millions on billboards and TV commercials. In fact, Slack didn't even have a chief marketing officer. The founders simply made sure to engage the press early on, and whenever they got a good write-up, they shared it with their most influential friends who posted it to their followers and so on.

Whenever I look at a startup, I like to see early signs that the story will resonate with the media. Is there something special about this startup that will strike a chord with journalists? Is the startup able to ride or, better yet, encapsulate a trend? What will bloggers say when writing about the startup? How will this startup speak to a sizable segment of the population? If the answers to these questions align with the value the startup is offering its customers, there's a decent chance it will be able to break through with its message.

But don't get fooled. The media can write about some pretty silly stuff, too. Not every trend will turn into a unicorn. I remember when the social app Yo launched. All it did was allow users to send their friends the word "Yo!" That's it. It was such a stupid idea that it caught everyone's attention, rocketed to the top of the App Store, and garnered an ungodly amount of coverage. Eager to cash in, some naïve investors hopped on the bandwagon, investing $1.5 million into the startup. Sure enough, this turkey didn't fly.

Media attention alone doesn't mean a startup will succeed, but if a startup has a solid team, product, and vision, the effect of media on its ability to grow fast can't be underestimated.

Skeletons in the Closet

MOST STARTUPS HAVE SKELETONS IN their closets, and it's the investor's job to open up every closet door before buying the house. One time, I was in the middle of due diligence when I asked to see the agreement assigning the intellectual property to the startup. I was led to believe the IP belonged to the company, but it turned out this wasn't the case at all. The CEO had kept the core IP under his personal name, and he hadn't divulged this to anyone. In fact, he had misled us, which bordered on fraud. I lost all respect for this entrepreneur, refused to introduce him to investors, and severed our ties to the company.

When an investor is performing due diligence on your startup, please don't hide anything. It's far better to be open and honest, even if you feel it may kill the deal. After all, your reputation is at stake. If you leave out important details that are relevant to the future potential of your company, that's the equivalent of lying to the investor. Everything must be transparent if you're going to build a long-term trust relationship. Eventually, all the details will emerge, so hiding important facts will only come back to haunt you. I can't stress this enough. Investors are about to become your partners in the business, and the last thing you want is partners who feel betrayed.

Another thing to watch out for is the interviews. During the due diligence process, smart investors won't limit themselves to looking at your documents. They will ask to meet with your key team members individually and talk with them. Often, they will ask the same questions to each member of your management team and compare notes to make sure all the stories add up. This is how they uncover problems with your business. With this in mind, you need to prep your team and make sure everyone is on the same page. The last thing you want is a miscommunication or misunderstanding to set off alarm bells in the investor's head.

To stave off competition for a hot deal, many investors will ask the entrepreneur to sign a nonbinding term sheet before entering into due diligence. This way they can lock in the deal while leaving the door open to walk away if they happen to find anything questionable. This can place the startup in a weak position, because as soon as the term sheet is signed, all the competing investors must be told. Momentum comes to a grinding halt, and the pressure is off. The lead investor no longer has to move quickly. Now it's a waiting game, and if the lead backs out of the deal, for whatever reason, it can cast a huge shadow on the company.

This is why the whole due diligence dance needs to be carefully orchestrated, from both the startup's and investor's perspectives. My advice to startup founders is simple. Before signing any term sheet, you should disclose everything of substance. Don't leave anything in the closet for investors to find. The earlier you do this in the process, the better. It not only builds trust; it tends to have less of an impact. The same fact presented near the beginning of the process, when the investor is still undecided, doesn't have nearly as much impact as when the investor is on the verge of committing to the deal. That's when even small details can tip the balance.

You should also keep a copy of every agreement your company has ever signed in a cloud folder, like Dropbox or Google Drive. Be sure to include a copy of the cap table (a spreadsheet listing a company's equity capitalization), articles of incorporation, patents, trademarks, hiring agreements, and all other pertinent documents in this one folder. When investors are interested in moving forward, you can simply email them the link and password. It makes it so simple.

I've seen a deal fall apart because the startup had its paperwork spread all over the place. Some of it was on old laptops, and other paperwork was missing entirely. It took weeks to get this information to the investors. By that time, several of the interested parties had moved on. Investors are notoriously fickle, and they had found other shiny objects to chase. Remember, VCs see so many deals that if one appears difficult, their attention naturally shifts to the next startup in line.

I know some investors will sign a term sheet even before they're sure they want to invest in order to lock out the competition. Then they drag their feet because they're still undecided and often make some excuse to back out of the deal. This is why you should have a clause setting a timeline for due diligence. There needs to be a firm end date, and if the investor misses that date, there should be a penalty to pay. When I was trying to raise capital for my second startup, we ran up $40,000 in legal fees only to have the deal fall through when the investor changed the terms on us at the last minute. I wish I'd had a clause in our term sheet covering this.

Have a clause setting a firm end date for due diligence,
with a penalty to pay if the investor misses that date.

Keep in mind that most investors won't agree to any sort of penalty. That doesn't necessarily mean they have bad intentions. The top-tier VC firms often won't commit to binding term sheets or penalizations of any kind. It's just not something they do. In this case, you'll just have to make a decision. Do you walk away from the deal or not? It often comes down to trust. Can you count on the integrity of this investor? If you have doubts, maybe it's the wrong investor for you. If the answer is unclear, which it often is, then take your time. Don't rush into signing the term sheet. Do some of your own due diligence on the investor before moving forward.

What's the Fun Factor?

I'VE SAVED THE BEST PART for last: the fun factor. What do I mean by this? I mean that in my experience, companies that seem like they are having the most fun are, more often than not, good investments. I love it when everyone on the team is enthusiastic, enjoys working together, and believes in what they are doing. When I hear this from the employees, I know the management team is doing something right. Even if they haven't figured out their product-market fit yet, and even if they are struggling to close deals, teams that have fun together, stick together. It's like winning sports teams. They form an intangible bond that won't show up on spreadsheets or P&Ls (profit and loss statements), but is the magic formula that may help them overcome seemingly insurmountable obstacles.

A study from two scientists at the University of California, Berkeley found that sports teams whose players physically touch one another, whether hugs, slaps on the back, or high fives, have a higher probability of winning. When players show affection and bonding, it actually translates into higher scores. They've counted how many times players make friendly physical contact, and this correlates directly to the final outcome in the games they play. "Touch predicts performance through fostering cooperation between teammates," says Dacher Keltner, a professor of social psychology at the University of California, Berkeley. "You can communicate really important emotions like gratitude, compassion, love, and anger just through brief touches."[1]

In startups, it's the same way. That's why I pay special attention to the body language of each team member. Do these people really enjoy being around one another? Do they seem sincere? Or are they all in it just for the money? What are the team dynamics? Sometimes, I like to take the team out for a hike or observe them in a group activity where I can see how they interact. Maybe it's ultimate Frisbee, paintball, or whitewater rafting. Are they helpful and supportive of one another? How well do they communicate? Are they having fun together?

Emotionally connected teams are great investments. It's no accident that many successful startup founders are good friends before they start their companies together. A lot of the time, they've been coworkers at previous jobs or college roommates. They understand one another's quirks and have each other's backs. This is essential because doing a startup is so hard, both emotionally and financially, that having the support of a group can be essential to keeping the startup afloat when times get tough.

I remember when I was a boy and joined Little League Baseball, I was assigned to the worst team ever. Everyone on the team was just awful. The first two seasons, we lost nearly every game. It was like the movie *The Bad News Bears*, except that we were even less talented. I was among the worst on the team, which tells you just how naturally gifted at sports I am. I was so terrified of the ball hitting me that I would sit out in right field praying no one would bat it my way.

Even by our third season, not a single one of us had progressed to the upper leagues, which in itself was remarkable. Trust me. It wasn't the lack of trying. We all tried to advance. No one wants to be left behind in the junior leagues, but we all failed. That's how bad we were. So, we were stuck with exactly the same team as the previous two years. It was our final season. After this, we'd all be going to middle school and be too old for Little League. Coming back to our same bedraggled team and seeing everyone again was bittersweet. We knew it would be a repeat of the previous two years.

Sure enough, we lost our first game of the season by a huge margin. Then we went on to lose our second and third games. Our coach, desperate to boost morale, promised to take everyone on the team to Disneyland if we simply qualified for the playoffs at the end of the year. This certainly seemed like a safe bet to him, but to us it was more. It was his way of saying he cared. It was also a tangible goal. We had something to work toward. We didn't have to win the championship. We just had to qualify.

Over the next couple of weeks, something magical happened. We bonded—not in the way we had before, but in a deeper, more emotional way. We trusted one another and began to work together toward our shared goal of going to Disneyland. That's when we won our first game—not by much, but still, we won! That single win gave us confidence, and we went on to win our second game, then our third. With each win, we became closer—like a single unit, instead of a bunch of misfits thrown together. Our mediocre players suddenly weren't quite so bad. I even became a steady hitter. I stopped striking out and made consistent singles and doubles.

Just as we were gaining momentum, the unexpected happened. Our coach ditched us. He packed up and moved across the country to work at a Hershey's chocolate factory, leaving us without any replacement. You would think this would have slowed us down, but it didn't. It wasn't about our coach any longer. It wasn't even about Disneyland. It was about one another. We didn't need a coach. We were a team now, and we were winning together. A teammate's mother filled in as our temporary coach, and we charged ahead.

We kept on winning and winning and winning, right up until the playoffs. We not only qualified for the playoffs, we made it to the finals. In the end, it was us versus our archrival: the same team that had slaughtered us at the beginning of the season. Our coach still hadn't returned, so we didn't expect any trip to Disneyland. But we were determined to win the championship. We couldn't let one another down. And guess what? We crushed them! I can't express how good it felt for all of us to end Little League as winners, not losers.

This type of energy is what I look for in startups. If they've come together and love what they're doing, there's almost no barrier too big. I look for startups that operate like a winning team. I want to see that they are in it for one another and will do whatever it takes. These teams genuinely enjoy working together, and that sense of excitement and camaraderie rubs off on everyone they do business with. These are the companies I want to be a part of. I want to be on their team because I know, in the end, it's going to be an amazing experience. They may not win this time around, but if they keep at it, they can make it to the playoffs.

※

I look for startups that operate like a winning team; these are the companies I want to be a part of.

The company culture tends to overflow into the products and customer service. When people love what they're doing and care about one another, their products and customer interactions can't help but reflect that. Think of how much fun Google is with its crazy logo, fabulous offices, silly slides, and open atmosphere. Whenever I run into Googlers in Silicon Valley, they rave about how much they love their jobs. The ride-sharing startup Lyft also gives off the same vibe. The founders began by putting giant pink mustaches on all their cars, and they've continued to exude a sense of fun and caring that Uber lacks. Brian Chesky, the CEO of Airbnb, has also been obsessed with community and relationship building. In the early days, he made a point of visiting all his hosts and bonding with them. He even went so far as to rent out the couch in his home for $50 a night.

Boxed is another one of these startups. It's the e-commerce version of Costco or Sam's Club, but if you compare the websites, the fun factor extends beyond the playful logo and user interface. Chieh Huang, the millennial CEO, wants all his employees to love the company, and he's putting his money where his mouth is. He pledged to pay the college tuition fees for his employees' kids out of his personal equity. That's money from his own pocket—not the company.

"We were really poor growing up," says Huang. "It was tough times in Ohio when we lived there. My dad was between unemployed and just selling random knick-knacks at a flea market. My mom was a cashier at a Chinese food restaurant."[2] Education has been transformative in his family's life and his own success. That's why he wants to give the same opportunity to everyone in his company.

Huang hasn't stopped there. Boxed has implemented a policy of reimbursing employees up to $20,000 for life-changing events, like weddings. "It's not the cheapest program," admits Huang, "but then, we don't look like a typical startup." In their offices, there are no Ping-Pong tables, beer kegs, or free lunches. "We're frugal, and we use our money to fund what we think are really impactful and meaningful things."[3] This approach has allowed him to build loyalty, engender trust, and retain employees. So far, the result is that, after four years in business and a payroll exceeding two hundred, fewer than ten full-time employees have voluntarily left the company.

Southwest Airlines is famous for its highly motivated, fun-loving employees. That's why their customer service has been so much better than any of the other airlines. People there genuinely like their jobs. They are encouraged to speak out and be themselves. This all comes out of the company culture. Southwest truly values its employees, and everyone working at the company knows this. They care about their jobs because they know the company cares about them. This is reflected in every aspect of Southwest, from its management style and profit-sharing plan to the work environment, making it one of the most profitable airlines in the world for more than forty years.

L.L.Bean, the outdoor outfitter, also builds its loyalty by supporting and nurturing its employees. It is consistently ranked in Fortune's 100 Best Companies to Work For. When you walk into its stores, you can feel the positive energy. The fun factor is genuine. It's present in everything the company does, from its award-winning customer service to its famously high-quality products. The result has been a brand the customers and employees adore and a turnover rate of just 3 percent, which is rare in the retail industry. What's even more surprising is that L.L.Bean is more than one hundred years old. So, this rule doesn't just apply to startups.

Whatever the business, the fun factor can't be ignored, and that's why unicorn hunters place a premium on this elusive quality.

5

Scaling Up

Building a Billion-Dollar Business

N ow that we've covered launching a startup, fundraising, and venture capital, let's tackle what it takes to supercharge your growth. We'll explore how to find the best talent, bring in customers, and accelerate your business. We'll also answer questions like: How do you design a more creative workspace? Which marketing and customer acquisition strategies work best? What does it mean to have an exit strategy? And why is it important for startups to have an unfair advantage? By the time we're done, you'll understand the nuts and bolts of scaling your company.

The Art of Hiring

AFTER CONVINCING INVESTORS TO FILL up your bank account with cash, the first thing you need to think about is hiring. It sounds exciting, but it can become a real chore. You get buried in résumés, there are endless interviews, and finding the right person for even one position can be a huge time sink. The worst part is that it never ends. As you grow, the problem only becomes more acute.

To lessen the strain, you need to plan ahead, and that means taking the time to establish a hiring plan from the get-go. A hiring plan outlines all the positions you need to fill in the coming six months, the job requirements, the compensation you will pay, and your recruitment strategy. You should make sure to get board approval on the compensation packages right up front, which is much easier than on a piecemeal basis every time you need to hire a new employee.

After this, the hard work begins. I like to say that the most important thing a CEO can do is to bring onboard the right people. If you do this well, they will do the rest. Google founder Larry Page takes hiring so seriously that he insisted on signing off on every new hire. By 2015, he had vetted more than thirty thousand employees. "The most common feedback from Larry is that a candidate might not meet our hiring bar or that the creativity shown in a portfolio might not be up to snuff," wrote Laszlo Bock, former head of human resources at Google, in his book

Work Rules. "More important than the feedback itself is the message from Larry to the company that hiring is taken seriously at the highest levels, and that we have a duty to continue doing a good job."[1] This is because Page understands that, when building a world-class company, the most important thing is the people you choose.

Even if you have millions in the bank and your investors are pressuring you to scale up fast to meet demand, take a page out of Google's playbook. Don't rush hiring. Don't cut corners. It's far better to take your time and thoroughly vet every candidate. A good rule of thumb is to interview at least ten qualified candidates before filling any position. You cannot get a feel for the talent available if you interview too few people. After ten people, it's usually diminishing returns. That said, if you don't find the right person after ten interviews, hold off and interview more.

※

A good rule of thumb: Interview at least ten qualified candidates before filling any position.

Interviews are better done as a team sport. Don't leave it up to one person. The problem with relying on a single individual is that this person may choose to hire his friends over more qualified candidates. It's a natural inclination because he has a relationship with them, but it's counter to building a true meritocracy. Also, when scaling up, founders and managers often feel intense pressure to fill vacant positions. This can lead to subpar hires and hurts the company in the long run. That's why companies like Google use independent hiring committees to make the final decisions.

When setting up a hiring committee, it's good to create a list of criteria you expect from the employee. What skills are required for the job? What qualities do you prize most: honesty, attention to detail, ability to communicate clearly, past accomplishments? Here are the top five criteria I use:

1. **Ability to Learn**—The candidate must be able to quickly pick up new things and learn on the fly.

2. **Leadership**—Has this person been in a leadership position? What in the candidate's past demonstrates an ability to take charge?

3. **Humility**—Is this person humble enough to take other people's ideas into account? Does the candidate understand how to listen and collaborate?

4. **Ownership**—Does this person take responsibility and follow through?

5. **Expertise**—Does the candidate have the skills required to perform the job? This is especially important for highly technical positions.

It's best if the hiring committee members interview the candidates independently and write down their evaluations of each person, assigning a score from 1 to 10 to each of the criteria on the list. The scores can then be summed up in a final number. If you want to weight certain criteria more than others, you can tweak the formula. You'll find that, in the end, the sum of the scores proves a far more accurate indicator of the candidate's suitability for the job than going on gut feelings, as most people do when interviewing.

If you want to know more about this method, read the book *Thinking, Fast and Slow* by Daniel Kahneman. The book explains how our brains have evolved to make snap decisions about people, and these decisions are based on unconscious biases. We evolved this way over thousands of years. When our ancient ancestors were walking down a trail and came across someone from another tribe, they'd have to decide if the stranger was friend or foe within a matter of seconds. One mistake and . . . *wham!* Their DNA might not make it to the next generation.

For this reason, we're always scanning the faces of strangers to determine if we can trust them or not. The process is almost instantaneous, meaning we don't logically think it through. This is good for survival in a harsh world but not so good for judging how competent people are at their jobs. A study at the University of Toledo confirms this. They found that judgments made in the first ten seconds of an interview can predict the final outcome. This is called a *confirmation bias*. It's the tendency to search for, interpret, or prioritize information in a way that confirms one's beliefs or hypotheses. In other words, if our gut feeling says the candidate who walked in the door is right for the job, then for the rest of the interview, we subconsciously look for evidence that reinforces this hunch.

The result is that we tend to pick people with whom we feel comfortable. If they are from our social group, that's an instant plus. Good-looking people get more job offers and higher pay than ugly ones. Extroverts have an advantage over introverts. Men get chosen over women. White people are given preference over people of color, even when the person doing the hiring is a person of color. This is because these biases are part of our society and get propagated unconsciously. We don't even realize we're doing it. This means the best, most-qualified candidates often get passed over.

To prevent this from happening, we need to consciously analyze the data and disregard our first impressions. That's why a systematized process is necessary. It's important to prepare predetermined, unbiased questions and a way to analyze and rank the responses. It also helps to take detailed notes during the interview of all relevant factors and then have someone who has never met the candidate review those notes and form an independent judgment based on the established criteria.

After the interview, when checking references, you cannot rely on the people the job candidate suggests. They will almost always be positive. You need to find references not on the list, and that requires some detective work. Every time you check a reference, you should ask to be connected with other people who worked with the candidate in the same company but were left off the list. Don't stop there. You should also get on LinkedIn and search for people who can tell you more about the candidate's past.

While you're at it, also check the candidate's social media postings. The goal isn't to see if the candidate went wild one night at a party or what taste in music this person has; it's to uncover serious problems and prejudices that would affect job performance.

If this sounds like it will take up a lot of your time, you are right. But as I said, there's nothing more important you can be doing. Hiring the right people lays the foundation upon which your company is built. A series of bad hires, especially at the managerial level, can undermine and topple the best organization, while good hires accelerate growth.

70

Identifying Talent

I'VE GOTTEN BETTER AT INTERVIEWING employees over the years. When I started out, I was terrible. I didn't know which questions to ask or how to evaluate people. I now have specific criteria that I look for in new hires. As a general rule, I prefer to hire for potential over expertise. Expertise is good and often necessary, but potential is even more critical. This is because most startup jobs are in constant flux, especially at the early stages when the business is still being flushed out. What someone needs to know today may be irrelevant six months later. Everyone has to adapt quickly and constantly be learning.

For example, I may hire an engineer who is an expert in Microsoft SQL Server, only to discover that I need someone who knows MongoDB next month. Can this engineer adapt and learn, or am I out of luck? The same is true with most knowledge professions. There's always something new coming along. Technology never stands still. This means the people in a modern organization need to be constantly retraining themselves. With this in mind, here are the qualities I look for:

- **Self-Improvers**—The best employees are never satisfied with what they know. No matter how talented they are, they are determined to become better. They are constantly seeking out new courses, coaches, mentors, books, and other ways of improving themselves.

- **Natural Curiosity**—People who innovate on the job tend to be curious about everything. They can't help but ask questions and seek out the answers. This behavior correlates directly to their ability to solve creative problems.
- **Love of Learning**—People who value learning are always sucking up knowledge and new ideas. They don't see learning as a chore but as one of the great joys in life.
- **Driven to Succeed**—I like to hire people who are internally motivated to rise up the ladder. They're always striving to get ahead and taking on new challenges.
- **Feeling of Responsibility**—The best employees own their jobs. They feel accountable for their actions and will go to extraordinary lengths to fulfill their commitments.
- **Enjoy Their Work**—You can't be the best at something if you don't like doing it. People who truly love what they do tend to go further. They are the engineers who download the latest software development kits for fun on the weekends. They are the marketing managers who can't wait to try out new analytics software or launch an experimental campaign just to see if it works. They enjoy their jobs so much that work and play become one and the same.
- **Doers**—Most important, I like employees who are self-starters. They don't sit around waiting to be told what to do. They figure out on their own what needs to get done, and they take action.

When I interview candidates, I go deep into their past. I ask all sorts of questions. I want to know what they actually did on their previous jobs. I don't care if they were a vice president or junior project manager. It's what they've done and how they did it that matters. Did they take ownership of their job? Did they come up with a project on their own and drive it to completion? Were they able to get others onboard? How did they convince their coworkers, bosses, and outsiders it was worth pursuing? By delving into their past, I want to see evidence that they actually accomplished something out of the ordinary of their own volition. Those are the people who pay off in the long run.

71

Recruitment Strategies

LET ME JUST SAY THAT I'm not a big fan of outsourced recruiting. I don't think you can build a great company by relying on paid recruiters, especially those earning a commission. The recruiters' goals simply aren't aligned with yours. If they are being paid per hire, they are incentivized to bring you a candidate that meets your qualifications as quickly as possible. The longer it takes, the more it costs them. As a result, they often gloss over things that might prevent this candidate from getting the job. Some even coach the candidate on what to say. I strongly recommend you build your own in-house team that has the company's long-term interests in mind and understands your goals and culture.

One of the most effective ways to recruit great people is to tap into your existing employees and their social networks. Many companies offer bonuses to employees who recommend candidates who get hired. However, the problem with giving bonuses is that it sends the wrong message. Employees wind up recommending candidates just to get some extra money, not because they truly believe they're the best fit. Instead, you want every employee to help identify potential candidates because they have a vested interest in making the company a great place to work.

For this to be effective, start by emphasizing the importance of hiring the right people and how it's everyone's job to recruit new talent. It's important to take the time to explain the company's hiring needs and criteria. Update employees regularly on the hiring status. Google found that a simple monthly reminder on what jobs need to be filled helps boost participation significantly. You should also throw a party whenever someone is brought onboard, where you thank those who contributed the most time toward finding the new hire and highlight exactly what employees did during the recruitment process. This is how you can build a lasting recruitment engine.

The other part of recruiting that many people overlook is taking the time to understand what the candidate wants from the job. It's not enough to put the person through the process; you need to find out what the candidate values most. What does he expect from your company? What are his long-term goals? What type of work environment does he prefer? There's no point in hiring someone if it's not a good fit. He will just wind up leaving, and you'll have to start over again. Once you determine the candidate is right for the job, you need to make sure he understands why your company is the best choice.

※

It's not enough to put the person through the process;
find out what the candidate values most.

Remember, any excellent candidate will be in demand. You must give this person a good reason to join your company over the competitors. Often, this goes beyond compensation. It comes down to the candidate's long-term career goals, ideal work environment, social values, and personal needs. You need to address all of these. But you can't do that if you don't understand who the candidate really is and what this person cares about most.

When the candidate visits your offices, take the time to show her around. Get to know her in a casual setting. Share your vision for the company. Help her understand not only what you're doing but why it matters. Allow time for the candidate to explore the office and feel comfortable. Introduce her to your employees and give them a chance to chat. You'd be surprised at how few companies do this. For most companies, it's all about the interview. Remember, hiring is a two-way street. You are not just picking who you want; they have to pick you, too.

It's also wise to have candidates visit the office more than once before hiring them. Each time, make the visit more personal and relaxed. Take them out to lunch. Let them hang out in the open area and mingle with your team. Invite them to a company outing. Do whatever it takes to integrate them into the team even before they are hired. Then, when it comes time to negotiate compensation, they aren't just thinking about who will pay them the most but what it means to work for your company over others.

In the end, don't let money become the determining factor. Remember, a great employee is worth ten mediocre ones. If this person is truly the right fit for your company, you should be paying above average, not pinching pennies. It will not only seal the deal, but it will help retain the person over the long run. What you want are the best employees, not the least expensive, and it's worth investing in the best.

72

Firing Employees the Right Way

YOU CAN'T GROW A BUSINESS without making mistakes. We all trip up sometimes. No matter how careful you are, you will hire lemons. The key is acting quickly and decisively. By the time most managers admit to themselves that they hired the wrong person, it's six months too late. Let's face it: No one wants to fire someone. It's a painful process. It's hard on the manager and even harder on the employee. But looking the other way only creates problems. You may think your team will react negatively to a firing, but by the time you recognize there's a problem, you can bet that most of your team feels the same way.

Often, the worst thing you can do is try to keep someone in a position that he or she is not suited for. It gums up the whole system. Other team members can't do their jobs with someone incompetent or disruptive in the mix. Firing the person isn't a bad thing. It's often the only solution, and you'll find that it makes your team stronger, not weaker, when you do it right.

I'm not saying you should just fire someone for the first screwup. That's not good management. You need to find out why the problem happened and determine if the person is capable of learning from the mistake. A manager's job is to analyze and understand everyone on the team and how they can best work together. Screwups are seldom the fault of a single individual. They usually stem from a flaw in the process, miscommunication, or multiple people doing things the wrong way.

To address problems in employee performance, you need to view your company as a continually evolving system. With each iteration, new problems become apparent, and each member of your organization should participate in debugging them. You can always do things better, and for your system to improve, the employees need to step up and address the issues themselves. Your goal should be to get everyone to come up with solutions. Casting blame does not help. It just makes people defensive.

Instead, focus on the process, not the people involved. If it's a process problem, you can fix it. However, if it becomes apparent that a particular employee isn't capable of doing the job, you have a choice: Either change the nature of the job, or let the person go. Once you decide to let someone go, do not procrastinate. Take immediate action.

Here's the twelve-step plan:

1. Document everything the employee did wrong. As part of good management practices, you should have been doing this all along. Each time you gave this employee feedback on his performance, you should have written it down and communicated it to him. Don't just fire someone because you don't like him. You should have evidence that this person could not perform the work required. Otherwise, you are opening yourself up to a lawsuit.

2. Once all your paperwork is in order, you need to consider looking for a replacement. You may even bring the replacement in early and initiate training. This is often necessary in highly technical positions for which there is no redundancy.

3. After the knowledge transfer is complete, make an exit plan for the employee being fired. You should know exactly what you are going to do and how it is going to unfold. Don't wing it. Don't leave anything up to chance.

4. Are you going to offer a severance package? If so, you should tie that to a legally binding release form to be signed upon termination.

5. Schedule a time early in the week to carry out the termination. Don't do it just before the weekend. You need time to

communicate to the remaining employees why this is happening and what it means to them. If they don't understand, they may fear they are going to be next in line and morale may drop.

6. When conducting the termination, you should be direct and truthful. Don't try to make the terminated employee feel good. That's not helpful, and it will just confuse him. If you like this person so much, why are you firing him? You need to explain exactly why you made this decision and give him advice so that he doesn't make the same mistakes again. This is how you can help.

7. When explaining, focus on specific behavior. The terminated employee needs to understand exactly what he did that led to this decision.

8. Keep it short. Don't drag out the termination. That can get messy.

9. Take the time to answer any questions the terminated employee may have.

10. Don't waffle. If the terminated employee begs you for another chance, you cannot capitulate. You need to stick with your plan. You are firing this person for a good reason, which means you've tried everything you could to make it right. Now it's too late. Aborting the termination process will only cause more problems and create confusion.

11. Ask the terminated employee to pack up and leave on the same day. Remember, you cannot stop this person from communicating with other team members. People talk. But you need the terminated employee out of the office early in the day, so you have time to get everyone together and message them on why the firing took place.

12. If you planned in advance, you will have already scheduled an all-team meeting for the afternoon. When everyone is together, you need to explain what happened and why. Don't bad-mouth the terminated employee. That doesn't help. Be fair, honest, and compassionate. Answer any questions, and then send everyone back to work.

That's how to handle it. If you follow these steps, you'll actually find it's not so bad, and your team will wind up even stronger. As long as you are making the right decision for the company and not doing it for personal reasons, your remaining employees should understand and respect you for it.

73

The 22 Rules of Selling

NOW IT'S TIME TO EXPLORE the art of selling. You cannot scale a business without knowing how to sell. Selling lies at the heart of every startup, and the CEO is always the number one dealmaker. You need to bring home the bacon. When I started out, I never considered myself a salesperson. In fact, I hated sales. I didn't understand how to do it, and I was awful. But as CEO of several startups, I was forced to sell. I had to sell everything. I sold my vision to early employees in order to bring them onboard for equity and not cash. I sold my products to our first customers. I sold the shares in my company to investors. And I sold our story to the press.

Here's what I learned in the process:

1. Create a 360-degree model of your customers so you know exactly whom you're targeting. When someone walks in your door, you should be able to recognize instantly if that person is likely to buy or not. The more detailed your customer profile, the better.

2. Know your product inside and out. I don't care if you're not an engineer; you need to understand the technical details of your product. You need to understand exactly how it works so you can intelligently answer any reasonable questions. Spend time with

your team so that you fully grasp how everything fits together. What technology stack are your engineers using? What problems are you solving for your customers? What functionality does your product offer that competitors don't? What's on the product road map? If you can't answer these questions correctly, you'll wind up causing a lot of problems by selling something that isn't quite the right fit. I've seen this happen. The CEO should not make any promises to customers without knowing what can actually be delivered in a reasonable time frame. The best salespeople I know understand their products right down to the smallest minutia. That's why they close deals no one else can.

3. It's not enough to have a great product; you need to know what the other side of the table wants out of the deal. Whenever you're selling, there's what you want and what the other party wants. If you don't understand their needs, you'll wind up emphasizing the wrong things. The key to selling is making sure that all parties win, especially when doing large strategic sales. What are the people you're selling to interested in? Are they looking to fix a problem, gain a technological edge, impress upper management, or save money? Or do they have some other motivation for closing this deal, like earning a commission? You need to know this right up front, or it's like trying to run blindfolded.

4. Identify the decision maker early. You may be talking to someone who actually has no power to close a deal. I've seen startups waste a lot of time talking to the wrong people inside an organization, only to discover much later that there was never a deal to be had.

5. To make a strategic sale into a large organization, it helps to have a champion. This person believes in your product, understands its value, and will go out on a limb to get the deal finalized. Without an inside champion, most enterprise sales hit a snag along the way and wind up in limbo land. To avoid this fate, figure out who is going to be your hero, and then work as partners to push the deal through.

6. Sales isn't about talking. It's about asking the right questions. You cannot figure any of this out if you're just blabbing away about your product. You need to step back and listen to what your customers are saying. This is far more important than getting through your sales pitch. The more you understand about your customers and their needs, the faster you'll be able to move the process forward.

7. The best salespeople I know aren't focused on the money. They don't see it as their job to extract as much cash as possible out of their customers. Instead, they truly want to help their customers come to the right decision. They take the time to figure out what's best for the customer, and if a sale isn't a good fit, they will tell the customer not to move forward. This may sound counterintuitive. But over the long run, it builds trust, and nothing is more powerful than a relationship built on trust. If you make a point of always doing what's in your customer's best interest, even if it means less short-term profits, the customer will stick with you.

8. Selling is not about giving the same sales pitch over and over. It's a creative process. It's about learning and understanding what works for different customers in different situations. Whenever you give a pitch, you should be paying attention to the customer's reaction and adapting your presentation to their needs. The top salespeople are constantly iterating on their pitch, trying new things, and seeing what works. Remember, no matter how good you think you are, you can do better.

9. Don't be too aggressive. No one likes overeager salespeople. Chill. Try leaning back and talking to your customers in a relaxed manner. Let them come to you. Don't force what you want on them.

10. You've heard of the fast-talking salesman. It's not a compliment. Don't speak too quickly. Slow down and make sure the customer understands you. How you communicate is as important as what you say.

11. You can say whatever you like, but what really matters is the data. Can you back up your claims with solid evidence? Do you have proof that what you're saying is actually the case? A great salesperson takes the time to gather all the data possible and uses it as the foundation of any sales pitch. If your solution is cheaper, faster, more efficient, and easier to use, then you'd better have the numbers to back this up. Otherwise, you're just blowing hot air.

12. If a customer wants something, like a product feature, that your company doesn't offer, don't promise it without first consulting your team. This will just get you in trouble. Instead, take note of what the customer wants and say you'll talk to the team about adding it to the product road map. You don't have to give a specific date. Just acknowledging what the customer wants is usually enough. Later, you can get together with your team and figure out if it's worth implementing.

13. Rejection is part of the process. If you do sales, you'll invariably get rejected. Don't try to avoid getting turned down. This only leads to increased stress, anxiety, and depression. The way to become immune to this ego-crushing process is to embrace it. Make it a learning opportunity. Each time you get turned down, ask the customers to explain to you in detail why they can't move forward. If you take this approach, you'll soon find that rejection doesn't hurt so much. It's actually part of the process of extracting valuable information.

14. Don't attempt to change a customer's core beliefs. It's not that it's impossible. You can do it. It's just not worth your time. If someone believes that small cars are unsafe, trying to convert them into a small-car lover is going to take a huge amount of effort. Instead of wasting your time, it's far more efficient to sell that person a large car. After all, that's what the person wants. If you don't have any large cars to sell, send the person to someone who does. You'll lose this sale but can spend your time with more promising prospects.

15. Make your sales tangible. If you want to sell a product, let customers touch it. If they can't touch it, show it to them some other way. Use videos, PowerPoint presentations, drawings, or whatever you can to make the product come alive. Showing is far more powerful than explaining.

16. Great salespeople don't just sell what they have today; they sell the future. Create a timeline that visualizes where your company and products are headed. Explain to customers that if they buy into your solution now, they'll receive far more value down the road than going with competitors.

17. Qualify your leads. Make sure that the customer is ready to buy. No point in wasting time with someone who isn't prepared to move forward. Even before you meet, you should know the probability of closing. If it's low, focus on other prospects.

18. Many companies have an entire process for lead generation and filtering. The idea is to ask a lot of questions in advance. Sometimes this is done through an online survey; other times, through a chatbot, email, or live rep. Once you have the data, you need to quickly sort prospects into categories by likelihood of closing, and then prioritize the ones most likely to buy today.

19. Know your bottom line. If you are negotiating a large deal, it pays to know going into the deal what you can and cannot accept. In advance, you should get together with your team and decide what you really need out of this deal and what you cannot commit to. You don't have to communicate these to the other party up front, but everyone on your team should be onboard so you can structure the deal in the right way.

20. If a deal isn't working out, let it go. Don't chase after a lost cause. It doesn't matter if you invested several months into closing this deal. If it's not moving forward, push it off your plate. Sinking more time into a zombie deal seldom pays off. It may make you feel better to keep it alive, but it's just sucking up mental energy and resources. Better to put a bullet in its head.

21. Set up a sales pipeline. You can use sophisticated CRM tools or a simple shared spreadsheet. The point is to list out your

pending deals and prioritize them by key criteria, like their dollar value, strategic importance, long-term potential, estimated closing date, and so on. This will help you prioritize the deals that matter the most and track everything.

22. Last, you'll find that a small number of deals usually wind up bringing in the majority of the dollars. This is especially true for large strategic sales. Focus 90 percent of your energy on the transformative deals. These are deals that have the potential to advance your business to the next level. For example, if there are a hundred possible deals in your sales pipeline, sort them by probability of closing and overall impact on your business. If one deal will have two times the impact of all the others combined, you should prioritize this far above everything. In other words, don't give every deal equal time.

If you follow these twenty-two rules, you'll be far ahead of most salespeople I know.

74

Presenting in Public

AS A CEO, YOU'LL HAVE to present in public. It's almost impossible to avoid doing this. It's an essential part of growing your business. Even if you're painfully shy, as I used to be, you'll have to force yourself into the limelight and represent your company. For me, this began when I launched my first venture-funded startup. Initially, I had to pitch investors; then I was invited to speak at events; next came the TV interviews, radio shows, videos, and so on.

I was awful at first. I remember hearing the quaver in my voice. I couldn't control it, and that only made me more nervous. How did I overcome this? I simply persevered. I forced myself to take every opportunity to speak because I knew that was the only way to get over my anxiety. Today, you'd never know I was the shy guy who hardly spoke in class. I give more than fifty talks a year, and I feel totally comfortable. It doesn't faze me anymore. My advice to you is to just do it. No matter how awkward and horrible you feel, you'll eventually get over it.

In addition to stepping out of your comfort zone, try what's called *deliberate practice*, where you analyze everything about your performance and modify your speaking style to see what works best. Try experimenting with different techniques. Watch videos of speakers whom you admire and note what they do right. Ask for feedback from the audience and people you trust. You can even join a speaker's club, like

Toastmasters, or hire a professional coach. I never did this, but I know it can help.

Let me share some of the things I learned along the way.

Less Is More—Keep your talk short. Keep your points concise. Don't just blab away. Don't waste people's time. It's not about you. It's about them.

Practice and Forget—The way to deliver a flawless pitch is to practice, practice, practice, and then when you get onstage, forget everything. Speak from your heart. Don't try to regurgitate memorized lines. That always comes out stale. Just say whatever pops into your head. You know your business. You know exactly what your company does. Feel free to go off script. Just keep it real and fresh.

Go Wireless—Whenever possible, free up your hands by using a lavalier microphone. This allows you to use your body language. It's also more natural. If you can't get a lavalier, at least procure a wireless handheld microphone.

Use Body Language—Video yourself giving your pitch. Examine your posture. Are you standing up erect, or are you hunched over? Where are your hands? Don't be afraid to move. Be expressive. If you study the great speakers, they use their body to enhance their delivery.

Avoid Podiums—Even if there's a podium, you don't have to use it. A podium gets between you and the audience. It's better not to have anything separating you from whomever you're speaking to.

Make an Entrance—Pay special attention to how you walk onstage. This sets the tone. Walk briskly, take center stage, pause for a moment to capture the audience's attention, and then start speaking.

Vary the Pitch and Tempo—Nothing is worse than a monotone speaker. When you're giving a speech, mix it up. Slow down to emphasize key points. Raise your voice when you're excited. Lower your voice when delivering an authoritative message.

Pause for Effect—The silences are as important as your words. The pauses allow you to emphasize specific points. When you pause, you capture the audience's attention. They zero in on you. The longer the silence, the more the anticipation builds. Try it, and you'll see the power of the pause.

Compose a Symphony—Think of your talk as a symphony where you are the composer. Great symphonies rise and fall, speed up and slow down, always building toward a crescendo. They have a clear structure. Listen to Beethoven, Bach, and Mozart, and pay attention to how they constructed their masterpieces. Let them inspire you.

Surprise Your Audience—Don't be afraid to do something out of the ordinary, even bizarre. Maybe show an unexpected video, tell a funny story, or reveal an interesting prop. Do whatever it takes to get the audience's attention and wake them up. Just don't be boring.

Make a Single Point—When using PowerPoint, every slide should make a single point. Don't try to cram three points into one slide. It will just confuse your audience.

The Six-Word Rule—Never fill your PowerPoint slides full of text. I have a rule. No more than six words per slide. That should be your goal. The audience should be able to read the slide in a few seconds. If not, they're going to miss what you say and become frustrated. This is because people don't multitask well. They have trouble reading something on a screen and listening to a speaker at the same time. If you want them to hear you, the fewer words you have on-screen, the better.

Make It Visual—Fill your PowerPoint with stunning photographs and imagery that reinforce your main points. Get creative with illustrations, animations, videos, and 3D models. The more compelling you can make your visuals, the more the audience will remember what you say. People forget most of what they hear but not what they see. Retention goes way up when audio is tied to visuals.

Know Your Audience—Understand whom you are talking to. What is their background? Why are they attending your talk? What do they want to get out of it? The more information you can gather in advance, the better you can prepare.

Quality Content—Focus on providing high-quality, actionable information and ideas. Don't focus on selling something. Most people don't want to be sold anything and don't care about what you're doing. They care about what they are doing, and they want information that can help them. So, concentrate your talk on helping them solve their problems.

Be Bold—Don't be timid. Speak in a strong, clear voice. Attempt to exude confidence, even if you don't have any.

Don't Shout—Being overly forceful doesn't work. This is also something I need to work on. Passion has its limits. It's better to talk in a tempered, even voice. If you are passionate, your passion will show through but in a more natural way. You don't want to overdo it.

Speak Slowly—Don't talk too fast. People won't be able to understand you, especially if the audio system isn't up to par or you have a foreign accent.

Make Eye Contact—Connect with your audience. Make eye contact with at least one person. Find an attentive listener and speak to that individual. Each new, positive reaction you receive will imbue you with more energy. Ignore those people who are on their phones. They don't count.

Take Mental Notes—Study the audience as you speak. They are your real-time feedback mechanism. See what parts of your talk they respond to and where they seem confused or bored. Make mental notes so you can improve your speech the next time.

Always Be Iterating—Creating a talk isn't a one-shot deal. It's an iterative process. I never give exactly the same speech twice. I'm always working to improve. After each talk, I edit my slides, change the wording, cut things that don't resonate, and add new, fresh material. You should do the same.

Never Stop Experimenting—Try different things during every talk. Don't be afraid to mess up or go too far. In fact, you should push your boundaries. Crack some jokes and see how it works. Act playful or try being dead serious. Experiment with different techniques and content. The more variations you try out, the better and more original your talks will become.

75

Marketing and Customer Acquisition

SCALING A BUSINESS USUALLY COMES down to marketing and customer acquisition. The mistake a lot of startups make is that they simply don't try enough different channels to acquire customers, and that winds up limiting them. It's not enough to test one or two channels. A startup should be assessing at least one new channel every month. This is because the ground is constantly shifting. There are literally thousands of ways to acquire customers, and finding the best ones ahead of your competitors can make all the difference. If you can be the first to figure them out and exploit them, you'll have a significant advantage.

Make sure these basic marketing and customer acquisition strategies are on your hit list:

- Search Engine Optimization
- Search Engine Marketing
- Click-Through Marketing
- Hyperlocal Marketing
- Inbound Marketing
- Social Marketing
- Content Marketing
- Guest Posts
- Public Relations
- Guerrilla Marketing

- Video Ads
- Display Ads
- Email Lists
- Retargeting
- Strategic Marketing
- Affiliate Programs
- Cold Calling
- Customer Service as Marketing
- Viral Marketing
- Launching on New Platforms
- Trade Shows and Conferences
- Private Events
- Public Speaking
- Cross Promotions
- Traditional Advertising

In order to test various marketing channels, you first need to calculate the average lifetime value of your customers and make sure it's significantly more than the average customer acquisition costs plus cost of goods. If the math adds up, you're in business. The greater the margins, the better the marketing channel.

Your goal should be to try as many channels as possible as quickly as possible to see which ones yield the best results. You'll find that some channels are excellent when your marketing budgets are small, but they don't scale well as your budgets increase. Over time, channels that are effective will change. Some will tap out. Others will become too competitive. This is why you constantly need to be experimenting. Marketing is an ongoing process of discovery. It's not set and forget.

For these reasons, it's important to build a strong internal marketing team. You can't simply outsource it. You need the knowledge inside your organization, so you have an edge over your competition. That doesn't mean you shouldn't get outside help. You should always bring on fresh consultants and integrate them with your team for limited periods of time so your team can learn from them. If you do this, you can stay one step ahead of your competitors and gain a significant marketing advantage.

Designing Your Workspace

ALONG WITH GROWTH COMES NEW offices. Silicon Valley startups have a tradition of spending their venture capital on uniquely creative spaces. These workspaces are designed to not only look hip and make an impression, but they often rely on extensive research in the areas of neuroscience, sociology, and human behavior. The goal is to enhance collaboration, communication, and creativity.

"Through tests, we can understand the consequences of a particular design on the workers who are operating within it,"[1] says Andrew Heumann, a designer at NBBJ, the architectural firm that designed headquarters for Amazon, Google, and Samsung. For instance, how far you sit from someone determines the likelihood that you will interact with that person. Simply glancing at a coworker during the course of a day dramatically increases the probability you will engage with them.

"There's a lot of research coming out that higher ceilings promote higher performance in conceptual thinking, while lower ceilings are better for mathematical thinking,"[2] adds Scott Wyatt, a managing partner at NBBJ. Sound also plays an essential role in productivity. A little noise actually helps. Libraries tend to be too quiet. Studies have found that 70 decimals of background noise are optimal for most people. It's enough input to boost creative energy, but not so much that it disrupts concentration.

There's almost no element in a space that doesn't have some impact on how well your employees will perform. For example, warm light decreases stress levels and enhances cognitive performance. Another study found that by swapping smaller tables for larger ones in the cafeteria, employees were 36 percent more likely to interact with one another back in the office.

Cornerstone and Harvard Business School found that if employees sit next to the right people, their productivity can go up 15 percent. Pairing people with opposite strengths works best. They wind up collaborating and complementing one another. On the other hand, sitting next to a toxic worker who has a negative attitude significantly lowers productivity and increases the likelihood the employee won't remain in the company.

Steve Jobs was obsessed with office design. He took an active role in redesigning Pixar's offices. He wanted to make sure that executives and editors shared the same buildings. He didn't want them separated. He even tried to limit the number of bathrooms so that employees from all across the company would randomly bump into one another throughout the day. Studies have shown that serendipitous encounters at work equate to increased idea sharing and cooperation.

If you look at Apple's headquarters, you can see that Jobs designed it as a giant donut in order to create a flow where workers are forced to walk through one another's spaces on their way to and from meetings. The donut also allows for an open green space in the middle where workers can relax, have lunch, bump into one another, and hold activities. Jobs cared deeply about the flow of workers within the space because he understood that the more connections people make in any given day, the more information and knowledge are exchanged.

※

The more connections people make in any given day,
the more information and knowledge are exchanged.

A company can be viewed as a living organism where everyone is part of one giant brain. The more neural connections, the more creative and productive it becomes. This is the reason most startups in Silicon Valley have open space for employees to mingle. They want their employees to have casual exchanges throughout the day. It's a different dynamic than being in a meeting or walking up to someone's desk. When people are hanging out, they're more likely to talk about what they're doing in an open, relaxed manner. This can lead to information being exchanged that otherwise wouldn't be communicated. It also catalyzes new collaborations and friendships.

For the same reason, many tech companies have eliminated cubicles in favor of open seating. They want everyone to work together and make eye contact throughout the day. They don't want physical barriers separating them. Some offices have gone as far as forcing employees to change seating throughout the week so they wind up sitting next to different people in the organization almost every single day. The underlying hypothesis is that an organization will become smarter and more innovative with each new interaction.

The same thinking has inspired companies to create play areas, complete with the mandatory Ping-Pong and foosball tables. Nothing beats games for encouraging teamwork and bonding. Some startups have even installed miniature golf courses, massage chairs, and video arcades. These may seem frivolous, but they are intended to get employees to open up with one another and form relationships that go beyond work. It's this type of closeness that enables teams to come together and accomplish far more than the sum of their parts.

All this openness is good for collaboration, but it can take its toll on concentration. As three executives from Steelcase, the furniture maker, wrote in *Harvard Business Review*: "People feel a pressing need for more privacy, not only to do heads-down work but to cope with the intensity of how work happens today."[3] According to their research, there has been a 16 percent increase in the number of people who can't concentrate at their desks. This is the reason many startups are creating quiet zones. They want a safe place for employees to go when they need to think without being disturbed. But quiet spaces alone may not be enough.

Around 70 percent of US offices have low or no partitions. Some experts now believe that the shift to open office design was a big mistake.

A survey by enterprise software strategist William Belk found that 58 percent of high-performance employees need more private spaces for problem solving. Psychologist Nick Perham found that office noise impairs workers' ability to recall information and do tasks as simple as basic arithmetic. In addition, the lack of privacy and constant interruptions can create significant stress, impairing workers' productivity and leading to health issues. In Silicon Valley, this has led to a backlash from employees and a raging debate among experts.

A less controversial trend in Silicon Valley is bringing the outdoors inside. For the majority of human existence, people have worked outdoors, so it's not natural to spend nearly all our waking hours cooped up inside a building. This is why designers are working to mimic outdoor environments inside the office. They are adding plenty of open space, large windows, natural lighting, and greenery. They're even pumping in fresh air and using earth tones for the walls and furniture. Some companies are painting the ceilings blue because blue suppresses melatonin, the chemical that makes people feel tired. If a person looks up and sees blue, the brain tells them its daytime, even if it isn't.

I'm just scratching the surface of the science behind designing workspaces, but as you scale up your business, I hope this inspires you to think more creatively about your office and how it will affect your employees' performance and overall quality of work and life.

Watch Out
for the Platforms

MANY STARTUPS CHOOSE TO LAUNCH their products or services on one of the major platforms, like Amazon, Alibaba, Salesforce, Microsoft, Facebook, or WeChat. This is because the advantages are numerous. These startups can leverage a mature infrastructure, brand, user-base, and ecosystem to build their businesses. All of these combined can accelerate growth far beyond what startups can do independently, especially if the company is fulfilling a strong unmet need on the platform.

The problem comes when the startup grows large enough to get on the radar of the big boys. With their God's eye view of everything that goes on under their domain, they can quickly spot what's working and how valuable it is to their users. This can create a conflict of interest. While they are happy to have other startups innovating inside their ecosystems, they also want to control the most essential and lucrative parts, maximizing both the value they provide to their users and their own profits. This means if the product or service is deemed strategic enough, the platforms will either opt to purchase the startup or copy it.

If the acquisition offer is good, this shouldn't be a problem for the entrepreneur. However, if big guys lowball the startup or simply roll out their own version, that leaves the entrepreneur in a tough spot. It's almost impossible to compete head-on with bigger players on their home turf. They have enormous advantages. They can fully integrate any product or service into their platform in a way no third party can match. They have the implicit trust of their users and can reach out to them at virtually no cost. Let's face it: When your competitor owns the platform on which you're competing, the playing field is tilted so far against you that it's almost impossible to win.

So, what should an entrepreneur do? Avoid using anyone else's platform? Unfortunately, it's not that easy. Today's digital world is made up of these platforms. It's often impracticable to avoid using them and still remain competitive. Few, if any, startups are in a position to build their own social network equivalent to Facebook, e-commerce portal on par with Amazon, or CRM platform as robust as Salesforce. It's simply not realistic, and many of the best business opportunities depend upon platforms like these to succeed.

Just to give you an idea of the magnitude of these platforms, according to Pivotal Research, 84 percent of global digital ad spending (outside China) went through just two companies: Facebook and Google. Amazon now accounts for nearly half of all online product searches and e-commerce revenue in the United States. Salesforce is the market leader in the CRM, with revenues of more than $10 billion for the fiscal year ending in January 2018. That's an increase of 25 percent year-over-year. When most of the action is on the big platforms, it's no wonder so many startups choose to build their businesses on top of them, even knowing that all data associated with these services goes directly into the hands of a potential competitor.

Unfortunately, the risks to startups are significant. ProPublica investigated Amazon back in 2016 and found that its search algorithm often steers users away from bargains in favor of Amazon's white-label offerings. This hurts the merchants on Amazon's platform. Google saw how successful Yelp had become and now competes directly with it, featuring Google's own reviews in Google Search. By favoring its own content, Google is steadily eating away at Yelp's business. This is just one example of a more pervasive problem. In fact, the European Union fined Google $5 billion for alleged anticompetitive behavior. And if you think it's tough in the United States, it's no better in China, with Alibaba, Tencent, and Baidu dominating the markets in similar ways. Globally, the big are getting bigger.

Economists, like Marshall Steinbaum of the Roosevelt Institute, argue that these companies act as monopolies, stifling competition and suppressing the growth of startups. Facebook, Google, Apple, and Amazon "are developing a concentration of power that fosters the premature death of big companies and infanticide for small firms," says Scott Galloway, a professor at New York University's Stern School of Business and author of *The Four*. "A press release with 'Amazon' on it has the power to bring down the value of an entire industry within hours."[1]

Steinbaum claims these quasi-monopolies are a cause of the recent slowdown in startup creation in America. Facebook can see which startups are gaining traction and buy them out, as it did with Instagram and WhatsApp. If they don't sell, Facebook will simply steal their best ideas, as it did with Snapchat. Apple has denied updates to apps it doesn't like, such as Spotify. According to Ariel Ezrachi and Maurice Stucke, authors of *Virtual Competition*, the big guys put up a pretense of competition and tout free markets while acting to consolidate their monopolies.

Amazon, Google, Facebook, and Apple "have aggregated more economic value and influence than nearly any other commercial entity in history,"[2] claims Galloway. Together, they have a larger value than the gross domestic product of many countries, including France. They create relatively few jobs for their size, pay minimal taxes thanks to clever accounting, and are laser focused on squashing any serious competition. Think about it. If one of the big boys approaches a startup with an offer to buy them or crush them, what do you imagine the startup will choose? This results in earlier exits at lower valuations, which makes it harder for investors to get the returns they need to continue supporting new startups.

This, however, doesn't mean startups can't survive in a world ruled by giants. Plenty still succeed by carving out niches between the titans. They can also gain an edge by using new technologies that create value beyond the platforms. With each wave of emerging technologies, there are opportunities to create new economies and build the next generation of platforms. Amazon, Google, Facebook, and Apple aren't the final embodiment of e-commerce, advertising, search, social networking, and operating systems. There will be future innovations that take us far beyond what we can imagine today. Using cutting-edge technologies, like augmented reality, artificial intelligence, quantum computing, and brain-to-computer interfaces, companies will redefine how we interact, shop, and access information.

※

Startups can survive in a world ruled by giants by carving out niches between the titans.

All it takes is for one of the big guys to miss a beat while a startup lands there first and grows fast enough to build a defensible platform of its own. As we've seen in the past, the network effect is extremely powerful. Google, with all its users, data, and talent, couldn't compete with the upstart Facebook. Even though Google built a sophisticated social network of its own, forced millions of users to sign up, and orchestrated a wave of positive publicity, it failed to take off. No one cared. No one wanted it. Facebook was already there and had an iron grip on the users.

Remember when Sun Microsystems, Nokia, IBM, and Microsoft seemed to dominate the tech landscape? Only Microsoft is still a contender. Sun Microsystems became irrelevant, and Oracle gobbled up its remains. Nokia lost the smartphone wars. IBM gave up on hardware, then pivoted to services, and is once again struggling to redefine itself. Its latest incarnation is as an artificial intelligence platform, but that has yet to prove itself.

None of these former goliaths was able to anticipate and thwart the rise of Google, Facebook, Amazon, and Apple, so why should we expect this generation of giants to be any different? I remember when everyone was saying nobody could compete with Microsoft because it controlled more than 90 percent of the market share for PC operating systems. They could just add a feature or bundle their own version with Windows and put most software companies out of business. Low and behold, PCs aren't as important as they used to be. Mobile is in the ascendance, and Microsoft lost out to iOS and Android.

So, don't give up hope. You can still win at this game. It's always been tough for startups. It doesn't matter how far back you go in time; the little guys have forever been scrambling to outsmart and outmaneuver the titans without getting the life crushed out of them. In the same way that a few college kids gave birth to Microsoft, Facebook, and Google, so, too, will the next generation of giants be born. And if history is any guide, today's giants will become tomorrow's dinosaurs.

78

The Unfair Advantages

WINNING BUSINESS ISN'T ABOUT BEING fair. In fact, it's the opposite. Companies win precisely because they have an unfair advantage over their competitors. It's impossible to command high profit margins and dominate a market if your company is just like everyone else. Below, I've outlined various ways companies put up barriers to protect their businesses, block competitors, and control markets.

Network Effect—This is when the value of a product or service increases according to the number of people, companies, or other entities using it. Just look at social networks like Facebook, Snapchat, and WeChat. Their primary value is predicated on the number of people using their networks. Even if users want to switch, it's almost impossible to get all their friends to move to a new service at the same time, thus creating an enormous barrier for competitors.

Access to Data—Data is the real estate of the future, and there's a massive land grab going on. Everyone wants to own the most valuable data. If a company like Amazon can generate proprietary data and use it to offer superior products and services, it has a significant competitive advantage. Proprietary user data plays a crucial role in making Facebook and Google the largest and most profitable ad networks in the world today.

Capital—Simply having more money than competitors can give a company a tremendous unfair advantage. Look at the unicorns that raise hundreds of millions of dollars, and then use their huge war chests to acquire customers, lower prices, and drive smaller competitors out of business.

Technology—If a company's products are only incrementally better than everyone else's, competitors can easily compete on price and features. However, if a company's products are two, three, or four times better than competitors, it can dominate the market. This usually happens through developing new and superior technologies that competitors don't have access to. NVIDIA is a great example of this with its hefty R&D (research and development) budget and substantial lead in developing the world's best graphics-processing technologies.

Provide Most Value—Companies like Amazon excel at providing the most value to their customers. Amazon is always thinking of how to give its Prime members more than other e-commerce sites, including free shipping, faster delivery, lower prices, music, videos, e-books, and more.

Lock In Customers—Oracle is a master at locking in customers. Their software requires such a deep level of integration that, once a company adopts it, the switching costs become so high that competitors with lower prices, or even free services, still have trouble stealing customers away.

Marketplace—Companies like eBay have shown the power of a marketplace. If a startup can be the first to attract a critical mass of buyers and sellers, it wins. Buyers will always choose the market with the most sellers because this guarantees the lowest prices and greatest choice. Sellers will always follow the buyers. Once a company captures both, it becomes extremely hard for anyone else to replicate.

Define a Product Category—It's not enough to be part of a product category. The most successful companies own the category. That means their products become synonymous with the categories themselves. Take Kleenex. It became so popular that people still say "Pass me a Kleenex" instead of "Pass me a facial tissue." Apple did the same thing with MP3 music players. We still call it podcasting because the iPod ate the category. Likewise, Google dominated search to such an extent, we still say, "Let's google it!"

Industry Standard—Simply becoming an industry standard, like Microsoft Windows, can keep out competitors. Once everyone is using a piece of software, the value of that software goes up. Many companies have tried to launch new operating systems, and most of them have failed miserably. Microsoft counts on this, and that's why in third-world countries, it has allowed people to easily copy Windows for years. Microsoft said it was illegal but did nothing to prevent people from making those copies because it knew that becoming an industry standard was more important than short-term profits.

Economies of Scale—The larger a company gets, the more it can take advantage of economies of scale by optimizing everything from manufacturing to supply chains and distribution. Just look at Walmart and how it can drive smaller stores out of business.

Monopoly—We all know the power of a monopoly. The Standard Oil Trust is infamous. It had such a stranglehold on everything from the transportation to drilling and refining of oil that no one else could compete. When they moved into a new market, they could literally afford to keep dropping the price until their competitors went out of business. In the end, it was only the US government that curtailed their dominance, breaking up the company through antitrust legislation.

Patents—One of the strongest barriers to entry, especially as a company scales up and dominates a market, is its patents. There are constant patent wars between the big guys like Apple, Samsung, Microsoft, Amazon, and Qualcomm. Every major company relies on patents to fend off and hobble its competitors.

Relationships—Having relationships with key strategic partners and government officials can give a company a huge competitive advantage. Just look at how much Big Pharma spends on relationship building each year. Not only do they put money in the pockets of politicians, but they also spend enormous amounts of time, resources, and money nurturing relationships with doctors and hospital administrators.

Tap a Trend—When a company becomes synonymous with an emerging trend, it can ride the wave all the way to the bank. Just look at Lululemon, which built a clothing empire on the back of the yoga craze, or Blue Bottle Coffee, which rode the gourmet coffee trend all the way to a $500 million exit.

Government Policy—If a business is closely aligned with government policy, it can use this to fend off the competition. Just look at Baidu versus Google in China. Baidu played by the Chinese government's rules and used them to its advantage. Google didn't and got kicked out.

Speed to Market—If a company is the first to market with new technologies, superior products, or lower prices, it can keep its competitors off balance. Fast movers are the first ones to cut prices, upgrade services, release new models, and employ the latest technologies. By always keeping one step ahead of the competition, they dominate their markets. A great example of this is Samsung Electronics. They are continually pushing to be first with the latest tech. This is part of their core strategy for fending off lower-priced competitors.

Brand—Having the best recognized brand in a market can make all the difference. People buy what they know. If they're in a drugstore or supermarket, they're going to feel more comfortable buying from a brand they've seen before rather than a no-name competitor. This is true across all product categories. Once a company has built a dominant brand, it's hard for others to compete on an equal footing.

Media Attention—Getting press is a significant unfair advantage. If a company is always in the media, it's what people think of. Everything on the web is only one click away, from productivity apps to shaving cream. Whatever name pops into people's heads first is what they type. Amazon may or may not have the lowest prices and best service, but we hear its name so often in the press that it feels like the natural choice for shopping. Amazon Prime Day has even become a special event, equivalent to a summertime Black Friday, thanks in large part to media attention.

Celebrity Endorsements—Because celebrities have name recognition and fans, a single endorsement can work wonders. Just look at how Nike dominates its market by obtaining exclusive endorsements from top athletes around the world.

Domain Expertise—Companies that refine a complex process and accumulate more knowledge and expertise about their industry than anyone else can consistently outperform the competition. Just look at how long Intel has maintained its lead in the fiercely competitive world of semiconductors.

Trade Secrets—Coca-Cola has put up barriers around its business for more than 120 years by keeping its formula secret. What competitors don't know, they cannot copy.

Exit Traps—Many companies have kept customers locked in by lowering costs up front while charging sizable fees if a customer chooses to leave. Verizon and AT&T did this for years with their cell phone businesses. They offered steep discounts on phones if customers agreed to sign multiyear service contracts. The longer the contracts, the higher the barriers.

Partnerships—Having exclusive deals with key partners can block competitors out of key distribution channels. As I write this book, Netflix is offering its video entertainment services bundled with T-Mobile's phone service. In other words, T-Mobile customers get Netflix for free, making it harder to justify signing up and paying for Hulu, Comcast, HBO, or any other competitor.

Proprietary Consumables—If a company makes both the product and the consumables, it can increase profit margins and outspend the competition on marketing. Just look at Gillette's razors, HP's printers, and Keurig's coffee makers. The majority of consumers will opt for the default, which is to buy consumables that come from the product manufacturer, thereby locking competitors out of the most lucrative part of the market.

Learning Curve—Some products take a long time to learn, and once people are trained, they don't want to switch. Adobe has made a fortune selling software targeted at graphic artists, video editors, and other creatives. Customers have to invest their time to learn how to use these sophisticated products, and once they do, they are reluctant to switch to a competing solution.

Servitization—Companies like Rolls-Royce have transformed the jet engine business into a service, which makes it virtually impossible for competitors to get off the ground. Instead of charging outright for a jet engine, which isn't cheap, they offer it to airlines as part of a service package that includes maintenance and a business model where airlines pay by usage. This allows airlines to better control costs, while Rolls-Royce makes it difficult for competitors to break into the market. It's simply too expensive to replicate this model because of the combination of high up-front costs and long-term service contracts.

Ecosystems and Platforms—Building an ecosystem is one of the best ways to win. This is often called a *platform play*. It's when a company creates value by bringing third parties onto their platform to offer an array of additional products and services. Salesforce is a perfect example. It is no longer the best CRM solution. It's expensive, difficult to learn, and hard to implement, but it has a robust ecosystem that no one can match. There are thousands of developers on their platform offering all types of additional products and services that enhance the value, making it hard to beat and even harder to leave. WeChat is another super ecosystem, complete with everything from voice and messaging to payments, marketing, mini programs, and developer accounts.

Every entrepreneur needs to work toward obtaining as many unfair advantages as possible. If your startup doesn't have at least a couple of these, you'll have a tough time building a billion-dollar business.

79

Planning Your Exit

MANY ENTREPRENEURS BELIEVE THEY NEED to have an exit strategy. They think it's smart to plan the exit from the beginning. This is fine, but don't spend too much time worrying about this early on. Most startups change direction at least once in their first year, so spending a lot of time planning for an exit before achieving a solid product-market fit doesn't make sense. Whatever your idea is when you launch your company, it's probably not what you'll wind up doing.

In addition, before you launch your product, it's difficult to know all the players in your industry and understand why they may want to purchase your business. This is something best learned along the way. Only by running your business and understanding the ecosystem can you best figure out who are the most suitable acquirers, what they have to offer you, and what value you can offer them.

I personally like to work with entrepreneurs who are passionate about building world-changing companies that will last far beyond their tenure as CEO. When they think of an exit strategy, it's a long-term view. To them, an acquisition or IPO is simply a by-product of their efforts—not the end goal.

I've found that those entrepreneurs who are simply focused on flipping their companies to the highest bidder at the earliest possible moment don't perform as well. They usually have a quick-money mentality. They're looking to cut corners. They tend to ignore their customers, build cheaper products, and prioritize short-term gains over long-term growth. All of this means that if an acquisition doesn't materialize, they aren't in a position to compete and win. They'll just become one of many opportunists who missed the boat.

Another red flag is founders who begin scrambling to find an acquirer after their company hits a rough patch. Instead of dealing with the problems, they're looking for a way out. This happens all too often in Silicon Valley. When a startup begins shopping itself around, everyone begins to wonder why. What's wrong with this company? Are they about to go under? Is there a lawsuit? No successful entrepreneur wants to sell a winner that hasn't achieved its full growth potential. That's why the top companies sell at unicorn-like valuations. They're not looking for buyers and will only exit if the offer is too good to refuse.

Most people hear about the mega exits. They get all the press, while the smaller ones go virtually unnoticed. However, companies get bought for many reasons and the outcome for the founders and investors can vary dramatically. Below are four types of low-value exits that happen all too often in Silicon Valley:

1. **Acquihires**—The startup is purchased for its team, not its technology, market share, growth potential, technology, or brand. Often, it's big companies like Google, Facebook, Amazon, and Microsoft that will buy these startups because they want the talent. Typically, they shut down the products and services upon acquisition and integrate the team into their current initiatives. The valuations for acquihires tend to be sub $20 million.

2. **Fire Sales**—The startup is bought for rock-bottom prices because it's going out of business. Many times, the acquisition is predicated on grabbing the company's domain name, user data, software platform, or other assets.

3. **Zombie Disposals**—The startup is sold or merged with another company simply to remove it from a venture fund's portfolio. Every fund has a life span, usually ranging from six to twelve years, and if the startup isn't able to exit, it needs to be

liquidated. However, some startups refuse to die, and these are called *zombies*. They continue limping along without any growth potential. If a startup won't go away, it's often folded into one of the fund's more successful ventures or sold off to a suitable company that has a relationship with the VCs.

4. **Tech Acquisitions**—The startup is purchased for its technology. Depending on the tech, the acquisition values range from very low to extremely high. There are no rules here. It all comes down to the patents and strategic importance of the technology to the acquirer.

The startups that command top valuations tend to be those that have assumed a leadership position in their market and are poised for hyper-growth. This is why I tell founders not to worry about selling their companies. Worry about building an amazing business, and buyers will come chasing after you.

That said, if you enjoy thinking about your exit, it can't hurt to plan ahead. I know many successful entrepreneurs who put together an exit plan early on while still maintaining a long-term view. Here are some practical things you should consider:

- Make sure you have the right legal structure. In the United States, it's usually a Delaware C Corporation, but it could also be an S Corporation. If you're in China or some other country, you need to consider whether you plan to IPO inside your home country or on the New York Stock Exchange, NASDAQ, or some other exchange. Decisions you make early on can have a big impact down the road.
- Form strategic partnerships with the top companies in your industry. By collaborating with the bigger players and demonstrating your value, you will be on their radar.
- Stay visible. If you are present at industry trade shows, have solid PR, and get plenty of attention, your chances of finding a suitor will rise. The more of an impact you can make in your particular industry, the higher your odds.

- Leverage your investors and advisors. Tap them for introductions to possible acquirers. Ask them to help facilitate any deals.
- Build personal relationships with key decision makers in your ecosystem. Knowing someone makes an enormous difference. Acquisition talks often begin simply because two people genuinely like each other and want to work more closely together.
- As you grow your business, also develop your patent portfolio. It never hurts to have strong intellectual property.
- Treat your employees well. If acquirers are smart, they will talk to your employees as part of the due diligence process. If your employees bad-mouth the company, it can kill the deal.
- Keep your finances in order. Sloppy bookkeeping, accounting discrepancies, and financial problems can hamper the process.
- Act with integrity. Everyone talks to everyone, and your reputation matters.
- Last, you can try to hire an investment banker to shop your company around, but this gets expensive fast. And there's no guarantee of success. This works best for large companies with predictable revenues. It doesn't work as well for early- and mid-stage startups.

At the end of the day, being acquired shouldn't be your primary, or even your secondary, objective. Instead, stay laser focused on doing right by your company, employees, and customers, and the rest will take care of itself.

6

Rules to Win By

Growth Leadership

Leadership isn't any one thing. It's a combination of a diverse set of skills and abilities. Some people are born with these. Others will never make good leaders. But most of us fall somewhere in between. We must work hard, be aware of our mistakes, and continually strive to improve and learn.

In this penultimate section, I'm going to explain how great leaders set the tone for their company, define their vision, communicate with teams, and become a super boss. I'll tackle many practical questions, like: How do you effectively manage a board of directors? What do you do when you miss a forecast by a large margin? And what does it take to reach your full potential?

80

Leadership Essentials

I WAS A PRETTY POOR manager when I began. I used to be introverted. I lacked communication skills, and I became anxious when things didn't go according to plan. This was a lot to overcome. It meant that I had to change so many things about myself if I was to have any hope of becoming a successful leader.

It was difficult, but it wasn't impossible. Here are some of the most valuable things I learned along the way:

- Don't ignore hard problems. Only by tackling the company's truly difficult issues can you make progress.
- Don't count on shortcuts. Anytime you think a shortcut will work, think again.
- When things go wrong, don't shift the blame. Accept responsibility for any failures, and then work to make sure the same mistakes don't happen again.
- Give your team something they can believe in. Show them how they can make a difference and achieve something of lasting value.
- Encourage your team to speak out and express their opinions, even when their ideas conflict with your own.

- Recognize your team's hard work and reward them for it.
- Don't play favorites. This will only breed resentment.
- Surround yourself with A-players. Your core management team should be the best of the best.
- Get to know your team members. Find out what makes them tick. The more you know, the better you'll be able to guide them.
- Think of your employees' careers, not just their jobs. Help them plan and prepare for a future that goes beyond your company.
- Focus on results when evaluating performance. Don't be swayed by sweet talk, excuses, or appearances.
- Match your team members' natural talents with their responsibilities.
- If a team member can't handle the job, find a new position within your company that matches his or her abilities. If there is no position available, let that employee go.
- Don't expect people to change. They seldom do.
- Don't accept the status quo. Encourage your team to experiment and improve every day.
- Don't use fear to control your team. Fear will cause your employees to cover up the facts and blame others when things go wrong.
- Don't hoard power. Empower your team and let them own their jobs.
- Take the time to understand what each of your reports does on the job. You can't effectively manage people if you have no idea what they do.
- Stay organized. If you aren't the type to plan, surround yourself with others who can do it for you.
- Always speak the truth. If you try to deceive your team, you will lose their trust.
- Show your team members that you care. If they're in trouble and need your help, be there for them.
- Be accessible and available. Don't hide yourself away or put up walls between you and your team. The role of a leader is to be there when your team needs you.

- Don't just talk. Do what needs to be done. Your actions speak louder than any words.
- Be direct. Don't ignore problems. Talk to your team in a straightforward manner, even about the most sensitive subjects.
- Be aware of both your strengths and weaknesses. The better you know yourself, the more effectively you can lead others.
- Always keep your word. When you promise something, deliver on that promise.
- Keep calm, even in the most trying circumstances.
- Never lose your temper. Instead of getting mad, address the problem and move on.
- Act as a role model. Exemplify the behavior you want to see in others.
- Don't be pessimistic. Negativity breeds negativity.
- Have empathy for those around you. No one is perfect. Everyone makes mistakes.

81

Setting the Tone

WHEN A LEADER EMBRACES NEW ideas, removes barriers, and sets a positive, bold tone that encourages risk taking and experimentation, it changes how everyone on the team acts. It enables individuals to step out of their traditional roles and try things that were previously deemed beyond their reach. It helps team members to push their limits and overcome mental blocks, and it allows the company to invest in more ambitious, transformative projects that will have a lasting impact.

Some Silicon Valley startups eliminate words like "can't" and "impossible" because they constrain people's thinking. Even when an idea appears a little outlandish, everyone is told to keep an open mind and not to criticize. This doesn't mean every half-baked concept will gain support within the company, but it does remove the fear factor when employees come forward with ideas that might be considered extreme or unorthodox.

Being negative or even hostile to new ideas just closes off possibilities. With ever-advancing technology, much of what we thought was science fiction now appears within reach: asteroid mining, colonizing other planets, self-aware AI, quantum computing, nanorobotics, internet-connected brains, editing our own DNA, eliminating disease, and extending life indefinitely. In the coming decades, our new inventions will only further astound us. If a company wants to innovate, it has to create an environment where ideas are explored and tested, not just dismissed out of hand because they appear to be unfeasible.

✕

If a company wants to innovate, it has to create an environment where ideas are explored and tested.

When addressing your team, it's important to include everyone in the process. After all, the culture of a company starts with the CEO. If you want a true meritocracy where the best people and concepts rise to the top, begin by treating everyone as innovators. It's often the introverts and outsiders who don't speak much who have the most unconventional ideas. They are the ones you need to activate. Giving them the permission and comfort level to participate opens doors to ways of thinking you might otherwise never explore.

I admire leaders like Larry Page, Elon Musk, Jack Ma, Jeff Bezos, and Richard Branson, who dare to take big risks. They are constantly reinventing their businesses, and they seldom accept anything as unattainable, given enough time and resources. They are always asking: How can we do this? Why hasn't anyone tried it yet? What will it take to make it possible? Where can we go next? And who do we need on our team to get there? These are the questions you must pose to your team. You must set the bar higher. As Larry Page likes to say, "It's very hard to fail completely if you aim high enough."[1]

If you place limits on yourself and your thinking, that mindset will also limit your company's vision. You need to stretch yourself in order to open up new horizons for your company. This is where many traditional companies get stuck. Their leadership can't see beyond what they've done in the past. No matter how successful they are, the future will always be different. That's why it's imperative to wake up each morning and look at the world with fresh eyes, always imagining what could be, not what has been.

Setting the right tone doesn't end with words. What you say only goes so far. It's also important to be true to your words. When psychologists studied family dynamics, they found that kids model their behaviors, morals, and values not on what parents say but on what they do. The parents' actions always trump their words. Parents who say one thing but do another send the wrong message to their children. The same is true in your company. It doesn't matter if you talk about innovation, empowerment, and openness. Those words only mean something if you can back them up with clear actions. You must live your words.

If you want to have a culture where people are open to new possibilities, share their ideas freely, and support one another as a cohesive team, you want your actions to reflect this from the get-go. What are you doing to encourage your team to try novel things? How do you receive new ideas—even unwelcome ones? What criteria do you use to judge success and failure? Do you promote unorthodox thinkers? Do you reward team members who question authority? How do you react when people have ideas that contradict the direction you've set? This is a true test of your leadership.

As your company grows, you can think of how to manifest these ideas in tangible forms. It helps to set up a process that promotes dissenting ideas, discussion, and debate. It's important to make the process transparent so everyone can see how decisions are made and participate in fine-tuning the system. The only thing that matters is what actually produces results.

In the end, you are only a single individual. You cannot do everything yourself. You need to be able to rely on your team. So, even at the very beginning, when your startup is no more than two or three people, it's up to you to implant the right DNA into the team. It is also up to you to create an environment that fosters creativity, originality, boldness, and reflection. It takes a very special type of leader to build and nurture this type of organization, and it all starts with setting the tone. If you select the right people, provide the inspiration and support they need to do their jobs, and shine a light on the path ahead, they will do the rest.

82

Define Your Vision

EVERYONE TALKS ABOUT HAVING A vision, but what does that mean? Marc Benioff, the CEO of Salesforce, was obsessed with this from day one. When he was at Oracle, he struggled with the fact that there was no written business plan or formal communication process during their growth phase. During his new hire orientation, he even asked Larry Ellison, the CEO, what Oracle's five-year plan was. Ellison replied, "We don't have a five-year plan; we barely have a six-month plan."[1]

"What I yearned for at Oracle was clarity on our vision and the goals we wanted to achieve," says Benioff. "As I started to manage my own divisions, I found that I personally lacked the tools to spell out what we needed to do and a simple process to communicate it."[2] To address this shortcoming, he sought wisdom from personal development coaches, leadership gurus, and even spiritual mentors. This led to the formulation of his own management process, which he calls V2MOM. It stands for vision, values, methods, obstacles, and measures. Benioff scribbled his first V2MOM for Salesforce on a large envelope on April 12, 1999. Here's what it said:[3]

Vision

- Rapidly create a world-class internet company/site for sales force automation

Values

- World-class organization
- Time to market
- Functional
- Usability (Amazon quality)
- Value-added partnerships

Methods

- Hire the team
- Finalize product specification and technical architecture
- Rapidly develop the product specification to beta and production stages
- Build partnerships with big e-commerce, content, and hosting companies
- Build a launch plan
- Develop exit strategy: IPO/acquisition

Obstacles

- Developers
- Product manager/business development person

Measures

- Prototype is state-of-the-art
- High-quality functional system
- Partnerships are online and integrated
- Salesforce.com is regarded as leader and visionary
- We are all rich

The night before Salesforce's IPO in 2004, Benioff's cofounder, Parker Harris, handed him the original handwritten V2MOM envelope, framed. For years, this simple document had clarified what Benioff was thinking and allowed him to communicate it to the entire organization. The beauty of his V2MOM is that the same structure worked for every phase in the life cycle of his organization. Salesforce has continuously used this as their business plan, from the time they were a tiny startup to the present day, with more than thirty thousand employees spread across twenty-five countries. "V2MOM gave us a detailed map of where we were going," says Benioff, "as well as a compass to direct us there."[4]

I'm not saying you should copy V2MOM verbatim. Just use it as a guide to develop your own personal vision statement. You can start by answering these five simple questions:

1. What do you want to achieve?
   This is your VISION.
2. What's important about it?
   These are your VALUES.
3. How do you get it?
   These are your METHODS.
4. What might stand in the way?
   Here are your OBSTACLES.
5. How will you know when you have it?
   These are your MEASURES.

I believe all good vision statements should be personal. They should come out of your core beliefs. They should embody your values. Just pasting someone else's vision on top of your company won't cut it. It won't be authentic, and you probably won't use it for very long. It's important to take the time up front to think through not just where your company is headed, but what you want out of life and the type of organization you intend to build. How do you want your employees to view your company now and in decades to come? What should they care about, and how should they go about achieving these goals? If you can distill this down into an elegant format, as Benioff did, you're off to a good start.

83

Becoming a Super Boss

BEING A LEADER ISN'T ONLY about hiring talented people. It's also about getting the people you already have to work more effectively. Having a lot of money and a large team aren't enough. You need to know how to manage your employees in order to take your company to the next level.

Have you ever had a boss who felt compelled to control every aspect of the business? It's no fun, to say the least. Bosses like this are classic, top-down managers. They love hierarchy. They are the boss, and they want you to do things their way. They are always saying, "Do this! No, not that. Do it this way!" Whenever you make a mistake or fail to meet their expectations, they get upset.

In the end, most employees in this situation will either quit or wind up turning into zombies. They literally turn off their decision-making brain and wait for their manager to tell them what to do. It's easier and less risky. They won't get yelled at for making a mistake, and they don't have to take responsibility. Having employees who blindly follow orders is fine if they're working on an assembly line, but not if you need them to think for themselves. In the Information Age, having an innovative, creative workforce is essential. You need their brains fully engaged if you are going to outperform your competitors.

My advice is simple: Ask, don't tell. Every time you want to tell your employees what to do or how to do their job, hold back. Bite your tongue. Instead, you should be asking them: "Let's imagine you are producing an event. What is the best way to get your team to tackle the job?"

TELL: We're going to be producing a startup competition.

ASK: What type of startup event do you think would work best?

TELL: We need seating for a hundred people.

ASK: How much seating do you think we need?

TELL: Let's show videos of each presenter to the right of the stage.

ASK: Should we show videos of the presenters or something else?

TELL: Everyone will be given five minutes to present.

ASK: What do you think is the optimal time for the presentations?

TELL: Here's the plan we used last time.

ASK: How can we improve upon the plan we used last time?

By asking questions, you are compelling your team members to work out the problems for themselves. You may know a lot more about producing events than your employees do, but your goal should not be to dictate every step of the process. That's inefficient. Instead, you should take on the role of mentor and guide them through the process with your questions. Every time you ask them instead of telling them, you are activating their brains. You are forcing them to think for themselves. They need to come up with their own ideas and solutions. Suddenly, they own the job, and they are innovating alongside you.

You may be surprised to find that even inexperienced members of your team come up with ways of doing things that are better and more original than your own. Part of this is because they haven't done the work a thousand times, so they aren't blinded by the past. They may come up with an approach that seems unorthodox, or even unfeasible, on the surface, but often it's precisely those breakthroughs that enable startups to jump ahead of competitors.

At the very least, when they feel empowered in their jobs and have a strong sense of ownership, they're likely to work harder and longer without your prodding them. They will want to put in the extra effort because it's their plan, and they will want to do everything possible to make sure it won't fail. The same can't be said if it's the boss's plan.

But what if your team is about to make a big mistake? Do you intervene and tell them what to do? No. It's better to ask more questions.

- Why did you suggest this plan?
- Have you considered this possibility?
- What if this doesn't work?
- Do you have a backup plan?
- Can you come up with some viable alternatives?

If you probe deeply enough, you will not only better understand your team's thought processes, you will force them to think through the issues and come up with a solution, instead of relying on you to fix their problems. This is what great managers do. They train their team how to think. It's not about getting your team to do the perfect job. It's about getting them to become self-sufficient, and that requires them to understand how to analyze and solve complex problems. If you hired the right people, they will step up to the challenge. If you didn't hire people who can learn and think for themselves, that's where your problem lies.

Your ultimate objective should be to have a team that runs on its own. You simply point them in the right direction and let them go. That enables you to step back and focus on other things, which is how you become a super boss.

84

Managing Your Board

AS A COMPANY MATURES, LEARNING how to effectively work with a board of directors can be a challenge for entrepreneurs. Even if the founders retain control over the company, good communication is still essential. Board members expect to know what's going on with the company and want to be a part of the decision-making process. If you respect and trust all of your board members and you want them involved in helping you run the business, there probably won't be any issues. However, some entrepreneurs are used to doing things their own way and dread interference of any kind. This can lead to tensions.

Difficulties can crop up when the CEO tries to keep the board at arm's length by not sharing details or discussing the real issues. There can also be problems when board members see things differently or when the company hits a rough patch. Personality and communication styles can also play a big part. These underlying tensions can easily escalate into open hostility. That's why it is crucial for startup founders to adopt a strategy for dealing with their board from day one. Winging it does not work. Without a clearly defined set of principles, it's easy to fall into one of several traps that wind up destroying the relationship.

Here are some of the traps I've witnessed over the years:

Hype Trap—This is when a CEO inflates the achievements of the company to impress the board.

Sandbagging Trap—This is when a CEO makes goals appear harder than they actually are so as to look good when reaching them.

Concealment Trap—This is when a CEO deliberately tries to conceal problems with the company from board members.

Filtering Trap—This is when a CEO filters data so that it fits with the company's version of reality.

Defensive Trap—This is when a CEO adopts a siege mentality to keep board members at bay.

Passive-Aggressive Trap—This is when the CEO acts nice and friendly, agrees to do whatever the board wants, but then never follows through.

Mule Trap—This is when the CEO becomes mule-headed and refuses to do what the board wants without providing good reasons.

Bully Trap—This is when the CEO tries to dominate the board and intimidate members into submission.

Political Trap—This is when the CEO plays politics with the board, favoring some members over others in order to silence dissenting opinions and manipulate members.

I'll walk you through an example of how seemingly innocuous behavior can gradually lead to a dysfunctional board. It can begin with something as simple as a startup founder inflating the company's achievements in an attempt to look good. This is especially true for first-time CEOs who have become used to selling the vision of their startups. By constantly inflating expectations, the CEO can wind up in a precarious position. The problem comes when the company doesn't live up to the hype.

At first, investors may be unaware, but they aren't stupid. Over time, they will begin to realize the truth. Even if the CEO never tells flagrant lies or doctors the data, as board members become more conscious of the manipulation, trust will erode.

Most of the time, this is swept under the rug, especially if the company is growing fast and times are good. However, as soon as the startup hits a rough patch and the CEO's hype begins to cover up real problems, board members will begin to question the CEO's decisions and ratchet up the pressure. Many entrepreneurs believe that if they can just buy more time, they can fix the issues, so the lies grow in size. But this seldom works. With each lie, the CEO digs a deeper hole until it's impossible to get out. When the board finds out, all trust is lost, and there's no going back. It can quickly devolve into a siege mentality with the CEO actively battling board members as if they're the enemy.

Now keep in mind, it's not always the CEO's fault. This type of situation can emerge for a variety of reasons. Sometimes one of the board members is simply a jerk. Other times, there's a philosophical difference. Miscommunications and personality differences crop up all the time. In the end, though, the CEO must still deal with the underlying problems. It's far better if the CEO never falls into any of the traps I mentioned above. That's why I'm going to lay out fifteen guiding principles that highly effective CEOs use when dealing with the board.

1. **Be Honest**—Being truthful is the first and foremost principle. Make it a point to never lie. If board members find out you are lying, that only makes things worse, and even if they don't, it's a slippery slope. Board members must know what's going on in the company. It's their fiduciary responsibility, and it's your job as CEO to keep them informed. Even small lies can add up fast. It's far better to take the pain of revealing any mistakes, bad news, or screw ups than to push them down the road. It might seem daunting, but you will get used to being perfectly frank. And your board will appreciate it.

2. **Show Your Warts**—Don't cover up anything unpleasant. This goes beyond honesty. It's possible to conceal things without

lying, but this doesn't help. In fact, it just creates an unspoken barrier between you and your board. On the other hand, bringing your mistakes and weaknesses to the forefront not only builds trust but allows the board to help. If you just wasted a huge amount of money on a flawed marketing campaign, let everyone know what it cost your company. Maybe someone on the board can recommend another approach or bring in a marketing expert to improve the situation. If your product is full of bugs due to careless engineers, let everyone know. Explain the steps you're taking to solve the issue and ask for their input. If a competitor just came out with a superior product, don't pretend it didn't happen. Admit this and work on a strategy to counter it. This type of frankness brings everyone on the board together. You are a team dealing with these problems, not a lone CEO hiding them.

3. **Choose Carefully**—Don't put anyone on your board of directors you wouldn't want as your partner for life. If you have an investor you don't believe can be helpful but is demanding a board seat, don't take his money with that condition attached. Once someone is on your board, it's hard to remove them. It's far better to spend the time and effort up front to identify people you respect, trust, and want as your partners, rather than trying to get rid of a bad seed later on.

4. **Come Prepared**—Never go into a board meeting cold. You should know exactly what you want to talk about and have all the material prepared beforehand. You should send out these materials in advance so board members have time to review everything and form their thoughts before you meet. The board meeting should be about maximizing the precious time you have together. You should speed through the routine approvals up front and then use the bulk of the time discussing real issues, leveraging your members' experience, insights, and relationships, and dealing with the toughest decisions your business faces.

5. **Don't Sell**—Your job is not to sell the board on your vision, ideas, and progress. That's not why they are on the board. They

don't need to hear your pitch and buy into your dream. They already did that when they joined the board. Once they are on the board, their job is to help you steer the company in the right direction, and in order to accomplish this, they need information. You should spend your time informing them as accurately as possible and getting their input so, together, you can make the best decisions possible.

6. **Don't Act Defensively**—Remember, when board members criticize the company and bring up thorny issues, they are usually trying to help, not personally attack you. You need to separate yourself from your company. Your job is to find solutions to these problems, not defend them, and you can't do that if you are confusing the company's issues with your own.

7. **Meet Outside**—Have regular lunches and meetings with individual members outside of the official board meetings. This will help build your relationships and facilitate the exchange of valuable information. If you just meet once a month or once a quarter, in a formal setting, you will never really get to know and trust your board members. You need to spend time in a relaxed environment to truly get to know them. The more time you spend together, the better off you will be when things get tough, which will happen at some point.

8. **Manage Decisions**—If you are going to ask the board to make a complicated or controversial decision, you need to prep them in advance. That means meeting with the board members one-on-one, getting their input, and making sure you're all on the same page. You don't ever want to surprise your board. That's a recipe for disaster. You need to connect with each member, educate them on the problem, and understand if they have any objections. Sometimes your interests and the interests of your investors don't align. That doesn't mean you can't find a compromise, but it isn't always easy. It often takes time to craft the right solution, and the only way to do this is by carefully managing the entire process outside of the board meetings. Only after things are resolved should you bring it up for a vote. Then, there won't be any surprises.

9. **Keep It Short**—Board meetings should never go longer than three hours. Two hours or less is ideal. Meetings that run over not only become inefficient and unproductive, they lead to bad decision making. Everyone gets exhausted and cranky when stuck in long meetings. You need to get the best out of your board members, and that means keeping the board meetings succinct, focused, and highly productive.

10. **Timing Is Everything**—It's best to have your meetings in the morning when everyone is fresh. I think 9:00 a.m. to 12:00 p.m. is perfect. Make sure to provide snacks and coffee at the beginning. Afterward, you can have lunch together and enjoy one another's company.

11. **Simplify the Process**—Don't expect your board members to labor through detailed spreadsheets, legal contracts, or dense PowerPoints during the meeting. You need to simplify what's presented so it's easy to understand and discuss. If there are complex legal documents or other materials, they should be sent in advance. During the meeting, you will want to stick to the macro picture. This is a time to make high-level decisions, not get lost in the weeds.

12. **Don't Do All the Talking**—You should not be the one doing the talking during the meeting. The meetings should be run more like an open dialogue than a one-way lecture. You shouldn't spend a lot of time presenting. Instead, you should be asking key questions and listening most of the time. Your board members should be your most trusted advisors, and you want to get as much feedback and input as possible during each session.

13. **Follow Through**—It's not okay to promise something and then not deliver. This seems obvious, but some CEOs make commitments during a board meeting but fail to act on them, either intentionally or unintentionally. This is a mistake that breeds frustration and resentment among your board members. If you say you'll do something, make sure to get it done. Follow-through is critical if you want to maintain a good relationship. If you can't deliver, you'd better have a good reason.

14. **Don't Get Angry**—Anger takes two forms: Either it's a loss of self-control or an attempt to gain control over someone else. When you get upset and lose control of your own emotions, it's a sign of weakness. Strong leaders don't let their emotions overtake them. On the other hand, if you are using anger to bully someone into submission, then it's an attempt to gain control through force, not persuasion or logic. Even if you can browbeat board members into agreeing with you, it's a short-term gain with a long-term price to pay. You haven't changed their minds, and you've probably earned their ire.

15. **Own Your Mistakes**—If you or your team screws up, you need to own it. Shifting the blame to your team doesn't help. Everyone can see through this, and in the end, you're the CEO. So, it's still your problem.

If you follow these fifteen rules, you should be in good shape. You won't always have an easy time, but you should be able to navigate the rough waters without capsizing your ship. As a CEO, that's the best you can do.

85

Nothing Is Too Crazy

VISIONARY LEADERS TEND TO BE a crazy lot. Just look at Sir Richard Branson and everything he does. Being dyslexic, like me, he hates numbers. He claims to not even pay attention to the P&L. All he cares about is dreaming up and building new businesses, and he's not afraid to try anything. His company, Virgin Group, has tried everything from launching punk rock bands, like the Sex Pistols, to starting airlines, hotels, health clubs, bridal services, rugby teams, banks, film and TV studios, radio stations, magazines, online entertainment, mobile phone services, electric utilities, and space tourism, as well as manufacturing its own brand of condoms, cosmetics, vodka, colas, games, alternative fuels, and the list goes on. And he's done this on a global scale.

If this sounds like a lot, it's because, like all great entrepreneurs, Branson is a bit of a madman. He's always taking risks on and off the job. He drove an amphibious car from England to France. He crossed the Pacific from Japan to Arctic Canada in a hot air balloon. He climbed Mont Blanc, Europe's highest peak. He broke the world record for the fastest Atlantic crossing on a custom-built speedboat. He bungee jumped off the Palms Casino in Las Vegas, hitting the building twice while traveling one hundred miles per hour, and survived with only ripped trousers. He drove a tank down New York's Fifth Avenue. He kitesurfed across the English Channel. He also kitesurfed with a naked model clinging to his back, but not across any channels. I'm not sure which is riskier, but you'd have to ask his wife about that.

Elon Musk isn't quite the daredevil that Branson is, but he's just as big a risk taker when it comes to business. He launched several companies at one time, each with an audacious goal. SolarCity led the world in solar homes, Tesla paved the way for the electric car revolution that has swept the globe, and SpaceX's ultimate mission is to take humankind to Mars. If this isn't enough for one man, he's gone on to pioneer more mind-blowing projects, including Hyperloop, his vision for the future of high-speed transportation; the Boring Company, which will dig the tunnels for Hyperloop; Neuralink, a startup that hopes to integrate the human brain with artificial intelligence; and OpenAI, which hopes to keep artificial intelligence from destroying humanity. He's also a master at pulling stunts, from selling flamethrowers online to blasting a Tesla car into space.

I'm not saying you have to be as outlandish as Branson or Musk to be successful, but going a little gonzo doesn't hurt. Most visionary entrepreneurs push the limits of society and themselves. This is why they're able to see the future and make it happen. They aren't normal. They aren't like everyone else. Even those who seem tame on the outside, like Zuckerberg and Gates, usually have a rebel on the inside, which allows them to defy conventional thinking and chart their own course through life.

If you're going to truly test your limits, it often pays to cultivate the nonconformist lurking deep within you. See what your rebellious side has to say. You may be surprised at what you're capable of doing. Just because you've followed the rules your entire life doesn't mean you have to continue down that path. Start by breaking a few rules. You can be whatever you imagine yourself to be. There really is no difference between you and Musk or Branson, except that they dared themselves to do it and went through with it.

7

Startup Life

Follow Your Own Path

U p until this point, the focus of this book has been about building successful startups. Now it's time to take those ideas and apply them to yourself. I'm a firm believer that great entrepreneurs are both born and made. There are a lot of smart, capable people in the world, but the ones who consistently accomplish outstanding things throughout their lifetimes don't rely solely on their innate abilities. They take an active role in reinventing themselves, over and over again, as the world changes around them.

In the same way, you need to continually iterate and experiment on yourself, your company, and your life, so that you can take on larger challenges, attain better results, and help those around you achieve more.

How do you make the hard decisions? What path do you choose in life? If your path turns out to be a dead end, what then? Ultimately, it's not what happens to your company, or how wealthy or poor you become; it's how you deal with the problems along the way that will determine your worth as both leader and role model for others to follow.

Bouncing Back

I'D LIKE TO TELL YOU some stories about entrepreneurs who bounced back. These guys got run over by a steamroller but managed to get back on their feet and keep moving forward.

Greg Bonann certainly knows how it feels to be flattened. He had the dream to produce his own TV show about an elite squad of lifeguards on a mission to save the bay. The show was called *Baywatch*, and when it aired in America, it was a mega flop. The ratings were so dismal that it was cancelled after only one season. "It was a crushing defeat for me," says Bonann. "I'd spent years getting this show on air, only to be told one Friday that it was over. A few days later, I was back at the beach working as a lifeguard, feeling sorry for myself."

On Father's Day, his father asked him what he was going to do with the show. Bonann said, "Nothing." Since the TV network owned all the rights, he felt like there was nothing he could do. Undeterred, his dad told him to ask for the rights back. Bonann tried to explain that's not how it worked, but his dad made him promise to at least ask. So, on Monday morning, just to honor his Father's Day promise, Bonann called and asked if he could meet with the network executives.

To his surprise, they were willing to sell the show back to him, and they only asked for $1 because they weren't doing anything with it.

"After I got the rights back," says Bonann, "I went to Europe with the show and hustled every network to take the show, leveraging one country's interest against another's, until I began to get traction." He even gave the show away for free in China to build an audience. Two years later, once it had become a hit, he asked for a licensing fee. China wound up paying more for *Baywatch* than they'd ever paid for a single TV show.

"Finally, Americans began to take notice, but this time it was on my terms,"[1] says Bonann. *Baywatch* went on to become a worldwide phenomenon. Like most successful entrepreneurs, Bonann had learned how to bounce back, and it wouldn't have happened without his father's advice. We can all learn something here. Never let other people and circumstances out of your control defeat you. Just because you think there is no way forward doesn't mean it's so.

※

Never let other people and circumstances
out of your control defeat you.

When Adam Pisoni was just nineteen years old, he left college and moved to Los Angeles to launch his first company: a web design firm. He was young, naïve, and hopelessly optimistic. It was 1995, and the dot-com boom was underway. Everyone needed a website, and Pisoni was there to capitalize on it. He didn't mind working hundred-hour weeks, and soon he had thirty employees. His clients included big names like Honda and Sony, and annual revenue shot up to $2 million. He was on top of the world, until he wasn't. Just as he was scaling up, the bubble burst, and his world collapsed. All his big clients cancelled projects and slashed spending, while most of his smaller ones went out of business.

It was devastating. He had thrown his entire life into this startup, and now there was no way to save it. With no revenue and rising expenses, Pisoni was forced to shut down his company. "It felt like the loss of a family member and sent most of us into a depression that took some time to get out of," admits Pisoni. Unable to conceive of doing another business, he moved to the mountains. He chose Mammoth Lakes, a town not far from Yosemite National Park, where he worked at a snowboard shop for three years. It would be eleven years before he would get up the courage to launch another startup.

He bounced around, working as an engineer and getting back into technology. During that time, he connected with David Sacks, an early PayPal employee and a member of the famed PayPal Mafia. Pisoni joined Geni, a genealogy website that Sacks founded. They collaborated well, and Sacks asked if Pisoni would join him in a new venture. Its goal was to bring social networking to large corporations, and it would be called Yammer. Pisoni signed on as cofounder and CTO (chief technology officer). He was back in the startup game.

It seemed like they were set to catch the wave. It was 2008, and social networking was the craze. Every corporation wanted in on it, and they had the solution. The timing was perfect, but nothing is ever easy when it comes to doing a startup. They quickly found out that they weren't the only ones. Within weeks of launching, three new competitors had entered the market. A year later, there were more than twenty competitors. It was brutal, and growth came slowly. They were struggling.

Through it all, Pisoni kept calm. He'd done this before. He didn't have any illusions about how hard things could get. He kept his doubts and fears to himself. "One of the challenges of leadership in a situation with uncertainty is that there's a set of emotions as a leader that you can't share with people on the team," says Zack Parker, former director of engineering at Yammer. "You can never be visibly worried. Adam [Pisoni] did a phenomenal job of being the anchor around which the positive culture of Yammer could build."

Pisoni took the iterative growth mindset approach. Even though he knew the odds were stacked against them, he was determined to keep improving their product and eventually find success. He didn't put blind faith into anything. He viewed each new product feature and sales strategy as an experiment that probably wouldn't work but could teach them something. He encouraged his team to challenge everything, especially when it came to conventional thinking. "In everything we do," says Pisoni, "we have to assume we could be wrong. If we jump into things thinking we'll generally be right, we might move forward for too long without changing."

This type of approach allowed Yammer to adjust to changes in the market and shift strategies quickly. Yammer wound up moving from Los Angeles to San Francisco, where most of the action was. In the process, they encountered a culture shock. Silicon Valley was filled with rich kids and Ivy League types, while Pisoni and his team were the opposite. Adam Pisoni, Zack Parker, and Kris Gale, vice president of engineering, had all dropped out of high school. In response, they became more determined than ever to succeed. They wanted to prove their team could win.

Instead of 2x growth, they aimed for 10x. They also encouraged their customers to develop a more transparent, agile, and collaborative way of working. Pisoni knew that only the best products would survive in this market, and they had to be first or second. Third place didn't matter. The results came fast. They wound up rising to the top of the heap. To fuel growth, they brought in $85 million in venture capital on top of the $57 million they'd already raised. Head count rose to around 250, and they still weren't profitable. But it wasn't an issue. What mattered was staying on top.

That's when Microsoft stepped in with a $1.2 billion offer to buy the company. It seemed too good to be true. The startup was only four years old, and they hadn't even proved out their business model. Despite this, most of the team didn't want to sell. They believed in Yammer too much. It wasn't about the money. They were building something amazing.

"It was heartbreaking at the time," says Gale. "We were so invested in the Yammer vision, and we believed in what we were going to achieve long term so deeply that we were all pretty bummed. I think my first words to Adam [Pisoni] were something like, 'So this is it?'"[2]

Having failed in the past, Pisoni knew this was the right move. There were still huge challenges ahead of them, and with the backing of Microsoft, they could remove risk from the equation and lead the market. In hindsight, it was the right decision. Yammer added a lot of value to Microsoft, but it never achieved the adoption that everyone expected. Pisoni's struggles had helped him navigate each challenge Yammer faced and end up on top. As I write this, Pisoni is doing another startup because true entrepreneurs never fade away; they just keep bouncing back. This is the essential lesson every founder needs to learn. It's better to be made of rubber than steel.

Are You Too Old?

IT'S COMMON WISDOM IN SILICON Valley that the best startup founders are in their twenties. After all, Bill Gates, Steve Jobs, and Mark Zuckerberg were just beyond their teens when they started. The stereotype is that only the young can come up with new ideas and master technology. If you're thirty or older, you're over the hill. What people don't realize is that the facts don't support this. The National Bureau of Economic Research conducted a comprehensive investigation of high-growth startups and found that the stereotype of younger entrepreneurs doesn't match the data.

It may surprise you, but when it comes to the top 0.1 percent of highest-growth startups, the average founder is forty-five years old. That means a good number of these founders are in their fifties and sixties. If you go deeper, the numbers don't change much. For the top 1 percent of startups, the average age is forty-four, and for the top 5 percent, it's forty-two. The statistics show that younger entrepreneurs, despite having grown up in the digital age, are less successful than their more experienced counterparts. The report concludes that "younger founders appear strongly disadvantaged in their tendency to produce the highest-growth companies."[1]

Despite this, society continues to discriminate against older entrepreneurs. Many investors in Silicon Valley prefer to fund young teams. If someone with gray hair walks in the door, some VCs automatically turn off. Vinod Khosla, one of the Valley's top venture capitalists and co-founder of Sun Microsystems at age twenty-seven, once declared, "People under thirty-five are the people who make change happen," and "people over forty-five basically die in terms of new ideas."[2]

This type of flawed thinking is present in many tech companies. If you're over forty, you're sometimes referred to as a "graybeard." Most corporations in Silicon Valley put on a youthful façade with activities and benefits that appeal to millennials like rock climbing, kitesurfing, beer bashes, foosball tables, and all-night hackathons. Even the biggest corporations fall into the trap of believing youth is equivalent to innovation. A ProPublica investigation, published in 2018, found that IBM cut twenty thousand older employees over the past five years while sharply increasing the hiring of people born after 1980. Meanwhile, Google has fought a series of age-related lawsuits. One is a class-action lawsuit to which 269 people signed on. Hired, a recruitment platform, conducted a study showing that once tech workers turn forty-five, they tend to see the number of job offers fall and their salaries plateau. Ironically, this is right at the age when they are most valuable to a company, according to the data.

If you think Silicon Valley is bad, just look at China. Chinese companies don't even try to hide their ageism. If you search popular job sites, you can find tens of thousands of job postings explicitly asking for applicants younger than thirty-five. A Beijing tech startup went so far as to state that while it's willing to relax its requirements for education, it won't for age. And it's not just startups. It includes giants like JD.com, Ctrip, and Baidu. Helen He, a tech recruiter in Shanghai, sums up the prevailing attitude when she says, "Most people in their thirties are married and have to take care of their family—they're not able to focus on the high-intensity work. If a thirty-five-year-old candidate isn't seeking to be a manager, a hiring company wouldn't even give that CV a glance."

Because of the fierce competition, Chinese tech companies often expect their employees to work a 996 schedule: 9:00 a.m. to 9:00 p.m., six days a week. And you can forget about holidays. "Working in tech is like being a professional athlete," says Robin Chan, a Chinese angel investor and entrepreneur. "You work extremely hard from twenty to forty years old and hope you hit it big. After that, it's time to move on to something else and let someone younger try their hand."[3]

This type of attitude has gained momentum because we see a lot of successful startups founded by entrepreneurs in their twenties. What we don't take into account is that young people are launching startups in larger numbers than ever before. Because of the sheer volume, we are bound to see some successes. What we rarely hear about is the huge number of young people whose startups fail.

Another factor in warping our perspective is a youth-obsessed media. We seldom see stories of fifty-year-old entrepreneurs hitting it big, but if a teenager launches a mildly successful startup, it's news. Part of the reason for this is that it's impressive when a young person actually does something extraordinary, while it's not so interesting when an experienced businessperson accomplishes the same thing. Exceptional things make better stories, which leads to misconceptions. So, let me share a few stories of some silver-haired superstars to set the record straight.

In the dot-com days, Julie Wainwright joined a small startup called Pets.com. It was just two people and a seedling of an idea. As CEO, she took that company all the way to an IPO, only to watch it crash and burn when the bubble popped. The same day she decided to shut down the business, her husband asked for a divorce. If that weren't bad enough, Pets.com wound up becoming the poster child for failed startups in the dot-com era. She was crushed, to say the least.

"It failed, and I became sort of a pariah," says Wainwright. "I was the dumbest person in the Valley. It was a little tough." After that, she tried her hand at venture capital, but her true desire was to run another company. The only problem was that no one offered her anything worthwhile. As an older woman, there weren't a lot of options, and her track record didn't help.

"Man, this could be a really bad second half of my life," Wainwright says. "Nobody is going to give me my dream job, so I better figure it out myself." Despite being in her mid-fifties, she set out to launch another startup. She drew her inspiration from a shopping-obsessed friend who would search for luxury clothing from the secondhand rack in the back of fancy boutiques. Her friend wanted to make sure the goods weren't counterfeit. That's why she never shopped online.

Wainwright realized that if she could earn the trust of customers by guaranteeing the luxury goods weren't counterfeit, she would have a big business. In the United States alone, personal luxury goods are a $50 billion market. Armed with this insight, she launched The RealReal, an online secondhand luxury marketplace that verifies and guarantees every item is authentic.

It was a brilliant idea, but raising capital wasn't easy. Most of the VCs were young guys in their twenties and thirties, and they took one look at her and passed. "It was really, really hard," admits Wainwright. "I didn't have success until I reached a woman [investor]."[4] She wound up raising $173 million in venture capital from twenty-two investors over seven rounds. By 2017, The RealReal had 950 employees and did more than a half-billion dollars in revenue. In spite of her highly publicized failure, getting divorced, and turning sixty, Wainwright is on her way to another IPO, and none of it would have been possible if she'd told herself that she was too old.

Wainwright is far from alone. There are many more like her. At age forty, Lynda Weinman cofounded Lynda.com, an online education startup that sold to LinkedIn for $1.5 billion. At age forty-two, Chip Wilson launched Lululemon, a yoga apparel brand, and took it all the way to an IPO. It now has a market cap greater than $13 billion. At age forty, Herbert Boyer cofounded Genentech and sold it to Roche for $46.8 billion. In fact, throughout the history of tech, there were far more founders of successful startups over thirty than under. Charles Flint founded IBM at sixty-one. Robert Noyce was forty-one when he cofounded Intel. Bill Porter started E*Trade at fifty-four. Arianna Huffington launched the *Huffington Post* (now known as *Huffpost*) at fifty-five. And Evan Williams cofounded Twitter at thirty-four.

It's not just successful tech entrepreneurs who tend to be over thirty. Asa Candler founded Coca-Cola at forty-one. Amadeo Giannini conceived of Bank of America at sixty. Henry Ford started Ford Motors at forty. Sam Walton founded Walmart at forty-four. Bernie Marcus opened Home Depot at fifty. Martha Stewart was nearly fifty before launching *Martha Stewart Living* magazine. Vera Wang did not even begin designing clothes professionally until she was thirty-nine.

In the end, each of us has to be careful not to fall prey to stereotypes. The only way to overcome this problem is to educate ourselves and take action. When bringing onboard cofounders and employees, all of us need to be careful not to judge them by their gray hair and wrinkles. What they lack in youthful appearance, they can make up for in experience. It pays to take the time to understand how potential collaborators think and what they truly have to offer.

If you're an entrepreneur with gray hair, take heart. There are investors in Silicon Valley who get this. "A founder should be the type of person a team can respect and look to for guidance and leadership, and often that requires a certain degree of maturity that comes with experience,"[5] says Bob Goodman, general partner of Bessemer Venture Partners. This sentiment is confirmed in a new study by scholars at the Kellogg School, MIT, and the US Census Bureau. They found that fifty-year-old entrepreneurs are nearly twice as likely to have a runaway success as thirty-year-olds.

Clearly, innovation doesn't just happen in your twenties. It's a lifelong pursuit. Anyone at any age can have valuable insights that transform our society and reinvent industries. If you have the energy, ideas, and ambition to make something happen, age isn't your problem; it's your asset. Leverage your life experience and dive right in with the twenty-somethings. You have a superpower they don't possess, and that can make all the difference.

※

Anyone at any age can have valuable insights that transform our society and reinvent industries.

88

Giving Back

IT'S GREAT TO EARN A lot of money doing a startup, but it's even more important to give back. Marc Benioff, the CEO of Salesforce, not only innovated on the job but also on philanthropy. He pioneered the 1-1-1 model of integrated corporate philanthropy, whereby companies contribute 1 percent of equity, 1 percent of employee hours, and 1 percent of product back to the communities they serve. Parts of his model have been adopted by more than seven hundred companies around the world.

Benioff believes it's the entrepreneurs' responsibility to use their wealth to change the world, not only through business but through funding non-profit organizations. Businesses do certain things well, but they are different from nonprofits. They can't address problems where there is no market. Natural disasters, epidemics, mass starvation, war refugees, human trafficking, and a myriad of other problems are often better handled through nonprofits. This is why donating time, money, and resources to charities is essential.

In the same spirit as Benioff, Bill Gates has been bringing new ideas to philanthropy for some time. He has shown that it's as important to innovate in the nonprofit sector as it is in the for-profit sector. Through his foundation, he is harnessing new technologies to fight the spread of infectious diseases, empower women and girls, improve education, and protect the environment.

Like Gates before him, Jack Ma, the cofounder of China's largest e-commerce firm, Alibaba, announced that he would step down as chairman in order to concentrate on philanthropy and education. Ma has a history of giving. In 2014, he and cofounder Joe Tsai established a charitable trust focusing on health and the environment. This was funded by share options they personally owned, which represented around 2 percent of Alibaba's equity at the time. Ma has also invested 300 million yuan ($45 million) in rural education in China and established a scholarship program in Newcastle, Australia.

Carrying on a long tradition of philanthropy in the United States—which includes such towering figures as Andrew Carnegie and John D. Rockefeller—Gates, Buffet, Zuckerberg, and other high-profile billionaires have pledged to give away nearly all of their wealth in support of good causes. In doing so, they have become role models for startup founders around the world. I encourage all of you to aspire to their level of social consciousness. Even if you don't wind up a billionaire, there's a lot you and your startup can do.

I met Candice Wang in our Beijing startup program, and when she told me her story, I knew I had to include her in my book. She's a perfect example of a startup founder who combines entrepreneurship with social responsibility and personal passion.

After working and studying abroad for eight years, Candice returned to China and went to work as a volunteer for a nonprofit. A year later, a sudden accident struck her family, setting her on a new path. A contractor was demolishing a building next door to her family's house when one of the workers asked her father to check on something inside. As soon as he stepped into the building, the roof collapsed on him. Nearly crushed to death, he was buried under the rubble for hours.

Her father wound up losing one leg but gradually regained his health. In order to walk again, he needed a prosthetic leg. Candice began doing research and found out the best legs were made in Germany, but they were extremely expensive in China. Her family would either have to spend a small fortune or accept a much lower quality prosthetic.

After more research, Candice discovered the same prosthetic leg and treatment were available in Russia at less than half the cost. Arranging it all herself, she took her father to Moscow and got him the best treatment possible. In the process, she realized that millions of families across China, especially those in less affluent communities, were suffering with substandard treatments due to lack of access to information.

Candice couldn't stand the unfairness of this. When she contacted the overseas hospitals directly, she found out they were already paying the medical tourism companies a commission of 10 to 30 percent for their services, and they felt it was wrong for the brokers to double or triple the price on top of this commission.

That's when she decided to launch her startup, in order to bring more affordable healthcare to people around the world. Candice is exactly the type of entrepreneur I like to see. She is not only building a disruptive business with growth potential but also giving back. Fortunately, Candice is not alone. There are many other entrepreneurs out there working to make the world a better place. I hope you will be inspired to do the same.

89

Seeking Knowledge

IF THERE'S ONE THING YOU can do to increase your chances of success, it's to suck up as much knowledge as possible in all its forms. I'm not just talking about reading business books like this one. I'm talking about tapping into the latest thinking on diverse topics, ranging from emerging technologies and innovation management to behavioral psychology and user experience.

The most innovative thinkers alive today share one thing in common. They are constantly consuming vast amounts of information and exposing themselves to new concepts across a wide spectrum of disciplines. Brilliant minds like Sergey Brin, Astro Teller, Jack Dorsey, Charlie Munger, Ray Kurzweil, Dean Kamen, Brian Chesky, and Ray Dalio gobble up other people's ideas and use them as the raw material for their own breakthroughs.

The most innovative thinkers share one thing in common: They are constantly consuming vast amounts of information.

Most new inventions don't come out of thin air. They often come by taking an existing process or method from one discipline and transplanting it to another. This is why expanding your understanding of other disciplines is so important. Fortunately, we live in a hyperconnected world, where information on every topic imaginable is just one click away.

But don't just sit at your computer all day. Some things are better experienced in person than online. To truly appreciate art, viewing a work online doesn't compare to being in the room with it. You have to walk around a Rodin sculpture to truly appreciate it. Nothing beats having a seat at the opera, watching Shakespeare performed live, or listening to Neil Young in concert.

Don't limit yourself to art and science. Learning a new sport can teach you an incredible amount about teamwork, the human body, physics, and society. Mastering a language is another way to expand your mind. When you learn a new tongue, it not only allows you to better communicate, it also reveals the hidden aspects of the culture, history, and psychology behind the language.

Learning comes in so many forms. Try making a point of not filtering. Go to a medieval Gaelic poetry reading; take a class on Kundalini meditation; or download some traditional Malagasy music. New experiences often wind up being the most impactful because you may have had the least exposure to them. The further you venture outside mainstream culture, the more original and unexpected ideas you'll encounter.

※

The further you venture outside mainstream culture,
the more original and unexpected ideas you'll
encounter.

The beauty of the pursuit of knowledge is that it never ends. The more you learn and understand, the hungrier you'll become to infuse your brain with novel concepts and experiences while realizing that what you know is such a tiny fraction of what's waiting to be discovered.

Surviving a Startup

SETBACKS HAPPEN FOR EVERYONE. I don't want to call them failures. They only turn into failures when we give up. As long as we can pick ourselves off the ground and try again, they're just one more hurdle along the obstacle course of life. I've been an entrepreneur long enough to know that not everything goes according to plan. In fact, surprisingly little turns out the way an entrepreneur envisions. Whatever plans you have in your head, be prepared for them to go up in smoke, and you'll be fine.

Failing to achieve a goal isn't all bad news. A lot of the time, you stumble upon something better. If you're open to change, you'll find new opportunities along the way that you never could have anticipated. One of those surprises or setbacks is often what leads the way to a new discovery. Most of the greatest breakthroughs in human history were unplanned. Many were complete chance.

Take, for example, how Bell Labs discovered proof of the Big Bang Theory. Originally, the scientists thought the buzzing noise on their new antenna was being caused by pigeon poop. It was a real problem. They tried everything they could to get rid of the buzzing, but it wouldn't go away. Only much later did they stumble upon the right answer, when Robert H. Dicke, a Princeton physicist who was theorizing about this, pointed out that they may have discovered the cosmic background radiation left over from the Big Bang. Of course, Bell Labs and its scientists took credit for it and won a Nobel Prize.

Similarly, unexpected events, including mistakes, led to the discovery of penicillin, X-ray images, LSD, microwave ovens, the pacemaker, Post-It Notes, potato chips, Coca-Cola, Teflon, plastic, radioactivity, Velcro, dynamite, anesthesia, stainless steel, smart dust, and a host of other inventions. The same is true in startups. Most entrepreneurs blunder onto a new business model, insight, or innovation that radically transforms their business. Often, this happens after a series of setbacks and failed experiments.

It's critical to understand that failure is part of the process. If you're trying to create something the world has never seen, you're going to hit obstacles, and some of those may be insurmountable. That means you just have to find another way around or change your focus entirely. The bigger and more audacious your goals, the harder it will be to get there. So, be prepared for a long, rough journey. And if you're under the illusion that dealing with setbacks is easier if you happen to be a famous billionaire, I can assure you that's not the case.

※

Failure is part of the process.

If you don't believe me, imagine how it feels to be kicked out of your own company after developing the most innovative personal computer in history. Steve Jobs experienced this. What's it like to be dragged in front of the US Congress and vilified on national television for compromising millions of people's data? Mark Zuckerberg can tell you. How agonizing must it be to watch your $90 million rocket explode? Elon Musk had to face this more than once, and this may only be the beginning of his travails if he's going to get us to Mars. The bigger you become, the worse it gets because more people are watching your every move and criticizing your actions. It's bad enough when you know that you screwed up, but when half the world is judging you, that's a big weight to carry.

Jack Ma, the founder of Alibaba, which is arguably China's most successful startup, failed not once, but twice, and that was just the beginning of his journey. His first company, Hope Translations, never made it off the ground. His second venture, China Pages, was also a dud. On his third try with Alibaba, he ran into more trouble and had to pivot. It's only when he adopted eBay's model and modified it to fit the Chinese market that he began to see some success, and even then, it was an uphill battle until he finally broke through with funding from Softbank and Yahoo!

Even visionaries like Marc Benioff, who had the right idea from the very beginning, have trouble when they are launching their companies. When Benioff first went out to raise capital for Salesforce, he approached every venture capitalist who would listen to him. "I had to go hat in hand," says Benioff, "like I was a high-tech beggar, down to Silicon Valley to raise some money. . . . And as I go from venture capitalist to venture capitalist to venture capitalist—and a lot of them are my friends, people I've gone to lunch with—and each and every one of them said no."[1]

Finally, Benioff quit talking to VCs. He was unable to raise a single dollar from them, but if he'd given in to the negative feedback, Salesforce would never have gotten off the ground and he wouldn't have pioneered cloud computing. Instead, he looked for alternative funding sources. After a lot of hard work, he managed to raise enough money from angel investors to take Salesforce all the way to an IPO. Today, it's a $160 billion company.

Rejection is often more the rule than the exception. Venture capitalists may be smart, but they don't have a crystal ball. They aren't necessarily any better at predicting the future than anyone else. The list of famous entrepreneurs who had to turn to alternative funding sources to get started is a long one. It includes Steve Jobs, who had to take out a $250,000 bank loan; Michael Dell, who worked out of his dorm and had to borrow $1,000 from his family; Bob Hewlett and David Packard, who started out in their Palo Alto garage with just $538 in capital; and Bill Gates and Paul Allen, who bootstrapped Microsoft after dropping out of college. Those are just a few of the big names who had to look for other means of funding their big dreams.

It's hard not to doubt yourself when everyone rejects you, but overcoming extreme doubt is the job of a CEO. This is what happens when you're pushing the limits. You can't let them get to you. You can't crumble under the pressure. You mustn't listen to the naysayers. Your job is to push harder when things get tougher.

Remember, when other people tell you something won't work, they may not be seeing what you're seeing. Often, the more someone knows about a particular subject, the blinder this person can become to the future possibilities. This is because experts tend to think they know everything about their fields, and if it's something they haven't considered, it's automatically not possible.

Experts have another Achilles' heel. They have accumulated so much knowledge in a specific area that it's easy to get locked into the past. This is why many VCs pass on excellent ideas. They extrapolate based on their previous experiences, and this can lead them to wrong conclusions. If something didn't work in the past, it's easy to dismiss it as another one of those. When, in fact, the world has changed, and that failed concept from a few years back may now be capable of disrupting an entire industry.

YouTube, Dropbox, Amazon Fresh, Facebook, and the iPhone were all redos of previous ideas that had failed. Remember Digital Entertainment Network, Xdrive, Webvan, Friendster, and Palm? They were the original failures. The point is that success is often more a matter of timing than vision. The previous attempts had the right idea but were too early, or they missed out on critical elements.

As an entrepreneur, instead of trying to eliminate failures, you should mentally prepare yourself for an endless series of disappointments, wrong turns, and outright disasters. You will make plans, build things, and watch them crumble. Then you will make new plans and build more things, until, if you persist long enough and are lucky enough, you will stumble onto something that magically takes flight, defying all expectations.

This is what I see time and again when I'm working with startups all over the world. It doesn't matter who you are or where you're from; it's always a similar story. Only you can push through those invisible barriers that are holding you back, attempt to rise above what's possible, avoid making the same mistakes others have made, and go on to make your own blunders as you charge down that chaotic, twisting, bumpy road we call entrepreneurship.

That is how you survive a startup.

Notes

Epigraphs

1. Daniel Morrow, "Steve Jobs 1995 Interview NeXT Computer," https://vimeo.com/31813340 (accessed June 17, 2020).
2. Elon Musk, "StartmeupHK Venture Forum—Elon Musk on Entrepreneurship and Innovation," https://www.youtube.com/watch?v=pIRqB5iqWA8 (accessed June 17, 2020).

Chapter 1

1. Monte Burke, "At Age 25 Mark Cuban Learned Lessons about Leadership That Changed His Life," *Forbes*, March 28, 2013, https://www.forbes.com/sites/monteburke/2013/03/28/at-age-25-mark-cuban-learned-lessons-about-leadership-that-changed-his-life/ (accessed June 17, 2020).

Chapter 3

1. Shane Snow, "What It's Like to Eat Nothing but This Magical, Healthy Ice Cream for 10 Days," *GQ*, January 28, 2016, https://www.gq.com/story/halo-top-ice-cream-review-diet (accessed June 17, 2020).

Chapter 5

1. Eugene Kim, "Parker Harris: The Little-Known Nice Guy Who Helped Turn Salesforce into San Francisco's Most Powerful Tech Company," *Business Insider*, February 16, 2015, https://www.businessinsider.com/parker-harris-salesforce-cofounder-profile-2015-2 (accessed June 17, 2020).

Chapter 8

1. Yvon Chouinard, *Let My People Go Surfing: The Education of a Reluctant Businessman* (Penguin Press, 2005).
2. Amy Feldman, "Costco for Millennials: How Chieh Huang Built Boxed, a Mobile Juggernaut with $100M+ in Revenue," *Forbes*, October 19, 2016, https://www.forbes.com/sites/forbestreptalks/2016/10/19/costco-for-millennials-how-chieh-huang-built-boxed-a-mobile-juggernaut-with-100m-in-revenue/ (accessed June 17, 2020).

Chapter 17

1. Guy Raz, "Patagonia: Yvon Chouinard," *How I Built This with Guy Raz*, December 25, 2017, https://www.npr.org/2018/02/06/572558864/patagonia-yvon-chouinard (accessed June 17, 2020).

Chapter 18

1. "Slack's Founder on How They Became a $1 Billion Company in Two Years," *Fast Company* (reprinted from *First Round Review*), February 4, 2015, https://www.fastcompany.com/3041905/slacks-founder-on-how-they-became-a-1-billion-company-in-two-years (accessed on June 17, 2020).

Chapter 26

1. K. Huang, M. Yeomans, A. W. Brooks, J. Minson, and F. Gino, "It Doesn't Hurt to Ask: Question-asking Increases Liking," *Journal of Personality and Social Psychology* 113, no. 3 (September 2017).

Chapter 39

1. Susan Adams, "Little Passports' Founders Desperately Wanted VC Cash. Luckily They Got Zero," *Forbes*, November 2, 2016, https://www.forbes.com/sites/susanadams/2016/11/02/little-passports-founders-desperately-wanted-vc-cash-luckily-they-got-zero/ (accessed June 17, 2020).

Chapter 41

1. Matt Linderman, "Bootstrapped, Profitable, & Proud: GitHub," *Signal v. Noise*, August 3, 2010, https://signalvnoise.com/posts/2486-bootstrapped-profitable-proud-github (accessed May 17, 2020).
2. Kathleen Elkins, "Daymond John: 'Quit Your Day Job' Is Garbage Advice—Here's the Secret to Success," CNBC, June 8, 2017, https://www.cnbc.com/2017/06/08/daymond-john-says-never-quit-your-day-job.html (accessed June 17, 2020).

Chapter 43

1. Rachael Micallef, "McCann Japan Appoints World's First AI Creative Director," *AdNews*, March 29, 2016, https://www.adnews.com.au/news/mccann-japan-appoints-world-s-first-ai-creative-director (accessed June 17, 2020).

Chapter 44

1. Lydia Dishman, "Betabrand's Building a Business on Balderdash and Memes," *Fast Company*, September 30, 2011, https://www.fastcompany.com/1783906/betabrands-building-business-balderdash-and-memes (accessed June 17, 2020).

2. "What Is Cards Against Humanity?" https://cardsagainsthumanity.com/ (accessed June 17, 2020).

3. Kim Janssen, "Cards Against Humanity Raises $2.25 Million to Fight Trump's Border Wall, Promote Card Game," *Chicago Tribune*, November 15, 2017, https://www.chicagotribune.com/news/ct-met-cards-against-humanity-1116-chicago-inc-20171115-story.html (accessed June 17, 2020).

Chapter 47

1. "DollarShaveClub.com—Our Blades Are F***ing Great," March 6, 2012, https://www.youtube.com/watch?v=ZUG9qYTJMsI (accessed June 17, 2020).

Chapter 48

1. Susan Adams, "How a Millennial with No Business Experience or College Education Created Streetwear for the Masses," *Forbes*, April 14, 2016, https://www.forbes.com/sites/forbestreptalks/2016/04/14/how-a-millennial-with-no-business-experience-or-college-education-created-streetwear-for-the-masses/ (accessed June 17, 2020).

Chapter 51

1. "How Dave Goldberg of SurveyMonkey Built a Billion-Dollar Business and Still Gets Home by 5:30 PM," *First Round Review*, http://firstround.com/review/How-Dave-Goldberg-of-SurveyMonkey-Built-a-Billion-Dollar-Business-and-Still-Gets-Home-By-5-30/ (accessed June 17, 2020).

2. Julie Bort, "AppLovin, a 115 Employee, Profitable Startup That Never Raised Money from VCs, Sold Itself for $1.4 Billion," *Business Insider*, September 27, 2016, https://finance.yahoo.com/news/applovin-115-employee-profitable-startup-154917743.html (accessed June 17, 2020).

Chapter 55

1. Robbie Abed, "This Chicago Duo Sold Their Protein Bar Company for $600 Million. 6 Lessons You Can Take from Them," *Inc.*, October 31, 2017, https://www.inc.com/robbie-abed/this-chicago-startup-sold-its-protein-bar-company-for-600-million-to-kelloggs.html (accessed June 17, 2020).

Chapter 64

1. Rob Walker, "The Guts of a New Machine," *New York Times Magazine*, November 30, 2003, https://www.nytimes.com/2003/11/30/magazine/the-guts-of-a-new-machine.html (accessed June 17, 2020).

2. Tom Kelley and David Kelley, *Creative Confidence: Unleashing the Creative Potential Within Us All* (Currency, 2013).

Chapter 65

1. Guy Raz, "Dyson: James Dyson," *How I Built This with Guy Raz*, February 12, 2018, https://www.npr.org/2018/03/26/584331881/dyson-james-dyson (accessed June 17, 2020).
2. Guy Raz, "Dyson: James Dyson."

Chapter 68

1. Tiago Fonseca, "High Fives Correlation with Team Bonding and Success," *Fox Sports Stories*, October 27, 2017, http://foxsportsstories.com/2017/10/27/high-fives-correlation-with-team-bonding-and-success/ (accessed June 17, 2020).
2. Amy Feldman, "Costco for Millennials.
3. Susan Caminiti, "A Dream Boss Who Pays for His Workers' Weddings and Their Kids' College Tuition," CNBC, June 7, 2017, https://www.cnbc.com/2017/06/06/boxed-ceo-chieh-huang-offers-generous-employee-benefits-to-keep-talent.html (accessed June 17, 2020).

Chapter 69

1. Richard Feloni, "Why Google CEO Larry Page Personally Reviews Every Candidate the Company Hires," *Business Insider*, April 8, 2015, http://www.businessinsider.com/google-ceo-larry-page-on-hiring-2015-4 (accessed June 17, 2020).

Chapter 76

1. Laura Entis, "The Science of Office Design," *Entrepreneur*, January 27, 2014, https://www.entrepreneur.com/article/231035 (accessed June 17, 2020).
2. Laura Entis, "The Science of Office Design."
3. Christine Congdon, Donna Flynn, and Melanie Redman, "Balancing 'We' and 'Me': The Best Collaborative Spaces Also Support Solitude," *Harvard Business Review*, October 2014, https://hbr.org/2014/10/balancing-we-and-me-the-best-collaborative-spaces-also-support-solitude (accessed June 17, 2020).

Chapter 77

1. Jeff Bercovici, "Apple, Amazon, and Google Want to Help Small Businesses Succeed—But Not Too Much," *Inc.*, May 2018 Issue, https://www.inc.com/magazine/201805/jeff-bercovici/big-tech-monopoly-startup-competition.html (accessed June 17, 2020).
2. Ben Schiller, "This Is How We Take Power Back from Facebook (And Every Other Monopoly)," *Fast Company*, March 21, 2018, https://www.fastcompany.com/40508850/this-is-how-we-take-power-back-from-facebook-and-every-other-monopoly (accessed June 17, 2020).

Chapter 81

1. Liza, "Larry Page Leadership Profile," Leadership Geeks, January 25, 2017, http://www.leadershipgeeks.com/larry-page-leadership/ (accessed June 17, 2020).

Chapter 82

1. Robert Glazer, "Marc Benioff Says This 1 Tactic Is the Key to Salesforce's Success. Here's How to Use It." *Inc.*, November 5, 2018, https://www.inc.com/robert-glazer /marc-benioff-says-these-4-principles-are-key-to-salesforces-success-heres-how-to -use-them.html (accessed June 17, 2020).
2. Alison Elworthy, "MSPOTs: The Secret to Focus and Alignment," ThinkGrowth, February 17, 2017, https://thinkgrowth.org/mspots-the-secret-to-focus-and -alignment-4a1510d9b3db (accessed June 17, 2020).
3. Marc Benioff, "Company Alignment: The Salesforce Secret to Success," *Salesforce Blog*, April 2013, https://www.salesforce.com/blog/2013/04/how-to-create -alignment-within-your-company.html (accessed June 17, 2020).
4. Marc Benioff, *Trailblazer: The Power of Business as the Greatest Platform for Change* (Currency, 2019).

Chapter 86

1. Brian D. Evans, "Every Successful Entrepreneur Has an Almost-Failed Story. This New Podcast Wants to Share All of Them," *Inc.*, May 25, 2017, https://www.inc .com/brian-d-evans/every-successful-entrepreneur-has-an-almost-failed-story -this-new-podcast-wants-.html (accessed June 17, 2020).
2. Jeff Kauflin, "Adam Pisoni's Path to a $1 Billion Exit: A Rational Fear of Failure, an Irrational Belief in Success," *Forbes*, June 29, 2016, https://www.forbes.com /sites/jeffkauflin/2016/06/29/adam-pisonis-path-to-a-1-billion-exit-a-rational -fear-of-failure-an-irrational-belief-in-success/ (accessed June 17, 2020).

Chapter 87

1. Danny Crichton, "New Research Shows Successful Founders Are Far Older Than the Valley Stereotype," *TechCrunch*, April 10, 2018, https://techcrunch.com/2018 /04/10/new-research-shows-successful-founders-are-far-older-than-the-valley -stereotype/ (accessed June 17, 2020).
2. Vivek Wadhwa, "The Case for Old Entrepreneurs," *Washington Post*, December 2, 2011, https://www.washingtonpost.com/national/on-innovations/the-case-for -old-entrepreneurs/2011/12/02/gIQAulJ3KO_story.html (accessed May 17, 2020).
3. Loknath Das, "Over 30? You're Too Old for Tech Jobs in China," *Bloomberg Businessweek*, May 2, 2018, https://businesslogr.com/30-youre-old-tech-jobs-china / (accessed June 17, 2020).
4. Catherine Clifford, "It's Never Too Late to Succeed: How This 60-Year-Old Founder Took Her Business from Zero to $500 Million in 6 years," CNBC, July 20, 2017, https://www.cnbc.com/2017/07/20/a-60-year-old-entrepreneur-took-her -business-from-zero-to-500-million.html (accessed June 17, 2020).
5. Dave Hochman, "4 Factors VCs Consider When Deciding to Invest in a Founder," *Entrepreneur*, May 26, 2016, https://www.entrepreneur.com/article/273332 (accessed June 17, 2020).

Chapter 90

1. Ron Miller, "Benioff: Every VC in Silicon Valley Turned Us Down," *TechCrunch*, April 9, 2018, https://techcrunch.com/2018/04/09/benioff-every-vc-in-silicon -valley-turned-us-down/ (accessed June 17, 2020).

Index

About the Author

STEVEN S. HOFFMAN, or Captain Hoff as he's called in Silicon Valley, is the CEO of Founders Space, one of the world's leading incubators and accelerators. He's also an angel investor, limited partner at August Capital, serial entrepreneur, and author of *Make Elephants Fly*, the award-winning book on radical innovation, and *The Five Forces*, an extraordinary journey into the minds and ideas of the people and the technology poised to reshape our world.

Hoffman was the founder and chairman of the Producers Guild Silicon Valley Chapter, served on the Board of Governors of the New Media Council, and was a founding member of the Academy of Television's Interactive Media Group. In Silicon Valley, Hoffman founded several startups in the areas of games and entertainment, and worked as mobile studio head for Infospace, which published the hit mobile games *Tetris*, *Wheel of Fortune*, *Tomb Raider*, *Thief*, *Hitman*, *Skee-Ball*, and *X-Files*.

Hoffman has a bachelor of science from the University of California in computer engineering and a master of fine arts from the University of Southern California in cinema/television. He currently resides in San Francisco but spends most of his time in the air, visiting startups, investors, and innovators all over the world.